Lucky Pommie Bastard

DON McNAUGHTON

Copyright © 2020 Donald McNaughton

All rights reserved. No part of this book may be reproduced, published, performed in public or communicated to the public in any form or by any means without prior permission of the author.

ISBN: 978-0-6450188-1-3 (pBck)

 A catalogue record for this work is available from the National Library of Australia

DEDICATION

Sgt Roy McNaughton 1943

In memory of my parents Roy and Anne McNaughton, the Trimble Lancaster crew and all the men of Bomber Command who died or risked their lives and their health to defeat fascism in World War 2. May they be remembered.

Bomber Command Memorial, London summer 2014.

Illustrations

The front cover is a photograph of the UK Battle of Britain memorial flight Lancaster taken at Duxford, UK during the 2018 Flying Legends Air Show.

Dedication – Sgt Roy McNaughton 1943.

Bomber Command Memorial, London summer 2014.

The Back cover photograph is of the Trimble crew on a visit to the Lancaster factory at Castle Bromwich, Birmingham in late February 1944.

Fig. 1.	RAF Spilsby Memorial – June 2018.
Fig. 2.	The Welch crew – Durnbach CWGC cemetery, Sep 2020.
Fig. 3	Gunner Trainees and staff, 2AGS Dalcross, Scotland, Apr-May 1943.
Fig. 4.	68MUG Course, 2AGS, Dalcross, 15 May 1943.
Fig. 5.	Hannover railway station, Autumn, 1945.
Fig. 6.	Hannover Air Raid Bunker – transformed into flats, Sep 2020.
Fig. 7.	Roy (Mac) and Jack, Darlington, 1943.
Fig. 8.	Trimble crew whilst with 207 Squadron.
Fig. 9.	Graves of five of the Heap crew – Berlin CWGC, 2018.
Fig. 10.	Naughty Nancy over Brunswick.
Fig. 11.	Trimble crew under Uncle Joe Stalin after the Leipzig raid, Waddington, Feb 1944.
Fig. 12.	The Trimble crew photographed at Castle Bromwich Aircraft factory, Feb 1944.
Fig. 13.	HK535 – First Lancaster from the Castle Bromwich Factory.
Fig. 14.	Inscription on the back of the factory photo of HK535, presented to Roy McNaughton.
Fig. 15.	Wedding of Roy and Anne, 18 Nov 1944.
Fig. 16.	Packing for Oz, August 1961.

CONTENTS

	Acknowledgments	i
	Glossary	ii
1	MUGS AWAY	1
2	NANCY'S WAR	16
3	PATHS TO BOMBER COMMAND	27
4	OPERATIONS OVER GERMANY	48
5	THE TOUR MOVES ON	58
6	NOT SO LUCKY CREW	71
7	LUCKY CREW	80
8	THE LAST OPS	101
9	AFTER OPS	115
10	TEN POUND POMS	132
11	NEW ARRIVALS	139
12	WE WILL CALL AUSTRALIA HOME	157
13	JUST HOW LUCKY?	174
	Resources	189
	Appendix Trimble Crew Operations	191
	About the author	220

ACKNOWLEDGMENTS

My first thanks go to my wife Liz McNaughton, for putting up with the long process of head in book, head in internet and me off in another world, sometimes mentally and sometimes physically. A big thank you goes to Vic Trimble's daughter Judy Nickles and the Trimble family for allowing me access to Vic Trimble's letters home and his logbook. Also thanks to Jim Marles for a long afternoon chat that allowed me to ensure that chapter seven is accurate. Thanks also to my brother Alan who provided information from his memory and records and located issues where my memory had failed. A few things he let me get away with! He also read and criticised the first draft along with my wife Liz and carried out a penultimate edit. My thanks also go to my old RAAF mate Mark Pemberton who went through an early version with a critical aeronautical engineer's eye. His knowledge of World War 2 aircraft sorted out a few issues and his suggestions were all useful. Thanks go to Steve Morton for helping me out with the photograph on the cover, to Jens Uwe Grabow for Hannover photographs and Luca Bizzocchi and Michela Giuliano for Durnbach photographs. Thanks also go to my children Lachlan and Caitlyn who ploughed through the final version of the book to find all my errors. Those errors that are left are my responsibility. A big thank you goes to Stephanie Sandford for putting together the website. Finally, my thanks go to my parents for bringing us little Pommie Bastards out to Australia in 1961.

GLOSSARY

AIRCRAFT TYPES

Anson — Two engine training aircraft widely used throughout the British dominions.

B-17 — Four engine US built bomber aircraft. Heavily armed in comparison to RAF bombers and used in daylight bombing raids. Bombing load approximately half that of a Lancaster bomber. The RAF used them in Coastal Command and adapted them for specialist roles. They were used in 100 Group as RCM aircraft.

Beaufighter — Two engine aircraft used in a night fighter, intruder, ground attack roles by the RAF.

Defiant — Boulton-Paul Defiant. Single engine "fighter" aircraft with a rear gun turret. Failed as a fighter and converted to night fighter and then gunner training roles.

FW190 — Focke-Wulf 190. A German single seater fighter aircraft introduced mid war and used also as a night fighter.

Halifax — British four engine night bomber that was not as successful as the Lancaster. It was not as powerful, had a slightly smaller bomb load than the Lancaster and could not take bombs greater than 2,000 lbs. Its loss rate was higher than that of the Lancaster but the crews liked it because it was roomier and allowed greater opportunity for bailing out. The survival rate for shot down Halifax bombers was 29% versus 11% for the Lancaster.

Hurricane — British single engine fighter used in the Battle of Britain.

Ju88 — German Junker 88 twin engine aircraft with multiple roles as bomber, intruder and night fighter.

Lancaster — British four engine heavy bomber equipped with powerful Merlin engines. The most successful British bomber of the war. Bomb load greater than the Halifax and it had a bomb bay that could take 4,000 lb Cookies and could also be adapted for 6 and 10 ton bombs.

Manchester — British twin engine bomber that was a forerunner of the Lancaster. It lacked powerful enough engines (Vulture engines) and was withdrawn from operations in 1942 and even from training in 1943.

GLOSSARY

Martinet	A British single engine plane purpose designed as a tug to tow targets for gunnery training. Introduced early in 1943.
Me110	German Messerschmitt twin engine multi-role aircraft used as a night fighter.
Me410	German Messerschmitt twin engine night bomber and fighter with a range that allowed it to bomb the UK and harass returning bombers.
Mosquito	British all wood twin engine aircraft used as a fast light bomber, night fighter and intruder.
Oxford	British twin engine aircraft used for advanced pilot training.
P38	Lockheed P38 Lightning – A twin boom US fighter aircraft used in photo-reconnaissance and fighter bomber roles.
P51	North American P51 Mustang – A single seater long range fighter and fighter bomber built originally for the RAF.
Spitfire	British single engine fighter used in the Battle of Britain and throughout the war. A very successful fighter that went through many iterations to make it faster, better armed and more powerful.
Stirling	British four-engined bomber that was underpowered and suffered heavy losses before being withdrawn from night bombing and used in a variety of other roles.
Tiger Moth	Single engine biplane used as a training aircraft in initial flying training.
Wellington	British twin engine bomber that saw service throughout the war in many roles. It was initially the main strike bomber of the RAF until the introduction of the four engine bombers.
Wirraway	Australian built single engine training aircraft

ACRONYMS & OTHER TERMS

A/C	Aircraft
AFC	Air Force cross awarded to commissioned and warrant officers for "an act or acts of valour, courage or devotion to duty whilst flying, though not in active operations against the enemy"
A/G	Air Gunner

Airborne Cigar (ABC) Radar system used to jam German night fighter controllers.

Batman An airman or airwomen assigned to an officer or officers as a personal servant.

Cookie 4,000 lb blast bomb carried by Lancaster bombers.

CWGC Commonwealth War Graves Commission

DFC Distinguished Flying Cross, awarded to commissioned and warrant officer aircrew for "an act or acts of valour, courage or devotion to duty whilst flying in active operations against the enemy."

DFM Distinguished Flying Medal, awarded to non commissioned aircrew. Equivalent to DFC.

DSO Distinguished Service Order, awarded for distinguished conduct under enemy fire. Usually for people in command positions.

E/A Enemy aircraft

EATS Empire Air Training Scheme

Flak General term for anti-aircraft fire. Comes from the German word **Fl**ugabwehr**k**anone (Aircraft defence cannon).

Fl Off Flying officer

Flt Lt Flight Lieutenant

Flt Sgt Flight Sergeant

GEE British radio guidance system. A chain of transmitters was used to send signals to a/c borne receivers. Signal time delays were used to determine the a/c position. The Germans eventually jammed GEE but it was used throughout the war as a navigation device for returning aircraft.

Gp Cpt Group Captain

H_2S A British radar scanning system that was used to scan the ground from the air and locate targets.

HCU Heavy Conversion Unit. An RAF unit formed to train crews on four engine bombers after initial training on two engine bombers.

IAS Indicated Air Speed

GLOSSARY

KIA   Killed In Action

LFS   Lancaster Finishing School – Advanced training school for Lancaster crews.

Link Trainer   An early form of flight simulator that was used throughout the war as part of pilot training.

MI9   British Directorate of Military Intelligence Section 9, which was responsible for organizing and supporting resistance groups over Europe to assist evading aircrew. They also informed and trained RAF aircrew in evasion techniques.

MONICA   A tail pointing radar system operating at 200 MHz to detect enemy aircraft. The Germans developed FLENSBURG to combat it and MONICA was withdrawn in July 1944 when it was recognised, after a Flensburg equipped Ju88 was captured, that the Germans were using the MONICA signal for detection of bombers. Serrate Mosquitos were subsequently equipped with MONICA to attract and detect night fighters approaching from behind.

MUG   Mid Upper Gunner

NAAFI   Navy, Army and Air Force Institutes who were responsible for running clubs, bars, shops and cafés for servicemen. Officers were not supposed to use NAAFI facilities.

Newhaven   A target marking system where the dropping of target indicator flares was controlled using the H_2S system.

OBOE   A ground based radio transponder system where the signal emanated from the aircraft rather than the ground. It was used for blind bombing often by equipment on a Pathfinder Mosquito, which would then direct the bombing of other aircraft. Mosquitos were used because they could fly higher, thus extending the range of the OBOE system.

OP/s   A shortening of Operation/s that was used commonly in the RAF and is used throughout this book.

ORB   Operational Record Book

OTU   Operational Training Unit. A unit where aircrew formed crews and trained for operations on a/c such as the Wellington

OTU sortie   Operations carried out by crews from OTU for training. They were usually leaflet drops, minelaying trips or ops to softer targets.

Parramatta	A target marking system where ground based target indicator flares were dropped blind. If they were directed by OBOE they were termed "Musical Parramatta".
Pathfinder	An aircraft of the Pathfinder force, which was a specialist target marking force.
PFF	Path Finder Force. Specialist Squadrons formed to lead and direct attacks and mark targets for the main bomber stream.
Plt Off	Pilot Officer
POW	Prisoner Of War
PRU	Photographic Reconnaissance Unit
RAAF	Royal Australian Air Force
RAF	Royal Air Force
RAFVR	Royal Air Force Volunteer Reserve
RCAF	Royal Canadian Air Force
RCM	Radio Counter Measures such as Mandrel – A jammer to counter the German early warning radar systems. Also German speaking radio operators who would confuse night fighter operations.
RNZAF	Royal New Zealand Air Force
Serrate	A radar device designed to lock on to the German night fighter radar system. It was carried by British Mosquitos and Beaufighters that mingled with the bombers.
Second Pilot	Most pilots new to operations were sent on an operation with an experienced crew as an extra pilot to gain experience. Early in the war bombers had two pilots but for man power reasons the second pilot was replaced by a flight engineer.
Sgt	Sergeant
Sqn Ldr	Squadron Leader
Tallboy	A six ton bomb designed to explode underground. It was carried by specialist Lancaster squadrons.
TI	Target Indicator
U/S	Unserviceable
USAAF	United States Army Air Force.

GLOSSARY

WAAF Women's Auxiliary Air Force

Wanganui/Whanganui A target indicator flare(or flares) that hung in the sky and were dropped blind. If they were directed by OBOE they were termed "Musical Whanganui".

Window Strips of aluminium foil dropped from bombers to confuse enemy radar. The size used depended on the wavelength of the radar that was to be confused.

Wg Cdr Wing Commander

WO Warrant Officer

WOP Wireless Operator

XIB British 4lb explosive type "X" incendiary bomb. There were numerous types of incendiary bombs used with a variety of chemical contents. They were generally 30lb or 4lb devices, the smaller ones often in clusters.

1   MUGS AWAY

With movement orders clutched tightly in hand, the three newly minted sergeants leapt off the back of the RAF truck, tossed their kitbags over their shoulders and surveyed the chaotic scene that greeted them. Inverness train station, despite the late hour, was a heaving mass of mostly uniformed humanity jostling for position before the arrival of the Edinburgh bound train. After their 16 weeks in the RAF moving from one training base to another the three youngsters were experienced travellers and wised up to bureaucracy, so they knew that they would most likely be occupying a train corridor for the upcoming journey. Nevertheless, hoping that their newly acquired status as sergeants and air gunners would snaffle them a place further up the seat pecking order, they assumed a confident air and approached the movements' clerk. A short conversation with the elderly clerk was it all it took to dash their hopes and inform them that the train was also running late. Their glum expressions elicited some gentle advice from the older man.

"Best bet for you lads is to be off to the NAAFI (Navy, Army and Air Force Institutes) truck and grab a cuppa and a bun, you'll be havin' a long wait. The lassies there will look after yers." They were indeed well looked after, with their brand new sergeant stripes and gunners badges attracting admiring smiles from both the young lassies and the more elderly matrons running the NAAFI.

It was May 1943 and RAF bombers were the principal instrument of attack against Nazi Germany, a regime at last on the back foot. The aircrew were consequently admired heroes in the eyes of the British public, and since graduation from their mid upper gunners (MUGs) course and removal of their white training bands and epaulettes, they had immediately joined the elite of Bomber Command. Three of 16 course graduates, they were on their way to Peterborough, the closest railway station to Cottesmore, home of Bomber Command No 14 Operational Training Unit (OTU). The newly minted air gunners had one thing in common, they had all just turned 19. Roy McNaughton, or Mac[1] as the other two knew him, was the youngest and had turned 19 just 10 days earlier. The three hailed from geographically diverse parts of England and from different social strata, Mac from Darlington in Durham, Fred Tunnicliff from Brighton in Sussex and Jim Seddon from Worthington in Lancashire. Despite their differing backgrounds, they had become firm friends after being thrown together for air gunner training and sharing a Nissen hut at RAF Dalcross.

A few minutes after midnight, the Edinburgh bound train entered the blacked out station and even before it ground to a halt people were leaping on board through doors and clambering in via windows. By the time the gunners managed to board there was little room available, so they straddled their kitbags close to a carriage door and settled in. With a shout of "All Aboard" and a whistle from the guard, the locomotive steadily powered forward, accompanied by the hiss of escaping steam and quickening puffs through the smoke stack. Before long the sound and movement settled into a soothing rhythmic clickety-clack as the train reached its cruising speed and then trundled on steadily through the night. The three mates passed the time by chatting about the idiosyncracies of their recent instructors, the crazy Polish pilots and their fellow trainees, before moving on to talk about home, family, girls and what the future might hold. After living close together for six weeks and experiencing three months of RAF discipline and training, they already felt part of a team, but were nervous about the next steps that would lead them to bomber operations over Germany.

Throughout the night, the train stopped irregularly, at sidings for passing traffic, at stations for passengers, and often for no apparent reason, so they witnessed the sun rising over the North Sea just before they pulled into Edinburgh's Waverley station. The air was crisp as they jumped off the train and made their way to tea and porridge at the NAAFI. Breakfast was served by a young NAAFI woman with a strong Scottish brogue. Her accent was just a little softer than the Inverness accent that they had grown used to in Dalcross, so they had no trouble understanding her and swapping banter. Over breakfast they mused about what might happen in the coming days. "Whaddya reckon Mac, how the

---

[1] Roy is referred to throughout as Roy, Mac or Dad depending on the context or the author's whim.

heck do you pick a good skipper, or how does he pick you?"

"Howay man, they'll alriddy have rear gunners so Fred here jist gits a coupla pints in for some rear gunners and we git the gen outa em."

"Trust two ikey Northerners to come up with that plan. How about the three of us buy a few of 'em beers and we take it from there?"

"OK Fred, yer on, when we get to Cottesmore let's just chat up a few fellow gunners."

Late in the morning, the London train was ready for departure and once again they perched in the corridor on their gear and dozed as the enclosed atmosphere became warm and fuggy with the smell of enclosed humanity and the ubiquitous tobacco smoke. As they pulled into Darlington station a couple of hours later the other two looked quizzically at Roy.

"Tempted to get off and see the folks Mac?"

"More tempted to get off and see the girl who moved in up the road just before I left home. I wouldn't mind getting to know her, but I guess it will have to wait until my next leave."

Finally, in the early evening after the usual long wartime stop-start journey and feeling stiff-jointed and woolly headed, they disembarked at Peterborough and searched out the bus transport to the nearby base. The shuttle bus was heaving with raucous aircrew and ground crew returning after a day out in town but they were made welcome, despite being the butt of jokes about new sprogs. Dropped off at the Sergeants' mess they waited in the ante-room to be allocated digs. The mess bar was crowded with noisy aircrew so they agreed to meet up later to try out their strategy for crewing up.

Fifteen minutes later they were back, perusing the crowd at the bar and working out from the wing badges who amongst the throng were gunners. A lively threesome with Air Gunner (A/G) badges at the far end of the room caught their eye. All three were dressed in the dark blue RAAF uniform of Australia. Mac pointed them out.

"Hows aboot those three Jim, the Aussies at the end?"

"Why not, from what I hear Aussies are all supposed to be good blokes, let's go".

Jim, the most confident of the three, led the way through the noisy crowd and they approached their prey. "Hullo lads, can me and me two mates buy you a pint?" The closest of the three Aussies gave them a quick once over and decided a free beer was fine.

"G'day fellas, my oath you can." With a grin, the Aussie stretched out his hand to Jim. "You must be new MUGs, we've been expecting a few to show up. The good looking one here is Ken from Sydney, the old fella is Charlie from Perth and I'm Jack from sunny Queensland."

"Ay, this is Mac and Fred and I'm Jim." Jim ordered six beers while they swapped details about how they had all arrived at Cottesmore. The Aussies had endured a long and convoluted trip to England and with more beer under their belts they talked the most. The Englishmen learnt that Ken Glover was married with a daughter approaching her first birthday and that Jack Lawrence and Charlie French were unattached. The three had arrived in England by ship the previous November and they were very happy that the weather had at last warmed up a little. Moaning about the lousy English weather was always one of the first topics with Aussies who had trained under sunny blue skies at home. After more small talk and what he considered an appropriate length of time, Jim Seddon broached the real topic.

"Are you blokes all crewed up?"

Jack settled back in his chair, took a sip of his beer, glanced at the newcomers and slowly considered his answer. After a final thoughtful pause, he summed them up as probably OK and answered.

"Yep, we're all settled so far, but we're on the look-out for mid upper gunners." He leaned backward a little more and pointed behind a group of navigators to a couple of figures also dressed in the dark blue uniform of Australia but with the full wing badges of pilots. "Those two Aussie sergeant pilots over the back there are ours. The short arse one is Vic Trimble, he's OK apart from the occasional flaming lousy landing." Ken Glover chuckled and joined in. "The big fella is my skipper, Artie Heap, nice and careful and perfect for gentle landings." Charlie French also piped up. "My skipper is another Aussie bloke, John Welch, he's such a gun pilot they made him an officer, so he's over in the officer's mess with the toffs."

"Ay, well, it seems you Aussies stick together, any more Aussies in your crews we should know about?" Jack answered for them all.

"Vic and I are crewed up with three English blokes, Artie and Ken have an Englishman, a Scotsman who doesn't seem to speak English and one Aussie. Charlie's one of four Aussies in his crew. Charlie is a WOP (wireless operator) so their lone Pommie is their rear gunner, Pop Whetton, poor old fella, it's past his bedtime so he's fast asleep now." After another half hour of chat, mostly one on one and getting to know each other, the Aussies decided that the three MUGs were definitely OK and told them they would let their skippers know that they had found three likely mid upper gunners. Their first operation being successfully completed, the three tired MUGs drifted off to bed not realizing that their individual fates had now been decided, simply by which of the three

Aussies they had connected with over the beer. Mac had swapped yarns with Jack, Jim with Charlie and Fred with Ken.

Crew details were settled soon after breakfast the next morning after introductions to the Aussie pilots, so within 24 hours of arriving the three MUGs had found homes with Roy (Mac) joining Vic Trimble's crew, Fred Tunnicliff joining Artie Heap's crew and Jim Seddon, John Welch's crew. By mid-afternoon the three six man crews of nine Australians and nine Brits were already airborne and practising low level bombing and cross-country flying in the clapped out twin engine Wellington bombers used for training. The Wellington bombers normally had a crew of five and lacked a mid upper gun turret. The MUGs consequently occupied the front turrets normally used on operations by the bomb aimer and sometimes swapped roles with the rear gunners. For five weeks, they flew two or three times a day out of Saltby airfield, a satellite field of Cottesmore. On these training flights they honed their skills, developed routines and built teamwork and mateships. The occasional days and nights off flying, lectures and ground exercises usually entailed a trip to Nottingham, where the Australian aircrew were allocated to the houses of families who had volunteered to provide Commonwealth troops with a home away from home. Vic and Jack had become close friends with the Bose and Cox families, so their English crew mates often tagged along and made themselves at home as well.

By 20 June 1943 the three crews had completed their training. With more than 80 hours flying time together they had gained confidence in night flying, gunnery, low and high level bombing and mock raids. Over this period of intense teamwork, they learnt a great deal about each other, swapping stories about their civilian lives, families, girlfriends, wives and friends. Strong bonds within crews and between crews naturally developed through the stress of training, relaxed nights in the bar and outings to the local towns and villages, with the gunners in particular forming a close network. At the end of their fifth week at Saltby/Cottesmore the MUGs and their crew mates gathered in the crew room, milling around with all the finishing crews and waiting for the crucial postings to be pinned up on the notice board. Jack Lawrence pushed his way to the front after the adjutant had posted them, read the list and came back with the news. "Good news fellas, Trimble, Heap and French are all posted to 1654 conversion unit so it's Lancs for us all. Bloody bewdy! And we've got a week of leave before we get there."

Over tea in the mess, the five sergeants of the Trimble crew chatted about how they would spend their week of leave. For the three English lads Roy, Ron Nixon (wireless operator) and Bill (Ginger) Aldworth (bomb aimer) it was a golden opportunity to head home and see the family, but the two Aussies had to think about where to spend the week. Like most Aussies far from home, they envied the English aircrew being able to just pop home on leave. Vic declared to the others that he would head for London, spend some time at the Boomerang club and try to catch up with some of his old mates. Roy turned to Jack.

"I'll be gann'n home Jack, ow bout you come along?"

"Thanks Mac, that would be great, I'll tag along for a few days."

"Reet then."

The following day the two gunners and Ron Nixon headed north by train to Darlington and five days of relaxation. Ron and Roy both lived in Durham, and Ron was heading home to Hetton-le-Hole. On the same train, but in first class, was their navigator Flying Officer (Fl Off) Arthur Herriott who was heading home to South Shields just north of Darlington. Purely by accident three members of the Trimble crew lived with 30 miles of each other. As usual, Roy, Ron and Jack were crammed up against a corner of the carriage and in the daylight, the green fields and trees of early summer England meandered past the window.

"Gee, Mac, the country is beautiful this time of the year, just like a Brisbane winter, a fella could almost live here when it's like this."

"Aye Jack, but oop ere in winter its damn cold. Long john country." Jack remembered the long, cold winter he had experienced in the south around Bournemouth and grinned at Roy.

"Too right mate, you should chuck yer long johns and come and live in sunny Queensland, no need for 'em there." The idea touched a nerve and planted a seed in Roy's mind and he replied, only half jokingly.

"If we get through our tour of ops, I might just have to do that Jack."

In Darlington Roy and Jack relaxed at home, chatting to Roy's younger brothers and sister and helping out in the garden, where the family raised rabbits and guinea pigs and grew strawberries, beans, lettuce along with potatoes and carrots. Jack enjoyed a week of total relaxation in a homely atmosphere and devoured Mrs Mac's afternoon teas with a line up of apple pies, scones, biscuits and cakes, whilst Roy kept a close look out for the girl next door but one, who according to his sister Eva, was Anne, or Nancy to her parents and was 21 years old.

His first sighting of Nancy was a dispiriting one when she arrived home on the first evening accompanied by an American colonel. How could a sergeant compete with a colonel and a well paid American one to boot? Maybe his air gunner's badge and the RAF blues would compensate. As it transpired, although his future wife was accompanying the colonel to movies, dances and music, she considered the American far too old to be a serious romantic link, so when she caught site of the RAF sergeant next door she was interested. Could he be the gawky young carrot top that she had noticed last December? Well hadn't he changed! With sister Eva as a co-conspirator, Roy managed to meet Nancy and by the end of the week they were off to the movies, with Jack tagging along. Their interests matched so well that by the time Roy and Jack hopped on the train to return south, they had agreed to write to each other and keep in touch. At the end of what seemed to Roy a very short week, he and Jack caught the train south to Doncaster and changed to Lincoln, the heart of bomber country. From there it was a local train to Swinderby where a bus took them to RAF Wigsley, the home of the 1654 Heavy Conversion Unit (HCU). Here they would develop the skills required to operate on bombing raids in a seven man Lancaster bomber.

At Wigsley the three crews were allocated British flight engineers, the only members of the crew not directly chosen by the pilot or by consensus. Jim Marles, the Trimble crew engineer, was, like many of the others, just 19 years old. Jim hailed from Banbury, a small town near Oxford. He had just completed two months of flight engineer training at St. Athan, near Cardiff. On 6 July 1943, the seven young men of the Trimble crew met up in the crew room with Fl Off Ferguson, an experienced bomber pilot, who was to start their conversion training.

"Welcome to Wigsley lads. Today you have the pleasure of flying a Manchester bomber." They all groaned, the Manchester was the two engine forerunner of the Lancaster and renowned for being underpowered and an underperformer with its troublesome Vulture engines. Its unfortunate reputation was well known throughout Bomber Command and the aircraft had been removed from operational duties 12 months earlier because of heavy losses. They were now infamous for their ability to kill novice aircrews. Ferguson took in their glum looks, smiled and continued.

"It has the same airframe, cockpit layout and functionality as the Lanc, so if you can handle this aircraft you can handle a Lancaster. I will take you up and you can all get used to its performance. When we land squadron leader (Sqn Ldr) Petty will take over and check you out."

A hectic afternoon followed as they carried out the first three of the 21 training exercises carefully designed to build their skills and teamwork as rapidly as possible. The three exercises required four hours of flying, three take-offs and landings with three different instructors. The final flight was the longest and consisted of a bombing exercise on the Wainfleet range. Two days later, after a day off for relaxation and now with four hours of dual instruction, Vic and the crew were seen off on their fourth flight, a solo, by Sqn Ldr Petty. Before they clambered into the aircraft he uttered some sage advice.

"Remember Vic, if you lose an engine, pick out somewhere to put it down. A Manchester can't stay up on one engine so you won't have much time." For an hour, they flew an uneventful cross-country exercise before heading back to Saltby with Lincoln cathedral spire as their landmark. After a smooth landing, they were greeted in the crew room by Sqn Ldr Petty.

"Well done, that's the last time you will have to take a Manchester up, it's Lancasters from here on." All seven aircrew sighed deeply in relief. They hadn't enjoyed the underpowered Manchester, which seemed to struggle its way through the sky and looked forward to flying its Merlin powered, four engine big brother.

It was four days later that they eventually carried out their first dual flight in a Lancaster and they were soon up once or twice a day working their way as a crew through the 21 exercises that culminated in a successfully completed "bullseye". Most exercises involved cross-country navigation exercises and/or bombing and gunnery, with three exercises aimed at evading fighter aircraft. The bullseye was a five or six hour cross-country night flight to an aiming point where they photographed the target as evidence that they had successfully navigated their way to and from a distant point. Navigator, Fl Off Arthur Herriott, supported by the other crew feeding him information from radio bearings and sightings, showed his skills by successfully guiding them around rural Britain with few hiccups.

After 40 hours of day and night flying on the Lancaster, they were declared proficient, and posted to 207 Squadron, RAF Langar, Nottinghamshire. The Heap and Welch crews finished their training around the same time and proceeded to 207 the day before the Trimble crew. On their last night, 9 August 1943 the Trimble crew celebrated late into the night in the closest pub, happy that they were heading off to operations with the Heap and Welch crews, but somewhat apprehensive about what the future held. Everything they had heard about operational losses to date told them that their chances of surviving a tour of 30 ops was slim, and the most dangerous period would be the first five or six ops when they were still inexperienced.

Early next morning, the Trimble crew, most nursing hangovers and awaiting transport to RAF Langar, were quietly drinking tea at the NAAFI. Vic gestured to them to gather around, and spoke seriously.

"Ok, fellas I just want to lay some ground rules for us as a crew. As I see things, the best chance we have of getting through a tour is to be in tip-top condition for flying, to stick to our training and to work together and support each other. Looking at us all now, I wouldn't want to be taking a kite up. So, whilst on ops I want no heavy drinking, no carousing. We get leave every six weeks so we can play up then. On the squadron it will be drills, practise and concentration on the job. I need you all to agree so that we are in it together. OK?"

The six others glanced at each other and nodded assent. Jack Lawrence spoke for them all.

"OK, skipper, we're all happy with that. After last night I couldn't face the grog for six weeks anyway."

Vic, only a flight sergeant (Flt Sgt) but the crew captain, looked over questioningly at Fl Off Arthur Herriott, their navigator. Arthur gave one of his cheerful grins and nodded his head in agreement. "OK skip, we're all in".

Shortly afterwards a WAAF corporal appeared in the NAAFI and shouted "All those for Langar, the bus is ready". Just 30 minutes later, the novice aircrew were dropped at their first operational station and allocated accommodation before being issued with the flying kit appropriate for their various roles. Artie Heap and John Welch had arrived the day before with their crews and the two pilots had just that morning arrived back from the previous night's raid on Mannheim, where they had tagged along as second pilots with two senior crews to gain experience.

Before lunch, the Trimble crew dropped into the crew room and discovered that Vic was scheduled to fly that night to Nuremberg as second pilot with Flight Lieutenant (Flt Lt) Ebert. Arthur Herriott was down to fly as second navigator with Plt Off Stephens and Jack Lawrence named as rear gunner with Sgt Moulton-Barrett. Three of the seven crew were to start their war immediately and that night they flew to Nuremberg on their first op. With low cloud over the target, the anti-aircraft fire (flak) was inaccurate and with few night fighters around, all 12 of the 207 Squadron Lancasters returned to base around 5.30am, some seven hours after take-off. For the three novices it was a relatively gentle introduction to night bombing over Germany.

Despite little sleep for the three who had been on ops, the Trimble crew were up the next afternoon carrying out a night flying test prior to another four hour cross-country bullseye night flight. After successful completion of their second bullseye, their names were chalked up on the board the next day, along with Artie Heap's crew, as one of the 13 crews to carry out the night's op to the distant target of Milan, a flight of some eight hours. They gathered in the crew room in late morning to carry out another night flying test in aircraft EM-T (T-Tommy)[2], all keyed up for the preliminaries of their first op together.

12 August 1943.
207 Squadron operations log:
Lancaster W4952 - I - EM-T pilot: Trimble - crashed on landing, Langar - all safe -: SOC (struck off charge) 23.8.43.

This succinct squadron Operational Record Book (ORB) entry three days after the Trimble crew were posted to B Flight 207 Squadron at RAF Langar marks the shaky beginning of a tour of ops for the crew. It was the first of many times their lives could have been cut short.

A mere 72 hours after joining an operational squadron they all walked away unharmed from overshooting the runway and flipping a Lancaster Mark II into a farmer's shallow pond following an otherwise uneventful night flying test flight. The aircraft T-Tommy was "struck off charge" (written off) after Vic did the unthinkable by landing downwind and running out of runway. The event showed that the crew still had a lot to learn to become fully proficient. Vic's logbook contains the signed admonishment entry by the flight commander of "Gross Carelessness", whilst the ORB entry "all safe" has a ring of relief. The Trimble crew thus had an inauspicious start to ops, missing their first scheduled bombing op. That night it was Artie Heap's crew who flew to Milan and completed the first full op of the three Aussie led crews, but with Jim Seddon in the mid upper turret replacing a sick Fred Tunnicliff. Jim Marles replaced the normal flight engineer in the crew of Flt Sgt Hall and successfully returned from his first op. So now four of the Trimble crew had completed an op before their tour as a crew finally kicked off officially.

The crash landing was at least the second of the nine or more lives that the mid upper gunner Roy used up in his 72 years. Fifteen percent of the RAF bomber aircrew who died did so in training accidents, so the least lucky aircrew members were those who did not even get to the starting line of an operational tour that usually consisted of 30 ops. In addition to the many training flights across country in day and night conditions, flight

---

[2] Lancaster a/c codes require an explanation. Aircraft were given unique numbers by the factory (eg. W4952 for the Lancaster they wrote off) and also coded by the squadrons with letters of the alphabet. The code letters for 207 Squadron were EM, so EM-T is termed T-Tommy for radio communication. After W4952 was destroyed, another a/c would have been designated T-Tommy. 463 Squadron code was JO, so JO-U was U-Uncle.

tests, gunnery exercises and practise bombing runs, two or three major hurdles were placed in front of new crews before their first op. One of these was a final fighter affiliation flight, where typically a Spitfire would simulate attacks to put the gunners through their paces and the pilot through evasive manoeuvres like the "corkscrew", an evasive action that doesn't take too much imagination to envisage. From the gunners' point of view, the major issue was working out the correct deflection during such manoeuvres so that they optimised the chances of hitting an attacking fighter by firing at where it would be when the bullets arrived. Deflection shooting was tricky enough in level flight but in a corkscrew required a great deal of practise to have any chance of success.

Another hurdle was the "Nickel Raid" which consisted of flying over Europe and dropping propaganda leaflets, usually on lightly defended French, Dutch or Belgian cities. The last hurdle was the "bullseye", a complex night navigational exercise of longer duration to simulate the problems faced by crews on an op. The Trimble crew completed two of these prior to ops but one of these that went amiss at Waddington, some 4 months after the Trimble crew finished their tour of ops, best describes the process and the obvious dangers in training.

Lancaster PD259 of 463 RAAF Squadron took off on a final night flying exercise prior to the crew starting ops. The exercise was a typical one that consisted of flying north west from Lincoln and over the Irish sea with two way points in Northern Ireland before heading to the north of Scotland and then proceeding back to Waddington south over the Cairngorms. The pilot, Fl Off Robert Beddoe, had already carried out 10 hours of night flying as a second pilot and the crew were highly regarded as proficient. They had transferred into 463 the day before from 83 Squadron. After the crew took off from Waddington, a depression west of Scotland moved east causing severe rain and thunderstorms in Scotland, weather that the crew were not accustomed to flying in. Their relatively straightforward flight went terribly wrong as they flew through the inclement weather over the Cairngorms at a briefed height of 25,000 feet and for reasons unknown their Lancaster broke up in mid-air and crashed. The wreckage was distributed over a large area of peat bogs near Kingussie, Scotland. All the crew, consisting of six Australians and one Scot, were killed.

The crew were an unusual age distribution given the average age of 21/22 for Bomber Command crews with three 21 year olds, one 23 year old and three members over 30, with the Scottish flight engineer a 37 year old. Even in the latter half of 1944 when the majority of new aircrew arriving at 463 Squadron were Australian, the flight engineer was invariably British because there was very little flight engineer training carried out outside the UK, with around 90% of flight engineers consequently being British[3]. The other six crew members had made the arduous wartime journey from Australia along with around 10,000 other Australians in order to fight with Bomber Command. After many months of training as pilot, flight engineer, navigator, wireless operator, bomb aimer, mid upper gunner and rear gunner the seven crew of PD259 had come together to take part in what was already an intensive bombing campaign.

Because of the remoteness of the crash and lack of resources during wartime, the Lancaster debris was simply gathered together and buried in the peat bog in order to prevent any over-flying aircraft from reporting an old crash. The six Australian crew, three of them married, are all buried in the Cambridge city cemetery, whilst the Scots flight engineer[4], is buried at Rutherglen, Lanarkshire. The quick burial of the wreck resulted in accidental preservation of the remains, which led to an expedition in the early 21st century by an RAF team to recover the parts. Consequently, a partial reconstruction of the aircraft can now be viewed in the Heritage Centre at RAF Waddington where the Australian squadrons 463 and 467 were based from late 1943 to 1945. Close to the crash site there is also a memorial consisting of a plaque and a single bent mounted propeller blade from one of the four Merlin engines that powered the Lancaster bomber. Navigator Frederic Walker was married just before leaving Australia and a child who was born after his departure from home was destined never

---

[3] In addition to the British flight engineers, a large number of other aircrew were not Australian. Numbers for 463 Squadron are not easily available but from 467 ORBs in November 1943, 82 of the 221 aircrew (37%) were Australian. In December 1944, 208 of 301 aircrew (69%) were Australian. The ground crew numbers for 467 were more consistent through the war with around 21% being Australian. There was also an average of around 50 WAAF personnel on 467 Squadron at any time.

[4] The Australian crew were: Flying Officer Robert Beddoe (21), from Elsternwick, Victoria; navigator, Flight Sergeant Frederic Walker (32), St Ives, NSW; mid upper gunner, Flight Sergeant Stanley Abbott (21), Cottesloe, West Australia; wireless operator, Flight Sergeant Terrence Dent (21), Walkeston, Queensland; rear gunner, Flight Sergeant Bevil Glover (23), Malvern, Victoria, and bomb aimer David Ryan (30), of Fairfield, Victoria. WO George Middleton (37) is buried at Rutherglen, Lanarkshire.

to meet his father. When as an adult that child found an old trunk in the attic after his mother's death, he discovered for the first time in his life evidence of his father's life. He subsequently visited Waddington and thanks to the efforts of the Heritage Centre people there learnt the tragic fate of his father and the rest of his crew[5].

Vic Trimble was diminutive enough that he had trouble reaching the foot pedals of a Lancaster, a shortcoming that his crew reckon partly contributed to flipping T-Tommy into the pond and made for many more "interesting" landings through training and over a full tour of ops. Vic and his crew arrived at Langar just after the major attacks that had focussed on the industrialised Ruhr valley region of Germany, or "Happy Valley" as the crews ironically called it, tailed off. In most history books, this is termed the "Battle of the Ruhr" and it was a period of high losses for Bomber Command. Their arrival was a couple of months prior to the start of the "Battle of Berlin" where the German capital, a difficult and distant target, was the major focus, so their tour of duty was carried out during the period of highest losses for Bomber Command. The whole crew were lucky enough to survive their Bomber Command tour in these grim high casualty 1943/44 days of World War 2, and smart enough to draw the line at one tour, so they all lived to generate new lives and new individual stories. Being a nerd who spent many years teaching kinetics to chemistry students, I could simply apply first order decay to work out the statistical chances of their operational survival from the average rate of aircrew losses. That seems rather impersonal, given that every one of the more than 125,000 Bomber Command aircrew were individuals who had a slightly different chance of survival.

For Roy (Mac) the main guiding thread of this book, the statistical chance of survival taking into account the 29 possible ops he carried out results in a 25.5% chance, so around a one in four. Given that 15% of those that died did so in training this further complication in the maths makes it around 22% so closer to one in five, and anyway Roy was always known in the Aussie vernacular as a "lucky Pommie bastard" when he wasn't a "bastard Pommie". Given that his last two ops were statistically the most dangerous at 8.9 and 11.9% loss rate he had an almost one in ten chance of not finishing either of those last two ops. Maybe that contributed to the decision by the Commanding Officer of 463 Squadron,

---

[5] Many thanks to John (Jimmy) Tarbox of the Waddington Heritage centre for leading me to this story and for the RAF for allowing me onto RAF Waddington.

Wing Commander Rollo Kingsford Smith, nephew of the more famous aviator Charles, to decide 28 or 29 was good enough for a full tour and so demonstrate to the squadron that it was actually possible for 463 crews to survive. Towards the end of this difficult period of heavy losses all crews who had completed over 25 ops were reviewed with the aim of determining which crews should finish their tour early. As well as a finishing crew being good for morale, experienced aircrew were desperately needed for training the increasing number of new crews, so some experienced crews were withdrawn early at this stage of the campaign. Apparently there were not enough crews finishing to fill the increasing need for training roles.

Maybe it was all down to continuous random chance anyway but perchance Rollo's decision alone made this book a possibility and this "little Pommie bastard" and his brothers Aussies. Anyway, thanks Rollo for that decision and thanks Vic, Roy and the rest of the crew for being smart enough not to take up the offer of a second tour with the Dambuster Squadron, 617 Squadron. 617 being the specially trained squadron that undertook the famous daylight raid on the German dams in May 1943 and became one of the specialist squadrons of the RAF, undertaking many dangerous ops. Experienced crews were often invited to join them. Many did and despite the high losses at 617, some survived!

After many years of trying to sweep Bomber Command and its actions under the table[6], attitudes have at last changed and the 125,000 aircrew of Bomber Command, including some 10,000 Australians, are commemorated with a memorial at the end of Piccadilly in Green Park, London. The 55573 (updated to 57862 in 2018) killed, were remembered

---

[6] At the end of the war, there was a change in attitudes to the wartime activities of Bomber Command brought about mainly by the famous raid on Dresden in February 1945. This raid was used like a political football, firstly as the war drew towards a conclusion and then during the cold war. Despite overseeing the strategy, Churchill and other political leaders essentially disowned Bomber Command and sheeted the blame to its leader Arthur Harris and by default the aircrew. The treatment of the aircrew has parallels in the treatment of Australian Vietnam veterans after their return home. Numerous books have been written from all sides about the strategy of Bomber Command and its successes and failures. Since the dismemberment of the Soviet Union and the opening up of more archives, there are now more balanced views and I recommend Frederick Taylor's book "Dresden" Bloomsbury publishing, 2004 for a balanced historical perspective on the subject of Dresden.

through 55573 red poppies dropped from the RAF memorial flight Lancaster on 28 June 2012, the day of the memorial dedication. The aircrew who died are remembered on headstones of Commonwealth war graves scattered throughout Europe, in British cemeteries or named on the RAF memorial at Runnymede alongside other air force personnel with no known grave. The Australian air and ground crew who died are also commemorated at the Australian War Memorial in Canberra. As of 2018, some of the experiences of both lost and surviving crew, ground staff and family members are recorded at the International Bomber Command Centre (IBCC) in Lincoln.

Around 34,000 aircrew completed a tour of ops, so there are more than 34,000 stories to relate about survival, success, failure and together they might tell where a part of the baby boomer generation came from. Of the *ca* 10,000 Australians who flew with Bomber Command 3486 died and *ca* 6600 survived. I hope this book helps to fulfil in part the wish of the surviving air and ground crews of 207 Squadron who served at RAF Spilsby. At the site of Spilsby airfield, the only evidence of their presence during World War 2 is an old hangar still used by a farmer and a difficult to locate memorial area with a stone that simply says:

"REMEMBER ME FOR I WAS HERE"

Fig. 1. RAF Spilsby Memorial – June 2018.

2   NANCY'S WAR

On the night of 14 August 1943 the Trimble and Welch crews carried out their first ops, an 8.5 hour trip to Milan and back. This was the second of three consecutive raids on Milan over three nights and the one that had the lowest loss rate. Only one of 140 Lancasters was shot down. On the third raid the following night, the Lancasters were attacked on the way home by German fighters over France and seven of 199 shot down. One of these was a 207 aircraft. This 3.5% loss rate was still low when compared with raids on German targets because the Italian cities were not as well defended as those in Germany. The Trimble and Welch crews both successfully completed this second Milan raid. Apart from an extremely long flight time and the gunners experiencing the intense cold for the first time, the op was relatively trouble free with light defences and a scenic trip high over the Alps ensuring their first raid was a gentle introduction to ops over enemy territory. The flak (anti-aircraft fire) was slightly heavier than during the first Milan raid.

14/15 August 1943 Milan
As a critical industrial centre of Italy, Milan was the target of continuous carpet bombing during World War 2. The city continued to be heavily bombed even after Marshal Pietro Badoglio surrendered to the allied forces in 1943, due to Milan being an integral part of Mussolini's Italian Social Republic puppet state, an important command centre for the German Army and a centre of heavy engineering. When the war in Italy was finally over on 25 April 1945, Milan was heavily damaged and entire neighbourhoods in the vicinity of the engineering works

such as Precotto and Turro were destroyed. After the war, the city was reconstructed and has again become an important financial and industrial centre of Italy. More than 30% of the buildings were completely destroyed and another 30% were so heavily damaged that they were demolished in the first years after the war. For the most part those buildings were located in the city centre and hundreds of historic buildings built over the previous 1,000 years were lost[1]

At an age when your average baby boomer or millennial had not long left high school, Roy was taking off on his first op as a mid upper gunner, perched in the top turret of a Lancaster bomber bound over the alps for Milan. He was to spend more than eight hours searching the dark sky for night fighters whilst confined to a tiny turret with his ears assailed by the unforgettable drone of four Merlin engines and in freezing conditions. Like most of his generation who fought in the war, he would never declare his feelings, fears, and desires when confronted with his World War 2 role. If the subject came up, and it rarely did, he would quickly deflect the topic onto stories about general life on an RAF base, mateship with the rest of the crew and the fun times that were part and parcel of air force life. Stories such as gifting laxative chocolates to other crews, going on leave with Jack Lawrence, travelling around wartime Britain by train and descriptions of the idiosyncrasies of some of the aircrew that he met.

The only time in my presence that he voluntarily introduced the topic of World War 2 was the occasion of a visit to Werribee Park, Victoria in the 1980s. The park is close to Point Cook airfield, the original home of the RAAF, where on some weekends classic World War 2 aircraft take part in air displays. As we admired the beauty of the Werribee Park rose garden a rumble could be heard in the distance and Dad gave a start "that is a Merlin engine, it's got to be a Mustang." Sure enough, a Mustang flew over shortly afterwards and Dad admired the aircraft and the engine noise, which he declared he could never forget. Listening to his occasional wartime descriptions as a child the impression that the ops he carried out

---

[1] The descriptions in bold of targets and operations throughout the book are derived mainly from the Bomber Command war diaries and supplemented from squadron ORBs and other records. Milan bombing general info derived from multiple web resources. See https://en.wikipedia.org/wiki/Bombing_of_Milan_in_World_War_II for greater detail.

were almost incidental to an easy-going air force life could have been an easy take home message.

Dad's stories and what he did not vocalize, did however spark an interest that led me into reading and re-reading in the 1960s every book on World War 2 air warfare available. Despite the glorification of the subject matter in books such as Paul Brickhill's "Reach for the Sky" and "The Dambusters" and the straightforward storytelling of Guy Gibson's "Enemy Coast Ahead", there were other books that encouraged a young mind to think more clearly about the effect of air warfare on the aircrew and the general population. Books such as Russell Braddon's "Cheshire VC", Don Charlwood's "No Moon Tonight", Ivan Southall's "They Shall not Pass Unseen" and Geoff Taylor's "Piece of Cake". These latter books raised the possibility that most aircrew must have been nervous, apprehensive, fearful and downright shit-scared. That the majority of them overcame these feelings to clamber time and time again into those compact metal boxes and follow through with each op, is possibly to the present young generation difficult or almost impossible to comprehend. An early baby boomer close enough to the times and with an interest in exploring 19th and 20th century history and social structure can possibly better place it in context and gain some limited understanding. I doubt whether reconstructions of the times on TV[2] placing the grandchildren of World War 2 veterans into Lancaster bombers or subjecting family groups to World War 2 conditions in "unreality" TV shows can succeed in doing the same. For the latest generations, at least such programs provide an avenue to encourage them to think about it all, wonder at how their forebears handled it, and place the history in an understandable context.

The fine details of how the original Trimble crew got together remain in part a mystery, but in the earlier days of Bomber Command the British had a policy of mixing Australian/Canadian/New Zealand and other Commonwealth aircrew with British aircrew and were reluctant to allow dedicated RNZAF, RCAF, RAAF squadrons to be formed. All three Dominion governments signed up to the Empire Air Training Scheme (EATS) where thousands of aircrew were trained in Australia, Canada, New Zealand and Rhodesia (now Zimbabwe) and then loaned to the RAF for the duration of hostilities. Normally a basic crew would get together at an OTU where a pilot would select his crew by finding out who he could get on with and who seemed to know what they were doing. The usual process was apparently to simply place all the prospective crew members together in a hall and let them sort it out themselves. Somewhat

---

[2] TV series: Bomber Boys: The Fighting Lancaster (2005–).

akin to the process at those terrifying teenage dances that persisted well into at least the 1970s where the males were expected to ask the girls they had never met before to dance. Make a bad decision and both parties were in for an awful night!

Vic Trimble must have chosen well and one imagines his first and obvious selection was his fellow Queenslander Jack Lawrence, the eventual rear gunner who arrived at 14OTU the day after him and shared the same mess. As one might expect, the RAF crew were a mixed lot with Arthur Herriott, the 22 year old navigator, who had been a government officer in South Shields, being the only officer until Vic was commissioned after a few ops. Apparently Arthur was better educated and spoke with a refined accent so under the British system of the time - officer material. On most training courses, the dux of the class became an officer, so it may simply have been that he was an excellent navigator and came close to topping his course. The other successful trainees all became sergeants, the normal minimum rank for trained aircrew. At the start of the war many aircrew were lower ranks and messed with the ground crews and station staff. It became apparent though that there was too much critical information being shared and so for security reasons all aircrew were given ranks that allowed them into the Sergeants' or Officers' messes and thus kept operational information more tightly guarded. The Canadian government tried unsuccessfully to go a step further and ensure all aircrew were of officer rank, reasoning that all aircrew took the same risks.

The flight engineer Jim Marles, hailed from Banbury, Oxfordshire where he was an estate worker and electrician on the staff at Broughton Castle, the ancestral home of Lord Saye and Sele[3]. The bomb aimer was Bill Aldworth, recently married, from Wandsworth, London and the wireless operator, Ron Nixon, from Hetton-le-Hole, Durham. Roy was an eagle-eyed, gangly youngster with great powers of concentration so would have possibly been a natural selection for pilot Trimble as mid

---

[3] He is a contemporary of the 21st Baron Saye and Sele, the fantastically named Nathaniel Thomas Allen Twisleton-Wykeham-Fiennes, who shortened the last bit to plain Fiennes – what a pity. I had the enjoyable experience of meeting Lord and Lady Saye and Sele whilst being shown over Broughton castle by Jim Marles in 2009. They were welcoming and completely down to earth with Lady Saye and Sele clad in what looked like hand me downs, while up a ladder changing a light globe and offering tea and cake. Jim and the Lord have known each other from an early age, first as playmates, then at school and eventually as ex military when they both returned to Broughton after the war. The lord was a major in the rifle brigade.

upper gunner when they had to select one at OTU. Trimble's approach to surviving the war was to optimize efficiency so he often had his crew undergoing training whilst many others relaxed. From all reports the crew carried out countless numbers of aircraft evacuation drills and dinghy drills where the time required had to be minimised to optimize survival. Each crew member had specific positions and roles that had to be completed in order, so drilling was the best way to ensure everything went well in an emergency. This rigour contributed, I am sure, to his crew surviving the first few ops whereas many inexperienced crews perished. Vic obviously believed in optimizing their chances of survival whilst many other crews just rode the statistics.

The easy relationship formed between the laconic Queensland rear gunner Jack and Roy, the miner's son from Durham, was to have a profound effect on my life and that of my brothers, three little Pommie bastards who became Aussies. The Trimble crew had close companions in the Heap and Welch crews, who had formed in a similar manner with the rear and mid upper gunners of the three crews, like Trimble and Heap, training together. It is highly probable that the flight engineers, who all arrived at the HCU the same day also already knew each other and similarly the two English navigators, both flying officers trained in Britain. It would seem the fates of these 21 individuals were intertwined before, during and after crew formation.

This first op would have been a long introduction to operational duties with over four hours flying each way in the cramped conditions of a Lancaster high over the Alps to approach Milan and then reversing the journey to get home. It seems to have been uneventful compared with many ops at that time of the war with only one aircraft out of 140 lost. Despite the long distance, Milan was looked upon as a slightly easier target with fewer fighter and flak defences than those experienced by the crews over Germany and a lack of fighter opposition whilst crossing the Alps. The bomb load was typical of this stage of the war with a 4,000 lb Cookie, designed to make a noisy destructive impact and cause structural damage and fear, accompanied by a major load of incendiary bombs designed to start fires by penetrating buildings damaged by the high explosives. For a new crew the successfully sighted target indicators (TIs) and the Pathfinder flares assisting navigation must have been a helpful introduction to ops.

The Bomber Boys TV programme[b] led indirectly to at least one insight into how my Dad and Mum (Nancy/Anne), and probably many others dealt, or rather did not deal, with their wartime experiences. The programme was aired in 2006 well after the death of my father but my mother watched it with a mixture of interest and reluctance. Nancy met my father just before he commenced his tour of ops, experienced almost six years of war in England and suffered bombings and strafing and all the deprivations of war. Despite this, after the programme she declared that at last she had some understanding of why my father could be short tempered and what was behind the many nightmares he suffered for years when he woke up in a sweat shouting "corkscrew, corkscrew". Corkscrew was the major bomber manoeuvre to avoid enemy night fighters and the gunner's main role in the aircraft was not to shoot down enemy aircraft but to sight them early and instruct the pilot over the intercom with "corkscrew port/starboard... now", the nautical terms being used ever since the development of aircraft. At this instruction, the pilot would aggressively throw the aircraft into evasive action. If the gunners actually engaged a fighter by returning fire then they were usually already in big trouble. The title observer/gunner originally used for this gunner role was probably a more appropriate term.

Mum had never asked Dad (or he didn't tell her) what his nightmares were about and it was the TV programme that at last informed her that the term was used when sighting a night fighter to get the pilot to take evasive action. This episode also gave me some further insight into how my mother dealt with her war experiences and with Dad, or rather how she could box those memories and experiences up, store them away and ignore them for so many years. Geez Mum if you had asked any of your sons (even me at 12 years old) they could have told you what "corkscrew" was all about and maybe made life a tad easier! Talking to my two brothers recently, none of us has any recollection of hearing Dad's nightmares, maybe not surprising for youngsters at the time. When we moved to Queensland in 1961 I slept in a room separated from my parents only by a double glass door and expect I would have woken up during his nightmares. I can only assume that by 1961 the nightmares had stopped. We three brothers all thought he was simply a volatile redhead with a heck of a scary way of getting mad when you had done something wrong in his eyes. I do not recall ever being clobbered by Dad, but those flashing green eyes and that scary fierce expression sure stopped me from pushing too many boundaries. My older brother Steve though seemed to lack the gene that allowed him to recognize Dad's flash points and he was often in trouble.

It was mainly in Mum's later years when she had lost interest in the current world that she started to reminisce about the exciting days of her youth. It certainly clarified in my mind that the years 1939-45 were the defining years of my parents' lives and nothing afterwards could match the excitement, fear, comradeship and general sense of purpose of the era. It also made me realize that the major reasons for our 1961 move from England to Australia were laid down in Bomber Command during World War 2. In her final decade of life, the subject of those war years and her remarkable memory for a lifetime of movies and music overrode any other subject that was introduced. Her ability to recall the names of even the bit actors in 1935-1970 B grade movies was amazing, and her last pleasure when subjected to almost total loss of vision and limited hearing, was to "watch" movies such as "Singing in the Rain". The DVD was merely a prop to stimulate her memory and so spend two hours of enjoyment in an otherwise difficult existence.

By the end of the war, Nancy, like many British civilians, had undergone a number of experiences with enemy aircraft, bombing raids, British bombers and armaments. In the early stages of the conflict, she lived in and around Sunderland, north east England, a major Luftwaffe target due to its shipbuilding capacity and heavy industry. Her father, William John Brown, was born in 1900 so was young enough to avoid the horrors of World War 1 but was conscripted in 1918 and became a member of the Rhineland occupation force in Germany. He became proficient in the German language and despite rules of non fraternization, gathered a number of German friends in Cologne during that period. His positive experience of the recent enemy instilled in him a belief that war was for the "bosses" and as a working man with no say in how the world operated he did not want to be caught up in any conflicts. In 1939 he was almost too old for conscription and was an electrician, so ostensibly in a reserved occupation that precluded him from military service anyway. Despite being an electrician, he had spent the pre-war years as a barman and then hotel manager in various towns and villages around Durham and surrounds. Early in the war he and his family (wife Hilda and daughter Anne/Nancy), lived above the Hendon Station Hotel beside the Sunderland docks where he was employed by a major brewery as hotel manager. He was also a volunteer firefighter, so was often busy during night raids fighting the resultant fires and rescuing casualties.

During early 1941 the family spent many long nights ensconced in the cellar of the pub listening to the unsynchronised drone of the German bombers overhead, the noise of anti-aircraft fire and the crash of bombs. After a while, like many others, they became tired of running down to the shelters and just remained tucked up in bed to let fate take its course. Nancy, 19 years old at the time, was employed at Binns, a department store in the town centre where she worked as a sales girl in the shoe department. Since leaving school at 14 she had worked in a dress shop and behind the bar in her father's pubs before moving on to Binns. On some evenings, accompanied by friends or alone, she would walk home from work through the bombing and continued to work at Binns until the Luftwaffe intervened more vigorously in her life.

Between 1941 and 1943 Sunderland was raided a number of times and the town bore the brunt of air raids on the northeast of England. The night of 10 April 1941 witnessed a particularly heavy raid that lasted through most of the hours of darkness. Nancy and a friend had decided to go to the movies that night, no doubt an American musical was playing, and the haunting wail of the air raid sirens interrupted the screening of the movie. The theatre management announced that the movie would continue for those who wished to stay, so Nancy and her friend settled down in the cinema rather than heading to nearby shelters or trying to struggle home in the short time before the bombing started. The movie soundtrack continued, accompanied by the crack of anti-aircraft fire, the pulsating drone of the engines of the German bombers and the explosive crashes and reverberations of bombing.

With the raid continuing late into the night, the projectionist simply started the movie again after it had finished and the manager announced that everybody could stay if they wished. At some point in the very early morning though, Nancy and her friend became bored with watching the movie for the second time and ran home through the bombing and debris in order to get some sleep before work. The falling bombs missed them and they managed a few hours of sleep before arriving at the Binns' building next morning to find a burning shell of a store. The Luftwaffe's incendiary bombs had destroyed their workplace and Nancy and her friend were now unemployed.[4]

At this stage of the war all civilians were under the control of the government so within a few weeks Nancy was conscripted/volunteered into the "Land Army" to help in farm production. She rather liked the look of such a job after seeing posters of smiling girls driving tractors and relaxing on the farm in the sun. The reality of farming life turned out to be rather different to the pretty poster pictures and she lasted less than two weeks in a role that required hard work carried out in extremely dirty conditions. She absconded from the job and declared later that she was "not suited to rural life!"

---

[4] The Binns store, which was the home store of a number of stores in the north of England and Scotland, was not reopened until 1953. Anne McNaughton did work for a short time in the Binns store in Darlington before starting work at Newton Aycliffe.

In one of the later Sunderland raids in May 1941, a parachute mine completely demolished a row of four houses in the street behind the Hendon station pub and her father "bailed out" of the heavily targeted Sunderland docks. After a period running the Kings Head hotel in Hetton-le-Hole just outside Sunderland, he was allocated to a position in a Royal Ordinance Factory at Newton Aycliffe near Darlington. According to Nancy, the parachute mines (often termed land mines) were particularly awful and unmistakable as they detonated with a massive noise. They were naval mines where a parachute slowed the descent, so that they remained above ground when they exploded. Typically, they had a clockwork fuse that lasted 25 seconds. Given that the above ground blast covered a large area, there was little chance of escape and the fearsome land mines could demolish half a street through blast effect. The dramatic effect of one detonating in the neighbouring street certainly convinced Jack Brown that there were safer places to reside than the Sunderland docks.

After extracting herself from the Land Army and leaving Sunderland Nancy became an "Aycliffe Angel", a munitions worker at the Newton Aycliffe factory where her father had also started work. She remained there until almost war's end and her job was to pack the shells into boxes and later to load cartridges into the ammunition belts. During the war a number of workers at Aycliffe were killed through accidental explosions, so it was by no means a safe occupation. Nancy spent a number of weeks off work with a badly burned face after an accident. The treatment was tannic acid jelly and bathing in bicarbonate of soda.

Darlington was a railway centre in a low valley and nearby Newton Aycliffe was in low boggy ground often covered in fog, a perfect place to sight a munitions factory. The Germans knew all about the factory and the importance of Darlington and Lord Haw Haw, the British/American traitor, often declared in his propaganda broadcasts that the "Aycliffe Angels" would be bombed. Despite attempting to raid both Darlington and Aycliffe a number of times, the Luftwaffe failed to find either and they were never successfully bombed. The worst accident at Newton Aycliffe occurred six days after the war ended, when eight people were killed in an explosion[5].

---

[5] The majority of the 17,000 munitions workers at Aycliffe were women. In Jacky Hyam's book "Bomb Girls" it is stated that the workers were strafed by the Luftwaffe but that the Germans never succeeded in bombing the factory. There is a report of a lone bomber that dropped a single bomb on the factory while it was under construction and one of the women workers recalls the

In Darlington, the Brown family moved into Mallard road, two doors up from the McNaughton family where she met the "young boy next door". When the "Gawky red headed kid" that she first noticed came home on leave the following year as a RAF gunner in a smart uniform, she gained a new appreciation of the "boy" who was 3 years her junior. They eventually married on 18 November 1944, well after Roy had finished his tour of ops. Just after their wedding day, they were staying in the upstairs room of a country pub when Nancy turned from the window to tell Roy about the pretty lights in the sky. She was shocked to be thrown to the floor by Roy, who had quickly recognised the tracer bullets emanating from a German Ju88 by now whizzing over the building. Either Nancy attracted trouble or these experiences through 1939-45 were common for the British civilian.

Nancy still had another major war-time event to experience. In the mid afternoon of an icy cold January day in 1945, on her way home from the munitions factory, she hopped off the trolley bus close to home in Darlington to hear the sound of an aircraft in trouble. A Lancaster bomber was low in the sky and seemingly heading straight for her. One of its wings was ablaze, the engines were obviously struggling and it was losing height as it flew towards the rapidly departing bus. As she ran towards home, she looked around and saw six figures leave the plane and deploy their parachutes. She was close enough to catch the eye of one of the crew as he floated down. The stricken aircraft roared over her head and she lay on the ground as the Lancaster seemed to hop over the last housetops of Lingfield Lane, the next street to Mallard Road, cartwheeled as it touched the ground and blew up in the field adjacent to the housing. The pilot was a Canadian, Plt Off William McMullen and one of the Lancaster's engines had overheated and started to burn as the crew returned from a cross-country training flight to the nearby RCAF air-base of Middleton St. George. McMullen stayed bravely at the controls as the crew bailed out and steered the plane away from the population centre of

---

planes overhead and having to go to the air raid bunkers a few times (https://www.bbc.co.uk/history/ww2peopleswar/stories/00/a8103700.shtml). Four workers were killed in a fulminate explosion in February 1942 and six in an explosion in 1943. Many others were killed or maimed and those working with TNT turned yellow. The explosions and deaths were kept a secret throughout the war, so determining exactly how many deaths and injuries occurred is not easy. Darlington did apparently have one bombing episode when in September 1940 a lone plane (probably lost) dropped incendiaries and high explosives on parts of the town. No one was killed or injured
(https://www.thenorthernecho.co.uk/opinion/latest/8407434.day-war-came/).

Darlington after the last man left the aircraft at just 500ft. The other six crew members survived baling out of the stricken Lancaster at a perilously low altitude. The town recognised McMullen as a hero and post war Lingfield Lane was renamed McMullen Road in his honour, with a memorial stone now located close to the crash site.

The following day as Roy and Nancy passed the Wheatsheaf pub, a favourite haunt of the Canadian aircrew, Roy, who was home on leave from Ireland, was granted a leave pass by Nancy to pop in and have a few beers with the six surviving McMullen crew members. No doubt he was aware of the need for the crew to debrief with a fellow Lancaster crewman, although he would not have expressed it like that. Besides, he enjoyed a chat and a beer, although a single pint would probably have lasted him the whole afternoon.

The other subject Mum would speak about was wartime rationing, which in Britain finally ended in July 1954. Luckily, unlike most at the time, neither of my parents smoked and they could trade cigarette coupons for food or clothing coupons to supplement those that were allocated to them by the government. My mother always declared that it was growing up in so many smoke filled, beer smelling pubs that turned her away from smoking and drinking. She could never abide the smell of fresh or stale cigarette smoke and stale beer.

3   PATHS TO BOMBER COMMAND

22/23 August 1944.
Leverkusen, situated on the outskirts of Cologne, housed the giant IG Farben chemicals factory, which was chosen as the aiming point for this raid. It was hoped that some of the bombs would hit this important industrial site. There was thick cloud over the target area and there was a partial failure of the OBOE signals. At this time Bomber Command were essentially trialling OBOE as a guidance technique with limited success. Bombs fell over a wide area; at least 12 other towns in and near the Ruhr recorded bomb damage. Three Lancasters and two Halifaxes lost, 1.1% of the force. The raid could only be described as a failure. Leverkusen was targeted twice more in 1943 with greater success.

COMBAT REPORT- Trimble crew
While in position 5106W 0617N on a course of 305°N at 0032 hrs at a height of 19,000ft one unidentified twin-engine enemy aircraft (E/A) was sighted on the port quarter down, at 700 yards; the enemy aircraft did not attack but as the Lancaster made a diving turn to port the mid upper gunner opened fire at 600 yards and closed at 400 yards when the E/A was lost.
No claims are made and there was no damage to the Lancaster as E/A did not open fire.
At the time there was no visible ground or searchlight cooperation and visibility was good with 10/10 cloud at 10,000 ft and half-moon.

This was one of a number of raids on Leverkusen over the course of the war, and was the first raid where the Trimble, Heap and Welch crews operated together, although MUG Fred Tunnicliff was still sick and replaced by a spare mid upper gunner. The three MUG mates had to wait another 24 hours to fly on the same op. Fred started his operational career with Artie Heap the following night on a raid to Berlin. On this raid on Leverkusen, the three crews took off one after the other and landed within 10 minutes of each other just under five hours later. The intelligence report of all three crews declared that the bombing was scattered and that the raid was not a success so even new crews seemed to know that the op had not gone well. On this second op for the Trimble crew an enemy aircraft was sighted, the crew's first interaction with the Luftwaffe. Despite the gunner's main job being to look out for fighters and instruct the pilot to take evasive action, which seems to have occurred, Roy also opened fire. This seems to have happened with the Trimble crew almost every time a fighter was sighted.

In 1943 there were two opposing schools of thought on the action to take when an enemy aircraft was observed. The top brass had the idea that an aggressive approach was best since it would scare off fighters and show the enemy that Bomber Command meant business. The more conservative alternative and textbook view was based on letting sleeping dogs lie so as not to disturb the fighter until it was apparent that the enemy pilot had observed your aircraft and was about to attack. On dark nights with high interception speeds, it was easy for an aircraft to pass close to another without observing it, or observing it too late to locate it again after flashing past. Hence the hope that the enemy aircraft would not be able to respond fast enough to be able to attack. Given the armament, speed and manoeuvrability advantage of cannon equipped night fighters, simply observing and watching it until it was obviously attacking was thought to give the optimum chance of survival. The official line was to allow each crew to make their own decision on which strategy to adopt. It seems that the Trimble crew were in the camp who believed in "have a go" and they opened fire on every occasion.

The first five to ten ops were the most dangerous, with inexperienced crews shot down at a much greater rate than for veterans. The Trimble crew escaped this first encounter with a fighter when they were still a green crew and it could count as cat's life number three for Roy.

27/28 August 1944
Nuremberg (Nürnberg), the city where the Nazis held their major political rallies, was the symbolic centre of Nazi power and an important manufacturing city for aircraft, submarine and tank engines. It was bombed numerous times from August 1943 to April 1945 and was the scene of many unsuccessful RAF raids

before it was almost totally destroyed in a January 1945 night raid which was followed up with daylight raids by the United States Army Air Force (USAAF). Hundreds of thousands of people were made homeless and thousands died. The marking for this raid was based mainly on H_2S. 47 of the Pathfinder H_2S aircraft were ordered to check their equipment by dropping a 1,000 lb bomb on Heilbronn while flying to Nuremberg. 28 Pathfinder aircraft were able to carry out this order. Nuremberg was found to be free of cloud, but it was very dark. The initial Pathfinder markers were accurate but a creep-back quickly developed which could not be stopped because so many Pathfinder aircraft had difficulties with their H_2S sets. The Master Bomber could do little to persuade the Main Force to move their bombing forward, because only a quarter of the crews could hear his broadcasts. Creep-back was a major problem caused by the natural inclination of the crews to let the bombs go as soon as they felt they were over the target. Given that they had to fly straight and level through night fighter infested skies with radar directed flak and searchlights probing for them it was an understandable inclination. 4.9% loss rate.

COMBAT REPORT Trimble crew
While in the target area, flying at 19,000' on an IAS (Indicated Air Speed) of 170 mph on a magnetic course of 354° three unidentified enemy aircraft were sighted between 00.57 and 01.00 hours.
The first was sighted at 600 yards on the starboard up and flew over the Lancaster. Both gunners fired short bursts.
The second enemy aircraft approached from the port quarter down. The rear gunner opened fire at 700 yards and the E/A sheared off.
The third enemy aircraft passed underneath the tail of the Lancaster from starboard to port. The rear gunner fired a short burst.
No claims are made for any of the attacks.
Each of the E/A carried a white light in the nose. At the time, visibility was good and there was no apparent ground cooperation.
MONICA was useless, owing to the number of enemy aircraft in vicinity, it was registering continuously.

The Pathfinder force consisted of experienced crews or crews who had excelled in training and were invited to join elite squadrons that were best able to identify and mark targets for the general bomber stream. They carried the most advance radar aids and the group leader was an Australian

Air Vice Marshall, Don Bennett. Generally, Pathfinder crews carried out 45 ops (including the 30 on their first squadron) although many did more than that. In addition to the airborne GEE and OBOE radar systems that were primarily designed as navigation aids, the Pathfinder force were mostly equipped with H_2S.

OBOE was the first aid introduced and used dual beams sent from a base station to guide bombers to their target and was accurate enough to use for blind bomb aiming. Because of the curvature of the earth, the range was limited, so although it proved useful during the Battle of the Ruhr, it was not useful for targets further into Germany and a different system was required. Additionally, OBOE relied on the radar beam being "reflected" from an aircraft so it could only handle a single aircraft, usually a high flying Mosquito to extend the range and fly above the German night fighters, who could also follow the beam.

GEE was originally designed as a radar based blind landing system that, like OBOE used the time delay between two beams to triangulate the aircraft position. Its range, like OBOE, was also limited to about 350miles, but the original beam emanated from the aircraft not the base, so the system could handle multiple aircraft. The OBOE system remained useful throughout the war because of its greater accuracy and because the British stayed a step ahead despite German jamming efforts. The GEE system however was successfully jammed over the target area by the Germans, so later in the war its primary purpose was to guide aircraft back to their base.

The H_2S system, unlike OBOE and GEE, consisted of a radar beam directed from the a/c at the ground so the return beam could be used to map the target area and directly control bombing by using it to drop marker flares with precision. The term GEE came simply from the use of a **G**rid in the technique, whilst the origin of the term OBOE was from the scientist who developed it. He thought the noise from the system sounded like that of an oboe. For security reasons none of the code words were meaningful acronyms that could give away the purpose of the systems. The origin of the term H_2S is controversial, but I prefer the explanation that somebody thought it stank so used the chemical symbol for the stinky hydrogen sulfide gas[1].

---

[1] See "Circumventing the law that humans cannot see in the dark: an assessment of the development of target marking techniques to the prosecution of the bombing offensive during the Second World War". Submitted by Paul George Freer to the University of Exeter as a thesis for the degree of Doctor of Philosophy in History in August 2017.

Two 207 Squadron aircraft did not return this night. One of those Lancasters was crewed by their good mates in the Welch crew.

Only three weeks after becoming operational the Welch crew were killed on their third op, the attack on Nuremberg. On this night the three Aussie led crews again took off within five minutes of each other but only the Trimble and Heap crews returned to Langar. Lancaster LM334 piloted by John Welch was shot down in the Nürnberg - Lohe area of Germany by Leutnant Johannes Hager of the II. / NJG1 night fighter wing. Hager was an ace with 48 kills. All the crew of four Aussies and three Englishman died and they are buried in the British and Commonwealth War Cemetery at Durnbach, south of Munich. Navigator Hugh McCulloch left behind a grieving widow, Marjorie. This was the Trimble and Heap crew's first experience of the loss of a group of close mates. At the post op intelligence debriefing they would have been aware that two aircraft had still not landed, one of them containing their mates, but would have hoped that they had landed elsewhere. On waking in the late morning, it would have been a saddening and sobering event when they discovered that their mates were listed as missing. After less than three weeks since arriving at Langar, four 207 crews had been lost. Facing up to the fact that the statistical chances of surviving 30 ops was extremely low, when an average of one crew was lost per op, would have been a daunting experience. The fact that John Welch was an excellent pilot would also have brought home the fact that the greatest ingredient for survival, especially in the early days on a squadron, was good luck.

Fig 2. The Welch crew – Durnbach CWGC cemetery, Sep 2020.

The reasons for these young men making their way into Bomber Command are many and varied, but the backgrounds and journeys of the Trimble crew are typical for the period 1943/44.

Family stories about Durham village life in the 1920s and 30s lead to a vivid image in my eyes of the local doctor arriving in the austere villages to attend to births, illness and deaths in a black Wolseley with huge headlights and running boards. It was well before the National Health system was introduced in the UK and knowing the impecunious state of the residents, he usually handed out sweets to the bairns and often exchanged his services for a freshly skinned rabbit, a bunch of vegetables or strawberries from the garden. It may be that too many 1970s nights absorbed in the TV version of James Herriot's "All Creatures Great and Small" has contributed to that image, primarily derived from family photographs and reminiscences, but given the time and place it can't be far off the mark. The bartering was a sign of the harsh living conditions and scarcity of ready cash, so entering the world as the second son of a coal miner working in the Durham mining village of Cornsay Colliery was a tough introduction to life. Roy was duly delivered at home on 3 May 1924 to Jack and Catherine (known as Reeney), examined the next day by the much revered doctor and pronounced fit and healthy. The doc was more than likely presented with a fresh rabbit and gruff thanks in an incomprehensible Durham dialect for his troubles.

In Germany at this time the Reichsmark was plummeting in value and Adolf Hitler was in Landsberg prison after his failed Beer Hall Putsch, dictating Mein Kampf to Rudolf Hess and detailing his evil intentions upon obtaining power. Not many people took much notice at the time and for most Germans the turgid Mein Kampf was unreadable when it became available in the bookshops. So, despite the clear direction of Hitler's intentions in Mein Kampf, he was allowed to move on with his plans and Roy and millions of others born around the same time were consequently destined for the battlegrounds. Hitler's activities also played a major role in my subsequent birth and that of my brothers as well as our conversion from little Pommie Bastards to Aussies.

Roy was one of five children out of eight to survive into adulthood, fairly typical numbers for the early 20th century. The eighth born, "little Eric", who had to be carried everywhere as a result of birth defects, died at the age of six and two girls, Irene and Mary, died soon after birth. Roy thrived on the village life until his early teenage years, learning to swim and tickle trout in the Browney, the local beck or river, attending the local village school, walking everywhere and keeping healthy on a diet supplemented with fresh garden vegetables, fruit and the home-bred rabbits. Early in life he used up one of his nine lives when one frozen winter he was propelled on a sled down the steep incline of a local street. The street crossed the main road at the bottom of the hill and little Roy lent back and gunned the sled down the hill expecting the road to be deserted, as it normally was in winter. To his dismay, a large truck was grinding its way slowly through the intersection and he went straight under the truck and out the other side. Luckily, the truck was struggling at reduced speed in the icy conditions so there was an element of control in the near disaster. This was the first of the many times that his life could have come to an abrupt end.

The meagre income of his father, a colliery hewer, was eked out by selling the garden produce as well as the seemingly constantly reproducing rabbits and cavies (guinea pigs). With money so tight, even at a tender age all the youngsters had to become proficient gardeners, a skill that kept Roy busy as school gardener between the ages of 12 and 14, and an interest that provided much enjoyment in later life. His first job as a young child was collecting dandelions to feed the rabbits.

Although the British education act of 1921 raised the school leaving age to 14, the skills of teachers in places like the Durham mining villages were limited, so for fast learners all knowledge was imparted long before graduation. With no thought or possibility of continuing education at secondary school, the lot of the smart kid was to continue at school as an unpaid gardener or become a truant until legally allowed to leave and start employment. Roy, at 12 became the school gardener and keeper of the school record books and accounts. These were simple and good days in Roy's memory, but for this baby boomer brought up on a diet of TV, another image derived from watching too many episodes of Monty Python pops up when considering his early life. The episode with four Yorkshiremen chatting about their penurious childhoods where they compete at to whose family was the poorest comes to mind "Aye, youse were looky, we wus so poor…"

For a 14 year old school leaver in such an environment the first job was of course with the mines where he joined others around his age and miners as old as 70 working away at the "Ballarat" seam. Even at this early stage of his life there seems to be an initial link with Australia, after miners returning from the Victorian goldfields of Ballarat who had worked the "Durham" seam in Victoria reciprocated in naming seams after their Antipodean forays. There was also a "Victoria" seam at Cornsay. Roy was the last member of his family to start life as a miner. His grandfathers were both miners in the Durham or Northumberland mines, as were most of his uncles.

In 1923, the year before Roy was born, there were 170,000 employed in the Durham mines and these numbers decreased rapidly between then and World War 2. The north east of England, with its focus on heavy industry, suffered more from the depression of the 1930s than most places in Britain, with shipyards closing en masse and the big engineering works slowing down. In Middlesbrough the completion of the Tyne Bridge in 1928 and the completion of the Sydney Harbour Bridge in 1932 for shipping to Sydney, saw large numbers of workers laid off from the huge Dorman Long steelworks. 1936 was the year of the famous Jarrow March with hundreds of workers from the Durham industrial town of Jarrow, where unemployment was a massive 80% after the shipyard and steelworks closed (Britain had 14% unemployment at the time), marching to London to protest against the social situation and demand jobs. The only booming industries in the cradle of the industrial revolution seemed to be the cinema and dance halls where large numbers of both were installed in the north east in the 1930s, so much so that in 1937 Darlington had more cinema seats per head of population than anywhere else in Britain.

The 1920s and 1930s were also the halcyon days of world record flying exploits and the greatest hero for English kids, and Roy, was the renowned Australian flyer Charles Kingsford Smith. In those days Australians were regarded by the British, and by themselves, as essentially British living down under and their triumphs had a major effect on English kids. Roy developed a strong desire to fly through the exploits of Charles Kingsford Smith and his posthumously published book "My Flying Life". This desire was reinforced by the appearance of aircraft at the local agricultural shows and fairs to provide joy flights, something that a miner's son could not afford. Little did he know that in a few years his commanding officer would also be a Kingsford Smith.

With their children maturing and all facing a bleak future with the slowing down of the mines, Jack and Reeney worked hard to achieve an alternate and better lifestyle and explored opportunities in the nearby market and industrial towns. They were on the ball there, with the Durham mines closing down completely in the 1950s long before "the Iron Lady" Maggie Thatcher forced an end to the British coal mines, so there was not even a grim future in places like Cornsay. Darlington, a market town on the Yorkshire border and a railway construction centre and transport hub was the choice for Jack and shortly after the outbreak of war, he acquired a job in Darlington with the London and North Eastern Railways (LNER) in their Darlington North Road workshop. Today the only remnant of this facility, which closed in 1966, is a small railway museum recalling the glory days of the first passenger railway in the world, the Darlington to Stockton line, containing Stephenson's first locomotive – "Locomotion" and celebrating the "romantic" days of steam locomotives and the long gone railway workshops. Other railway construction centres that were developed in the north east such as Shildon closed down in the 1980s and the Shildon workshops now contain a massive railway museum, part of the National Railway Museum complementing the even more comprehensive museum in York. Consequently, in 1939 at the start of World War 2 Roy was a 16 year old settling into town life in Darlington and working in labouring jobs at brickworks and roof tiling.

Around the same time half a world away in Cairns, Queensland Victor Herbert Trimble, born almost three years before Roy, had just finished high school at All Souls School, Charters Towers and at 18 had begun his working life as a clerk at the Cairns' branch of the New Zealand Insurance company. Vic was born in the small country town of Einasleigh, 450km south west of Cairns, Queensland. Shortly after his birth, the family moved to Mareeba, a larger town on the Atherton tableland, some 60 km inland from Cairns, and he attended the local primary school. His father, a successful local business man, could afford to send his children to boarding school, so Vic received a good education at All Souls. Like many Australians of his age, Vic had immediately joined the army at the outbreak of the war and was already a sergeant in the 51st Battalion, a militia unit based in North Queensland. Further south in Nudgee, Brisbane, John (Jack) Patrick McKenna Lawrence, 17 years old, had left school at 16 and was employed as an Engine cleaner and fireman on the railway system in Ipswich, Queensland.

Although the call up age for military service in Britain during World War 2 was 20, at the age of 18 males in the UK could volunteer for service in the RAF. Consequently in 1942 these teenagers turning 18 were the main source of aircrew recruits in Britain, all the eligible older members of society having already joined up for military service. Recruitment into the RAF Volunteer Reserve (RAFVR) had peaked in late 1940, a year into the conflict and Britain needed a new source of manpower to build the numbers required for air warfare. This need had been recognised even before the start of the conflict and EATS was set up at a meeting in Toronto in November 1939 to source aircrew from the Dominions. In May 1940 the first of the Australians under this scheme were sent to

Canada and by 1942/43 many of the new aircrew were starting to come through EATS, so large numbers of Canadians, Australians, New Zealanders and others from the Dominions were filling out the squadrons of bomber and coastal command. In Australia, there was an advertising and poster campaign with slogans such as:

This is a Man's Job – On To Victory – Aircrew wanted urgently.

Going Places? – How about YOU – RAAF Aircrew wanted at once.

The backdrop for these slogans was invariably a pilot in a fighter aircraft. The men the posters were aimed at were British by default and British by attitude and could volunteer at 18. Large numbers of recruits were attracted to the RAAF by the prospect of flying modern aircraft, being part of an elite, travelling to Europe and hopefully returning home an officer and set up for a good job, so there was also a long waiting list. Because of the waiting period and the long time in training, it was usually quite some time before they commenced ops in Europe. Australians and New Zealanders carried out their basic training and some aircrew training in their home countries and early in the war many were sent to Canada or Rhodesia for advanced training in the various aircrew musterings. The training scheme expanded as the war dragged on and in Australia the number of flying training schools increased from two in early 1940 to 26 in 1945, whilst the total number of RAAF schools of all types increased to 46. As the war progressed, the casualty lists from the RAF showed that the survival rate was horrifyingly low, but this did not deter the deluge of recruits.

Vic, although a sergeant in the militia, applied for aircrew and was eventually accepted for aircrew training. More than 80% of those who applied for aircrew training failed the rigorous medical, fitness and aptitude tests. After being sent home to wait for a position in the training program, he eventually enlisted in Cairns on 16 August 1941 and it was to be two days short of two years before he started operational flying. Vic was allocated the service number 414175, showing he was the 4175th Australian EATS volunteer of 1941. He was also typical of the recruits at that time, having a complete high school education and so strictly meeting the educational requirements for aircrew.

Like all Australian aircrew volunteers Vic enlisted for the duration of the conflict plus 12 months and being a Queenslander he was immediately sent to No. 3 Initial training school (ITS) in Sandgate (now in Brighton) a northern outer suburb of Brisbane, for two months of basic training, aptitude testing and classes in first aid, maths and air force law. At ITS around 15% failed the aptitude tests or exams so those that proceeded could indeed think of themselves as elite. By coincidence Roy, subsequently lived the last 7 years of his life in Brighton, Brisbane just 200 m from the site of this training base.

Having a good secondary school education and the necessary aptitude Vic was chosen for pilot training, promoted to leading aircraftsman (LAC) and transferred to No. 6 Elementary Flying Training School (EFTS) at Tamworth New South Wales (NSW), where prospective pilots underwent 50 hours of training on Tiger Moth open cockpit biplanes. The failure rate was up to 40% at that time but he was obviously pilot material and after almost four months of basic flying training was sent on to No 7 Service Flying Training School (SFTS) at Deniliquin further south in NSW for training on the Wirraway, an Australian built training aircraft. The 40% who failed the basic flying training and many others who failed the more advanced training were re-assigned and trained as air gunners, wireless operators, bomb aimers or navigators. At SFTS the student pilots started at intermediate level and moved on to advanced level with instrument flying, night flying, advanced aerobatics, formation flying, dive bombing, and aerial gunnery on the syllabus.

After only a month at Deniliquin at intermediate level Vic was posted to No. 3SFTS, Amberley, Queensland and stepped up to flying twin engine Avro Anson aircraft. After only a further three weeks, along with a fellow Queenslander, Arthur Heap, and a New South Welshman, John Welch, he was posted to No. 1SFTS, Point Cook, Victoria, the original home of the RAAF, for advanced training. The RAAF and RAF careers of Vic, Arthur and John were almost identical from this point on until part way through an operational tour with Bomber Command and they would spend the next 20 months mostly in each others company. The dates and postings in their RAAF records match almost exactly from being posted to 3SFTS until late 1943, apart from Vic being promoted to pilot officer on 13 July 1943, one day before Arthur, and John being promoted to pilot officer at the end of training in Australia.

John Welch (413918), from Newcastle, was 29 and had been working for a number of years as a salesman in the oil industry. Being older, he was an immediate candidate for officer. His above average flying ability and rapid completion of courses perhaps also contributed to him becoming a pilot officer rather than sergeant on graduation. One third of the graduating pilots were commissioned as pilot officers and the selection was based on maturity, skill and an interview system. The interview also favoured confident characters capable of self promotion so the cards were stacked against a quiet Vic becoming an officer.

Arthur Heap (414027), 20 years old and one of three brothers who all joined the RAAF, was from Esk, just outside Brisbane. He also had a secondary education and had been a government clerk in the Queensland State Government Insurance Office prior to enlistment.

By 26 July 1942, almost 12 months after joining the RAAF, Vic, Arthur and John had graduated as pilots and were ready for overseas service. It was to be around another 12 months before they started operational flying. By the time of his departure overseas, Vic had a "crime" on his record. He had been docked seven days' pay for being Absent Without Leave (AWOL) for 23.33 hours whilst based at Point Cook[2]. It seems the delights of nearby Melbourne kept him away for an extended period! John Welch had a similar charge on his sheet for AWOL. The three graduate pilots eventually embarked on 24 August from Sydney on the TS Westernland, a Holland-Amerika liner converted to a troop transport. The accommodation, as one might expect, was spartan and crowded. With the problematic transport situation during World War 2 it took Vic, Arthur and John until mid November to make their way to the UK. The route was a circuitous one, firstly to Perth where they embarked more EATS trainees, and then on to Durban before the ship was escorted to Cape Town. In Cape Town they spent two weeks billeted in tents at a transit camp in Retreat, just at the foot of Table Mountain. Here, whilst awaiting further transport to Britain, they drilled and exercised in the morning and explored the delights of Cape Town in the afternoons and evenings. After two weeks, they boarded the MV Highland Brigade, a former Royal Mail liner, and joined a convoy bound around the Cape to Liverpool via Freetown, Sierra Leone. The Highland Brigade then sailed independently to Avonmouth, the port of Bristol where they at last disembarked.

The three of them arrived at the No. 11 Personnel Dispatch and Reception Centre (PDRC) in Bournemouth on 18 Nov 1942 and from that point on were the responsibility of the RAF. They were three of 1123 Australian aircrew to arrive in November. Like many incoming aircrew, because of the large numbers of new arrivals, they then spent two months kicking their heels at the Metropole Hotel, enjoying the hospitality of the

---

[2] Many of the service records of RAAF personnel I have perused contain AWOL charges, so it seems the Australian reputation for not caring too much about discipline may be warranted. The AWOL episodes, whether for one day or a whole week, seemed to have absolutely no effect on promotion prospects.

English, attending dances, exploring the local pubs and the countryside, walking in the forests or along the beach front and finding girls. Later in the war when even larger numbers came out of the EATS scheme, some aircrew would spend up to six months at 11PDRC. Just a week after their arrival Arthur Heap, with his brother Edmund already in the UK with the RAF, managed to spend a few days in London to meet Edmund and explore the delights of the city.

No 11PDRC was set up specifically for incoming airmen from the Empire Training Scheme and gathered all RAAF aircrew, as well as Canadians, New Zealanders and other Dominion aircrew in hotels around Bournemouth. All who spent time there had fond memories of the English coastal town but also remembered the frustration of waiting, with two months the standard period of time spent there. German intelligence were well aware of this centre and in May 1943 a few months after Vic, Arthur and John departed, 26 German Focke-Wolf 190 aircraft carried out a surprise bombing raid on Bournemouth with the aim of killing as many airmen as possible. They destroyed the Metropole Hotel as well as many other buildings, killing close to 200 allied airmen residing in the Metropole. This raid and its results remained a state secret for a long time and it was not until 2013 that a memorial to those killed was erected on the site. Soon after the raid, 11PDRC was moved to Brighton, Sussex, again a coastal town with plenty of activities.

Vic and Arthur Heap were eventually posted together to No. 3(Pilot) Advanced Flying Unit (AFU), South Cerney just outside Cirencester in Gloucestershire, whilst John Welch carried out his advanced training at No. 15AFU at Leconsfield in Yorkshire. In a further coincidence, Roy spent 18 months living in Cirencester in the 1970s whilst working at the nearby Dowty aerospace industry. At the AFUs Vic, Arthur and John trained on Airspeed Oxfords, fast twin-engine aircraft that provided a stepping stone into flying either bombers or night fighters. After 10 weeks training at South Cerney both Vic and Arthur had many hours of flying under their belt on a variety of aircraft with Vic having 250 flying hours in his logbook when he was posted out. In addition to gaining more flying experience, the object of the training was to familiarize them with the vastly different English flying conditions. Rather than the blue open skies of uncrowded Australia, they had to contend with English weather, flight control systems for the crowded skies, instrument flying and many different navigational aids.

Vic was transferred to No 14OTU, RAF Cottesmore on 6 April 1943 accompanied by Arthur Heap and many of the rest of the course whilst John Welch was posted into Cottesmore from 15AFU on the same day.

Vic and Arthur had spent many months together training and socializing in the sergeant's mess, so were close friends by the time they were posted into Cottesmore. Being Aussies, John's officer rank would not have affected all three being close mates after so many months together. Vic had further blotted his copybook by losing his original RAAF pilot's logbook and required a new one, so unusually his logbook is an RAF edition rather than an RAAF edition. The Australian war memorial has a photograph taken on 6 April 1943 at South Cerney of 10 of the graduating pilots, including Arthur Heap. Of the nine identified pilots in the photograph only one survived the war. Vic, who was averse to having his photograph taken, believing it to be bad luck, was not in the photograph.

John (Jack) Patrick McKenna Lawrence, enlisted in the RAAF on 25 April (Anzac Day)1942, eight months after Vic and proceeded straight to 3ITS, by then in Kingaroy, Queensland, for the obligatory two months of basic training. Having completed fewer school years than Vic, he was selected for training as a WOP/A/G and progressed on to 3 Wireless and Gunnery School (WAGS) in Maryborough, Queensland. After five months of mostly WOP training at WAGS, he was posted to 3 Bombing and Gunnery School (BAGS), Evans Head in NSW for one month of pure air gunnery training using obsolete Fairey Battle aircraft.

Jack eventually embarked for the UK from Melbourne on 15 January 1943, arriving at 11PDRC Bournemouth two months later. In Melbourne, he was joined by a fellow trained rear gunner, Ken Glover of Hurstville, Sydney. Ken was a factory hand working for tobacco company W.D and H.O Wills before enlisting in the RAAF in December 1941, long before Jack. Ken had married just one week before joining up and had a daughter by the time of his departure for Europe. He had originally started training as a pilot and progressed to No 8SFTS before being rejected as a pilot and re-mustered for gunnery training.

By this stage of the war most RAAF personnel who trained in Australia travelled to England via the United States, so Jack and Ken travelled on the troopship USS Westpoint to San Francisco via Noumea. The Westpoint was originally SS America, a luxury liner built for a passenger complement of around 1,200. After conversion to a troopship, it held almost 7,700 troops so it would have been extremely crowded and uncomfortable. From San Francisco, along with other RAAF personnel, they enjoyed a luxurious Pullman train journey across America to Boston. From all reports, the individual sleeper carriages were a godsend after being squeezed into the converted cabins of the troopship. For a while, they cooled their heels at Camp Myles Standish, Taunton, Massachusetts and enjoyed the hospitality of the people of Boston before taking a train north to Halifax, Nova Scotia, Canada. From Halifax they crossed the Atlantic to the Clyde (Scotland) and were then transferred to 11PDRC Bournemouth.

WOP/A/G, Keeble Charles (Charlie) French, a 27 year old farmer from the small town of Northam, Western Australia arrived in Bournemouth two months before Jack and Ken and after eight weeks of specialist training was back at Bournemouth where the three gunners met up and progressed together through the Bomber Command system. Eventually the three of them were posted together to 14OTU, arriving at Cottesmore the day after Vic Trimble, Arthur Heap and John Welch. At this stage Vic, Arthur, Jack, Ken and Charlie were all sergeants so would have met up in the sergeants' mess and being fellow Aussies, probably stuck together. Unlike Vic and John, the others had all been good boys, or got away with being AWOL. Jack had taken almost a full year since enlistment to arrive at an OTU, so for an Australian gunner it took on average some eight months longer than a UK based gunner to start operational flying.

The operations record books of 14OTU show that all these Aussie mates would have missed taking part in a sports day to celebrate the anniversary of the formation of the RAF on 1 April and a "Wings for Victory" parade on 2 April. They would definitely have been part of the Anzac Day celebrations on 25 April, which were apparently "well received" by the Australian and New Zealand aircrew. The records proudly show that the station football team won the "Grantham Cup" for the third year in succession with an 8-2 result, most likely without the help of the Australians, who were more used to playing Australian rules football or rugby.

Soon after arrival, the process of crewing up began and all the new aircrew simply congregated in a large hangar for the day and sorted out who they would crew with. Vic and Jack eventually lined themselves up with three Englishmen: Navigator, Arthur Herriot; bomb aimer, Bill Aldworth; wireless operator, Ron Nixon; and the nucleus of five crew commenced the rigorous 12 weeks OTU training of a bomber crew on Wellingtons, flying out of the Cottesmore satellite airfield of Saltby. Their respective mates Arthur Heap and Ken Glover teamed up with another mate, Australian wireless operator Tony Boultbee, who had travelled from Sydney with them and also found themselves two other crew, Scottish navigator, Robert Gall from Edinburgh and an English bomb aimer, Daniel McCreadie.

John Welch found himself a number of fellow Australians. His chosen navigator was fellow officer Fl Off. Hugh John McCulloch, a 25 year old who had been a school teacher at the prestigious Caulfield Grammar School in Melbourne. He hailed from Ulverstone Tasmania, was in the militia prior to enlistment and had a BA degree. His medical grade had precluded him from pilot training but his education had ensured a quick route through to flying officer rank. McCulloch married just prior to leaving Australia. The wireless operator was Charlie French, and the bomb aimer Flt Sgt. Geoffrey Augustine Lynch, a 24 year old from the country town of Rochester, Victoria. The fifth member of Welch's crew was English rear gunner Sgt. Arthur Herbert Whetton, aged 32 of Hillingdon, Middlesex.

On 3 May 1942 Roy turned 18 and applied almost immediately for entry into the RAFVR as aircrew. He was following in the footsteps of his older brother Jack, who to avoid the prospect of being called up for the army had joined the RAF in 1938 when he turned 18. Jack spent the war in a ground-crew role ensuring aircraft were fit to fly and experiencing the loss of many aircrew who were friends. The selection boards looked at educational, psychological and physical attributes in their process and Roy, like his brother, would not have been selected for aircrew in 1938, because the educational level required by the RAF for aircrew had been an upper secondary school or technical school qualification. By 1942 man power issues had forced a change in this policy and the recruiting boards ignored the educational levels for otherwise good candidates. After three days of medical and dental examinations, eyesight tests, physical and aptitude tests at the Aviation Candidate Selection Board at Doncaster he was accepted for aircrew training and sent home to await instructions. Only around one in three candidates successfully accomplished the rigorous medicals and testing so he returned home to Darlington a very happy young man.

Many months later, just after Christmas 1942, a telegram arrived instructing Roy to report immediately to Doncaster. Hence, on the last day of 1942, after attending a final selection Board he enlisted in the RAFVR to become aircraftsman second class (AC2) McNaughton, 1590267. He was declared RAFVR medical grade I, recommended for training as an air gunner and medically fit for pilot, navigator or bomb aimer. Like all British and EATS volunteers, he had signed up for the duration of the war and was immediately presented with travel documents to proceed to No. 3 Air Crew Receiving Centre located at Abbey Lodge, adjacent to Lord's cricket ground, London. After a slow trip south by steam train he arrived at Kings Cross station, experienced his first trip on the London underground and arrived at Lords to join a large number of other raw recruits sourced from all parts of the UK. He was processed through what was by this stage of the war a very slick system, although as usual in the services, there were long periods of boredom and of waiting. Eventually he and 15 others were organised into a flight under the care of a corporal.

All the aircrew recruits rapidly received an extremely short haircut, numerous medical inoculations, uniforms, including the white flashes of a cadet under training, kit bags, their first taste of RAF discipline, and a lot of exercise in Regent's Park undergoing marching drill, running and calisthenics. Even at this early stage of training recruits mustered for air gunner were able to experience a working gunnery turret, which had been installed in December 1943 to complement the Link Trainers available for the pilots. The initial serious training was supplemented with copious amounts of entertainment and sport to help keep the recruits occupied and ensure that they were fit both mentally and physically. The unit's records at this time contain the many sports results for the month as well as details of concerts, films, lectures and dances along with records of courts martial, disciplinary actions and the capture of loose Italian Prisoners of War (POWs). Accommodation at Abbey Lodge was in very well appointed luxury flats in the area and the recruits messed in the Regent's Park Zoo cafeteria. For Roy and probably many of the recruits the food and accommodation was the best they had ever experienced. Roy and the others of his flight would have been given a copy of Air Ministry pamphlet 161, "You are going to be an air gunner", the first part of which describes the personal attributes that led to selection.

> *"You have been selected for training as an air gunner because, from what has been learned about you already, it is considered that you have the aptitude for this aircrew duty. It may interest you to know the points that have been borne in mind while your potential ability was being assessed. An efficient air gunner must have four main attributes. First a gift for rapid and accurate brain-eye-hand coordination; for in a matter of seconds he must be able to recognize an enemy aircraft, estimate its range by knowing its span and comparing it with the size of his ring sight, judge the position of the enemy aircraft in relation to his own aircraft, apply the simple rules of aiming, manoeuvre his turret to bring his guns to bear, and fire to hit the enemy. Second, he must be really fit, and have marked determination and fighting spirit. Third he must be able to keep calm and talk clearly to the crew-captain when his aircraft is in action. Fourth, he requires some mechanical aptitude for reasoning out, under difficult conditions, the causes of gun and turret faults and for rectifying them quickly.*

> *The interviews and tests that you have been through show that, after suitable training, you should be able to fulfil these requirements.*
>
> *When you become an operational air gunner the safety of your aircraft will, to a large extent, be in your hands. You will be the 'eyes' and the 'sting'. By your watchfulness you will be able to advise the pilot of the approach of an attacking aircraft; and then, for a few seconds, you may in effect be in control of the aircraft, for you tell the pilot what tactics he is to adopt. The task of the bomber aircraft, in which you are most likely to serve, is to reach the allotted target and to destroy it with bombs. If combat should develop, the complete success of the operation depends upon your watchfulness, and upon your skill in destroying or driving off the enemy.*
>
> *The object of this pamphlet is to prepare you for the training that you are to receive, to warn you of possible delays in training, and to advise you of the importance of each part of your training, no matter how trivial and unrelated to your final duty it may seem at the time."*

After 16 hectic days of being organised by the RAF in London, Roy was sent on to 14 Initial Training Wing in Bridlington, a seaside town in Yorkshire and a training centre specifically for air gunners. Here the aircrew were billeted in requisitioned houses by the sea, exercised and drilled on the seafront or in the parks, learned to shoot on the beach using clay pigeons as targets and sat through many lectures in various halls throughout the town. The prospective gunners also carried out dinghy drill in the harbour, swimming out with a Mae West life preserver, clambering in and out of dinghies in the cold water and then swimming back. The subject matter for study was contained in a 200 page standard RAF Notebook with chapters entitled: Air Navigation, Magnetism and Electricity, Law, Discipline, Administration and Organization, Hygiene and Sanitation, Definitions, The Principles of Flight, Airframes, Engines, Mathematics Problems for Revision. In the Australian edition (and I imagine the English as well) there was a special section: a 10 page simplified description entitled "Magnetism and Electricity for Gunners" replacing the challenging 123 pages and 30 lectures on the subject for other aircrew[3]. An inserted booklet on "How to learn Morse Code" was included. After four weeks of initial gunnery training at Bridlington Roy travelled north to No. 2 Air Gunnery School (AGS) at RAF Dalcross, Scotland, now Inverness airport, to be instructed in the more practical

---

[3] My thanks go to Doug Parry for giving me the RAAF edition of his training manual and other Bomber Command books. Doug was an air gunner on Wellingtons with Coastal Command and as of 2019 his memorabilia are presented in a display at the Melbourne Shrine of Remembrance.

aspects of air gunnery training.

At Dalcross, the raw air gunner trainees carried out Skeet (Clay pigeon) shooting to perfect aiming and timing, as well as instruction on static turrets and turrets on wheels or rails with ground-based moving targets. For Skeet shooting the machine guns in a turret were replaced with a single 12 bore shotgun and the gunners learnt to manipulate the turret and shoot. They learnt to strip and reassemble the .303 machine guns blindfolded, how to prevent and fix stoppages and were tested on simulators and moving targets. Eventually when declared proficient they were taken up for their first flight and a live firing exercise over the sea aiming at target drones, usually in a Boulton-Paul Defiant, an aircraft that first saw service in 1939 equipped as a fighter with only a rear firing turret. Soon after its introduction, it became apparent that although it was very good at knocking down bombers it was extremely vulnerable to German fighters and was withdrawn to take on the role of a night fighter. During 1942 a purpose designed night fighter, the Bristol Beaufighter, was introduced and the Defiants were relegated to target towing and air gunner training duties. They were powerful aircraft that could be thrown around the sky and when flown by the rather cavalier and bored training pilots invariably made most trainee gunners sick on their first flight. Most of the bored pilots were Poles who were more interested in fighting the Germans than flying trainee gunners. The turrets were equipped with cine cameras to record performance. In April 1943 purpose designed Miles Martinet target tugs were introduced and the Defiants started to be used as pure gunnery training aircraft. In the short period that Roy trained at Dalcross, a number of Defiants and Martinets were lost in accidents that also killed a number of pilots and trainees.

After successfully completing 68 Mid Upper Gunners (MUGs) course (part of No. 51 course) on 13 May 1943, some 18 weeks after enlistment, along with 15 others, Roy was presented with an A/G badge, promoted to sergeant and posted immediately to 14OTU, along with a number of others from 68 course. Looking through the ORBs of 2AGS, there was an average of around 85% graduation rate in this period of the war, although the exam marks for passing some elements were around the 40-60% mark to ensure that only the very inept failed. Out of 60 trainee gunners that started on 51 Course, 52 graduated as sergeant gunners. Roy, together with Fred Tunnicliff, from Brighton, Sussex and Jim Seddon from Worthington in Lancashire, travelled down to Cottesmore together and arrived at 14OTU Cottesmore some five weeks after Vic Trimble, Arthur Heap and John Welch had formed their crews. In the sergeants' mess they met the three Aussie gunner/WOPs and over a few beers were asked to join up with the Aussie piloted crews.

Being volunteers, aircrew could step away from the role at any time up to and including OTU, although remarkably few did so. Some found that the challenges of operational flying were not for them, whilst others had met a lifetime partner and reconsidered their future in the light of starting a family. A small number, despite the training system, were simply not suited to the role and were encouraged to withdraw. Once posted to a squadron, aircrew were no longer able to back out without the indignity of demotion to a menial job and a black mark against their name. Those that refused to fly on ops were labelled as "lacking moral fibre", and sent to Aircrew Disciplinary Centres for re-education. If they did not return to flying duties, they were stripped of rank and flying badges and either allocated menial tasks or joined the army.

Flying an operational bomber was a highly complex process which required a team of six, and later seven, learning how to combine as a crew until everyone was familiar with their role and capable of carrying it out automatically under extreme circumstances. Hence, there were a large number of repetitive exercises, particularly in navigation, fighter affiliation to learn evasive manoeuvres, signalling, cross-country flying, night flying as well as dedicated gunnery flights, high and low level bombing flights, dinghy drill and crash drill. The intense training was also dangerous, with an average of one flying accident per day according to the operational record books, with some of these fatal. The two most crucial crew members in training were of course the pilot, who was experiencing controlling a heavy multi-engine bomber for the first time, and the navigator, who could easily get them lost.

Vic and Arthur Herriott were a proficient team and on 20 June 1943 after around 85 hours of training on Wellingtons, the crew of six were sent on leave before starting the next stage of their training at RAF Wigsley and 1654HCU. The Heap and Welch crews were also declared proficient and transferred to Wigsley on the same day. The four engine bombers were much more complex than the twin engine Wellingtons and required a second person in the cockpit to relieve the pilot of some of the multitude of tasks. Early in the war, this was a second pilot but the luxury of those days had long gone and the second person was now a flight engineer, trained to take responsibility for controlling and monitoring the engines, aircraft systems, fuel reserves and if necessary to fly the plane in an emergency. The three crews each required a seventh member so they picked up three English Flight Engineers, Jim Marles from Banbury, Oxfordshire joining the Trimble crew, Bill Carter the Heap crew and Leslie Thomas Reynolds of Pontefract, Yorkshire the Welch crew.

Upon arrival at HCU all three crews were sent to No 5 Aircrew Commando School at Morton Hall to undergo three days of evasion training. The Heap crew of three Australians and four English/Scotsmen, the Welch crew of four Aussies and three Englishmen and the Trimble crew of two Aussies and five Englishmen were by now good mates after for most of them, months of travelling, training and socializing together. By the time they arrived at 207 Squadron and were assigned to B flight it was almost 12 months since Vic and Arthur had first met in Sydney and one week shy of two years since Vic had enlisted.

Fig. 3 Gunner Trainees and staff, 2AGS Dalcross, Scotland, Apr-May 1943. Roy McNaughton is second from the left.

Fig. 4. 68 MUG Course, 2AGS, Dalcross, 15 May 1943.

4 OPERATIONS OVER GERMANY

27/28 September 1943
Hannover: 678 aircraft - 312 Lancasters, 231 Halifaxes, 111 Stirlings, 24 Wellingtons. 5 B-17s also took part. 38 Bomber Command aircraft - 17 Halifaxes, 10 Lancasters, 10 Stirlings, 1 Wellington - lost, 5.6% of the force, and 1 B-17 also lost. The use by the Pathfinders of faulty forecast winds again saved the centre of Hannover. The bombing was very concentrated but fell on an area five miles north of the city centre. No details are available from Germany but RAF photographic evidence showed that most of the bombs fell in open country or villages north of the city.

1/2 October 1943
Hagen: 243 Lancasters and 8 Mosquitos. This raid was a complete success achieved on a completely cloud-covered target of small size, with only a moderate bomber effort and at trifling cost. The OBOE skymarking was perfect and severe damage was caused. Two Lancasters lost, 0.8% of the force.

COMBAT REPORT *Trimble crew*
In position 52° 23' N 05° 20' E at 20:58hrs, flying at 19,000ft on a magnetic course of 125° at an IAS of 160 mph an unidentified twin engine enemy aircraft, burning a white light in the nose, was seen on the port quarter, up, at 600 yards after a warning had been received by MONICA.
The enemy aircraft came in as though to attack and at 600yards a diving turn to port was made, both gunners opening fire until, at 500 yards the enemy aircraft

broke away to the starboard quarter down, without firing.
No claims are made.
Visibility was good above cloud and as previously stated, MONICA was working very satisfactorily.

Having been commissioned in July, Vic Trimble was now listed as Plt Off Trimble. On their fourth trip, a raid on Hannover, they did not encounter night fighters but were coned by searchlights, including a 200 cm master searchlight controlling three other searchlights to triangulate the aircraft position. Once isolated by multiple searchlights escape was extremely difficult and the radar controlled flak quickly focussed in on the single aircraft trapped in the multiple beams. The intense light beams also blinded the pilot and his crew, making control difficult. Often aircraft coned over the target where the flak was thick were destroyed, so their escape, which cost them 8,000 feet of height, can probably be put down to a combination of luck and the excellent flying skills of Vic Trimble. Hannover, the target, was an important rail, manufacturing and military centre which was bombed numerous times through World War 2 and was well within the range of even the early twin engine bombers. The day after war was declared, a lone Whitley bomber dropped leaflets over the city and major raids took place throughout the war. By April 1945, 90% of the city centre was destroyed, along with huge parts of the rest of the city.

The author ended up spending extended periods of time from 2007 in Hannover, carrying out research at the Gottfried Wilhelm Leibniz University, cycling around the city, drinking Hefeweissen bier in the Waterloo Biergarten and chatting to locals. From these many trips, it was apparent that the effects of the bombing still reverberated some 60-70 years after the war. The new Rathaus (town hall), an impressive castle like structure located in a pleasant garden setting and built during Kaiser Wilhelm II's reign, contains amongst other interesting objects, four detailed models of Hannover city at different times in history. The model of 1945, which consists of skeletal building remains and piles of bricks and rubble, brings home to the observer the massive scale of destruction brought about by combined RAF and USAAF bombing.

The only direct evidence now of all the World War 2 bombing is the Aegidienkirche, a bombed out church left as a memorial shell which also contains a peace bell donated by Hannover's apt sister city of Hiroshima. The "old town" centre, where the attractive and busy Christmas market now takes place, was entirely reconstructed using the facades of surviving buildings rescued from all over the city to complement the rebuilt "old" Rathaus (dating from 1410) and Marktkirche (market church), so appears at first sight to be an old medieval town centre. One of the oldest buildings is Leibnizhaus, the university guesthouse, where the façade dates back to 1499 and the building is named after the philosopher, scientist and mover and shaker of his times Gottfried Wilhelm Leibniz. The façade was simply transported from outer Hannover where it had survived the war with minimal damage. Leibniz played a major role in ensuring that the Hanoverian royals were installed as the royal family of England.

There are other occasional reminders of the destruction, with unexploded bombs often found when buildings are reconstructed or trenches dug. There are regular evacuations of parts of the city with the latest in May 2017 involving 50,000 people evacuated whilst a number of British bombs were defused. There was also a bomb removed from the airport whilst under reconstruction just days after President Obama's heavy 747 touched down on a section of rarely used tarmac containing that bomb. Any ensuing explosion would have been hard to explain if the bomb had gone off! In Linden, an up and coming trendy area near the university, a huge thick walled air raid bunker, still showing the scars of the war and now converted into flats, remains on one corner block. The construction is just too big and strong to remove economically and such huge rectangular monstrosities can be found throughout the major German cities. In Hamburg, a huge quadruple flak tower is one of the major landmarks that can be seen from the lookout at the top of St Michael's church tower.

During the war, various strategies were used to try to confuse or deter the bombers over Hannover and I found to my amazement on my first visit in 2008 that the physical chemistry building still had a black tar covered roof that was installed in 1941 so that light would not be reflected back to the British bombers overhead. The roof was eventually removed in 2016 when the building was finally modernised. The Machsee Lake, a huge artificial lake constructed by the Nazis in the 1930s south of the new Rathaus, was also covered in a range of artificial devices to disguise the lake's appearance and confuse navigation.

What the defenders could not disguise was the geometric layout of the Herrenhauser gardens, the English style Georgian gardens constructed by the Hanoverian electors north of the city and this remained as an easily recognised landmark. The royal family of England, direct descendants of the elector of Hannover and the head of the House of Braunschweig (Brunswick[1]), requested that the Herrenhausen Palace, the centre piece of

---

[1] The English and the RAF referred to the town as Brunswick and it is widely accepted. Braunschweig, the German name, has been used when in a German context. Hannover, the German spelling has been used throughout other than

the gardens built in 1640 not be bombed. However, as a result of the night carpet bombing carried out in World War 2 the palace was completely destroyed in 1943. If not for the rules of accession that demanded a male ruler preside in Hannover and so precluded Queen Victoria from the position, the RAF could have been bombing the royal family's own property. The Trimble crew certainly did not cause the extensive damage to the palace, given that on the night in question the bombs fell many miles from the city centre. The most damaging raid on the city took place the following month. The palace was reconstructed eventually between 2009 and 2013 and now again takes pride of place in the magnificent Herrenhauser gardens. Hannover is still well connected with England, evidenced by it being the rugby centre of Germany with the rugby pitches located just beside the formal Herrenhauser gardens – der Grosser Garten.

Other evidence of the RAF bombing is situated just to the west of Hannover where the Hannover Commonwealth War Graves Commission (CWGC) site contains the graves of around 2000 airmen killed in the surrounding area. This is one of the 31 CWGC sites in Germany and it is by no means the largest.

Fig. 5. Hannover railway station, Autumn 1945. (photograph taken by Margaret Bourke-White (USAAF). From Wikimedia Commons.

---

for Hanoverian.

Fig. 6. Hannover Air Raid Bunker – transformed into flats –Sep 2020.

The West German population of Germany have consistently been educated throughout their upbringing about the atrocities of Nazi Germany and the manner in which the Nazi party rose to power. One consistent message is that the German population were mostly complicit and that regardless of whether they actively supported the regime or not they allowed it to happen. Such ongoing education has had a profound effect on their attitudes to the allied bombing as well as on their general relations with the rest of the world and on their capacity to be proud of their country. It was not until the soccer world cup of 2006 in Germany that the German population felt comfortable enough to wave National flags and cheer wholeheartedly for their country and its anthem when most of those cheering were two or three generations removed from their World War 2 ancestors. The educated population have a much broader understanding of the history than the rest of the world and a better context for that understanding. It was reported recently on Australian TV that Lawrence Larmer, an ex RAAF pilot who flew Halifax bombers over Germany, wrote letters to the mayors of a number of German cities expressing regret and apologies for the innocent people who he may have killed in World War 2[2]. Nearly all of those mayors wrote to Larmer and

---

[2] https://www.stpats.vic.edu.au/old-collegians/legends-of-spc/laurie-larmers-

made the point that there was nothing to forgive and that the bombing was a necessary function of defeating the Nazis. They also pointed out how the German cities were regenerated after the war and how that was enabled and funded by the Allies.

If anything the Germans brought up in the West can be too apologetic. I once attended a conference in Wurzburg, a small city of virtually no strategic significance and with little industry that the RAF flattened in an incendiary caused firestorm on the night of 16 March 1945, not long before the end of the war and only three weeks before US troops occupied the city. The beautiful medieval central city was completely destroyed and some 5,000 people killed. The Germans at my table at the conference dinner in the historic Juliusspittal wine restaurant explained that of course it was a navigational error and the RAF were after the more legitimate targets of Nuremberg or Stuttgart further south. They simply did not believe that the Allies were capable of intentionally bombing such a target. I suspected otherwise but without knowing for sure kept quiet and later checked the records, where I found that it was indeed a planned raid on a previously untouched soft target that was easy to find and would burn well because the city centre contained a large number of compact wooden buildings.

A few years ago, I persuaded my Hanoverian scientific host and friend to accompany me to Wolfenbüttel, a small medieval town outside of Braunschweig that was reportedly virtually untouched by bombing. My desire was to explore an intact medieval town, a feature most Germans just take for granted. My friend was eventually persuaded that the trip was worthwhile when we happened across a festival in the town but he did insist that we first visit Braunschweig itself, which he said was also "virtually untouched by bombing" because it was the home town of Mathilde (Maud) the English born queen of Henry the Lion, Duke of Saxony and Bavaria. In the 12th century, Henry and Maud were under the protection of Henry II of England and so the story was that the tombs of both Mathilde and Henry were in Braunschweig cathedral and so the British continued their protection some 800 years later during World War 2. I certainly confirmed that the tombs were in the cathedral, but the historic boards explaining that 90% of the medieval centre was destroyed in World War 2 and then rebuilt, helped persuade my friend that the romantic story was simply a myth. Explaining that my Dad and his crew had actually bombed the town in one of the 42 raids that were carried out during World War 2 also helped in the persuasion.

story/

The lessons of history are easily lost and in the modern world of instant digital feeds the history can be rewritten on web sites that are simple to setup and unchecked. There are web sites that rewrite World War 2 bombing history with ludicrous claims that would have required an order of magnitude greater bombing offensive and laying the burden of death and destruction on the Allies alone[3]. These websites have arisen in parallel with the rise of the German right, which with some justification the "Westies" tend to blame on the lack of education of the "Easties" as to the causes and progress of World War 2. In East Germany the attitude after 1945 was to sweep World War 2 under the carpet as done and dusted and start again, leaving the general population, unlike those in the west, to grow up without a historic context for the next 50 years. The East Germans were taught that the Nazis were those that resided in what was then West Germany. Certainly, the AFD (Alternative für Deutschland) party gains most of its support in places like Saxony that were part of the old East Germany.

Hagen, the target of the raid a few nights later, is on the southern edge of the Ruhr and before this raid, was the only city of the Ruhr left intact after it had escaped the bombing through the "Battle of the Ruhr". Despite Vic Trimble doubting the success of the raid in his intelligence report, the city was destroyed on this night and suffered further damage later in the war through RAF and USAAF bombing. The Bomber Command war diary states: "This raid was a complete success achieved on a completely cloud-covered target of small size, with only a moderate bomber effort and at trifling cost." Hagen was then a small steel producing city some 325 miles from London where the OBOE directional radar system worked well despite the extreme range, resulting in a concentration of bombs on the city despite the cloud cover. The cloud cover also resulted in ineffective flak and the loss of only two Lancasters. Above the cloud, the fighters were active, and once again the Trimble crew encountered a night fighter, which fortunately broke off the engagement after the gunners opened fire. Their aircraft was equipped with MONICA, the backward facing radar system designed to pick up German night fighters approaching from behind. It seems to have worked well on this occasion giving them adequate time to prepare for interception.

---

[3] I suspect they have used the number of times air raid sirens were activated. When including bombers overflying cities to other targets and reconnaissance aircraft checking and photographing results, a factor of 10 would be easy to arrive at.

2/3 October 1943
Munich: 294 Lancasters of 1, 5 and No 8 Groups and two B-17s - to Munich. Eight Lancasters lost, 2.7% of the force. Visibility over the target was clear but the initial marking was scattered. Heavy bombing developed over the southern and south eastern districts of Munich but later stages of the raid fell up to 15 miles back along the approach route. Most of this inaccurate bombing was carried out by No. 5 Group aircraft, which were again attempting their 'time-and-distance' bombing method independently of the Pathfinder marking. The No. 5 Group crews were not able to pick out the Wurmsee lake, which was the starting point for their timed run.

A return flight time of around eight hours shows how far Munich was from the bomber bases, so despite it being a major industrial and transportation centre and the birth city of the Nazi party it was not a major target until late 1942 when the four engine heavy bombers came into service. The USAAF followed this raid up with a daylight raid and eventually by 1945, Munich was almost totally destroyed in a similar fashion to most major German centres. Like most large German cities, unexploded bombs are still found and in 2012, a 550lb bomb found under a nightclub had to be detonated in situ, causing great damage.

On this op 207 Squadron lost an aircraft on take-off in particularly traumatic circumstances[4]. The accident involved Flying Officer Jock Bremner, who had acted as an instructor with the Trimble crew on their first training flights after arrival at 207 Squadron. Bremner had invited his wife down to Langar for a weekend and they had spent the previous night socializing at the White Hart Inn with other crews and a few wives. Jock's wife was pregnant and along with the wife of the rear gunner in another crew, Ron Buck, she had been invited to watch the crews take-off. Bremner in DV184 O-Orange was the second aircraft to take-off just in front of Plt Off Drane's crew containing Ron Buck. Ron saw Jock's wife and her husband wave cheerily to each other as O-Orange started down the runway. As the aircraft passed the control tower Wing Commander Jennings, the commanding officer, observed that the coloured streamers of the pitot tube covers were still in place and alerted the flying control officer, who immediately fired off a red flare to abort the take-off. Bremner closed down his engines, but apparently upon realizing that he

---

[4] The basis of this story is derived from Ron Buck's contribution to "207 Squadron RAF Langar 1942-1943" – Barry Goodwin and Raymond Glynnewen. The crew are listed in CHAPTER 13.

was unlikely to stop before the end of the runway, quickly restarted the engines and attempted to take-off. O-Orange struggled to 50ft before the heavily laden Lancaster fell to earth and the 4,000lb Cookie blew up, killing all the crew.

The crews yet to take-off stopped their engines and rapidly left their aircraft in case any of the sensitive Cookies in their bomb bays went up in sympathy. Ron Buck reported that his crew sat around on the grass passing around cigarettes and watching the black smoke at the end of the runway until Wg Cdr Jennings appeared and declared that because O-Orange was not blocking the runway, all aircraft should now take-off. Six of the remaining crews, including the Trimble crew, now some 20 minutes late, took off and bombed Munich. These crews had to pass over the burning wreckage containing their dead mates as they took off. Three of the other crews cancelled. DV184O, the Lancaster destroyed, was the aircraft that Vic Trimble flew in as second pilot on his first op. The remains of four of the crew were never located and those four are commemorated on the Runnymede memorial. The other three are buried in their local churchyards in Britain.

The role of the pitot tubes is to provide airspeeds and without them an aircraft is essentially unflyable. Removing the covers is part of the essential check-list before boarding the aircraft for take-off and one wonders if the distraction of having his wife watching contributed to the crew's deadly mistake of leaving the covers on. For his wife and the other observers it must have been a horrific few moments. Bremner's crew were the last 207 fatalities at Langar and they had completed 17 ops before their deaths. One of Bremner's crew, flight engineer Sgt Robert Appleton, whose remains were never found, was like Roy, from Darlington. With a home town in common they were probably quite close. Ron Buck, the rear gunner in the Drane crew, was also a friend of Roy's and the two of them communicated later in life. Ron had something of a charmed life. Whilst at 207 Squadron, he was allocated by Wg Cdr Jennings to fly as spare gunner with a new crew on their first op. Knowing that new crews stood a much greater chance of not returning and wanting to stay with his own crew, he refused, and Wg Cdr Jennings sentenced him to two weeks at the Sheffield aircrew disciplinary centre for his actions. The replacement rear gunner who flew with the new crew instead of Ron died that night together with the six on their first op. The Drane crew were posted to 97 Pathfinder Squadron after 18 ops with 207 Squadron and Ron Buck completed 45 ops. Peter Drane's luck ran out in January 1945 when after 67 ops he was killed in a Mosquito when he clipped a hedge on landing.

7/8 October 1943

<u>Stuttgart:</u> 343 Lancasters despatched to Stuttgart. The first aircraft to be equipped with ABC, (known by the crews as 'Airborne Cigar'), from 101 Squadron operated on this night. The German night fighter controller was confused by the Mosquito diversion on Munich and only a few night fighters reached Stuttgart at the end of the attack; 4 Lancasters were lost, 1.2% of the force. The target area was cloud-covered and the H_2S Pathfinder marking developed in two areas.

Stuttgart was a huge manufacturing city spread out down a number of valleys and hence was a particularly important but difficult target for the RAF. This raid was one of the first to achieve some success. Despite a large number of raids, Stuttgart did not suffer to the same extent as most major German cities but was still a wreck by the end of the war.

Over Munich, the Trimble crew yet again encountered a night fighter, their fourth such experience in their first seven ops. It was not mentioned in the intelligence report, but from Vic Trimble's logbook, on the Stuttgart trip they landed at RAF Ford in Sussex short of fuel and flew back to Langar the next day. They had also been coned by searchlights over Hannover and had written off a Lancaster before their first Operation. To add to their own experiences, the Welch crew had been lost on the Nuremberg trip and they had witnessed the Bremner crew aircraft blow up in front of them. After this incredibly eventful start to their tour and surviving their first seven ops against the odds, they must have been wondering how they could possibly survive another 23 ops.

Incredible as it seems, by comparison a small number of aircrew reported after a full tour of 30 ops that they had never seen a night fighter, never been coned by searchlights and always arrived home unscathed after a raid. The Trimble crew seem to have been towards the opposite end of the luck spectrum though without being at the extreme end and joining those shot down. After their many lucky escapes in the first seven ops, the Trimble crew settled into a "routine" of just occasional troubles, losing an engine one night on their way to Berlin and then engaging a night fighter over Berlin on their 15th trip. This was followed by a near disaster after being shot up over Brunswick on the their 19th op and then by a landing at Tangmere in the south of England short of fuel after another long flight to Stuttgart on their 25th op. They raided Stuttgart four times and on return were short of fuel on two of those occasions.

5 THE TOUR MOVES ON

On 10 October 1943, 207 Squadron was stood down from operations and relocated to RAF Spilsby in Lincolnshire the next day. Fog then precluded ops at Spilsby until 18 October. The USAAF moved into Langar upon their departure.

20/21 October 1943
Leipzig: 358 Lancasters of 1, 5, 6 and No 8 Groups. 16 Lancasters lost, 4.5% of the force. This was the first serious attack on this distant German city. Weather conditions were very difficult - Bomber Command records describe them as 'appalling' and the bombing was very scattered.

Leipzig was a distant target in the east of Germany and one that had not been successfully bombed. It was Germany's fifth largest city, a centre for trade fairs and important as a large industrial centre, aeroplane construction centre and railroad hub. This raid was again not decisive and the city was finally attacked with great success and loss of life on 4 December 1943, when a firestorm was started. Leipzig was raided many more times by both the RAF and USAAF throughout the war.

10/11 November 1943
Modane: 313 Lancasters raided Modane.
Both Roy and Jim Marles took part in this raid with the Bill Baker crew. Arthur Herriott also went to Modane but as navigator with the Moulton-Barrett crew. Modane, a French railway centre on the Italian border, was attacked two nights running in an effort to shut down rail traffic. This was the second attack and it was hoped to close the tunnel

south of Modane. The results were similar to those of the first raid and it was not particularly successful.

18/19 November 1943
<u>Berlin:</u> 440 Lancasters and four Mosquitos were dispatched. Few German fighters intercepted the force. 9 Lancasters were lost, 2.0% of the force. Berlin was completely cloud-covered and both marking and bombing were carried out blindly; Bomber Command could make no assessment of the results. (They weren't very good - see Neillands[1]). The route out was a wide swing out over the North Sea and over the Dutch coast.

This was the first raid of what has been termed the Battle of Berlin and the first of eight trips to Berlin by the Trimble crew. Roy was unavailable and replaced by Sgt Codling for this first trip to Berlin. The Trimble crew did not actually make it to Berlin because of engine trouble and bombed an alternative target, the island of Texel, which housed a large number of German flak batteries. The sortie was declared complete in the squadron ORBs so counted towards the 30 ops necessary to complete a tour.

22/23 November 1943
<u>Berlin</u> attacked by 764 aircraft - 469 Lancasters, 234 Halifaxes, 50 Stirlings, 11 Mosquitos. This was the greatest force sent to Berlin so far but it was also the last raid in which Stirlings were sent to Germany. Bad weather again kept most of the German fighters on the ground and the bomber force was able to take a relatively 'straight in, straight out' route to the target without suffering undue loss. 26 aircraft - 11 Lancasters, 10 Halifaxes, 5 Stirlings - were lost, 3.4% of the force. The telling point of the raid and many previous ones was the 10% loss of Stirlings versus 2.3% of Lancasters and 4.3% of Halifaxes. The Stirling losses were unsupportable, hence their withdrawal from the battle. Berlin was again completely cloud-covered and returning crews could only estimate that the marking and bombing were believed to be accurate. In fact, this was the most effective raid on Berlin of the war. A vast area of destruction stretched from the central districts westwards across the mainly residential areas of Tiergarten and Charlottenburg to the separate suburb city of Spandau. Because

---

[1] The Bomber War – Robin Neillands, Overlook Books, NY. 2001.

of the dry weather conditions, several 'firestorm' areas were reported and a German plane next day measured the height of the smoke cloud as 6,000 m (nearly 19,000 ft).

Bomber Command decided to make a maximum effort on this operation because of favourable weather in England and unfavourable weather for the night fighters over Europe. The simple straight in - straight out route was also chosen because of the weather conditions. The strategy worked on this occasion. Rather than waves of aircraft of the same type, for the first time they mixed the aircraft types with the more experienced crews bombing first and the inexperienced crews bringing up the rear. New target marking techniques were also employed with sky markers in addition to ground flares. It was estimated that 175,000 people were bombed out on this night. The list of buildings destroyed or severely damaged included: the Kaiser-Wilhelm-Gedächtniskirche (the Kaiser Wilhelm Memorial Church) which is today, half ruined, half restored and a major monument and attraction in Berlin; the Charlottenburg Castle; the Berlin Zoo; much of the Unter den Linden; the British, French, Italian and Japanese embassies; the Ministry of Weapons and Munitions; the Waffen SS Administrative College; the barracks of the Imperial Guard at Spandau and; many industrial premises, including 5 factories of the Siemens electrical group and the Alkett tank works which had only recently been moved from the Ruhr to Berlin. The huge explosion seen by the Trimble crew and many others was the Nuekolln gas works going up. Hitler's private train was apparently also destroyed in this raid.

23/24 November 1943
Berlin: 383 aircraft - 365 Lancasters, 10 Halifaxes, 8 Mosquitos - to continue the attack on Berlin. The bombing force used the same direct route as had been employed on the previous night. The German controllers made an early identification of Berlin as the probable target; their single-engine fighters were gathered over the city before the arrival of the bombers and other fighters arrived a few minutes later. Fake instructions broadcast from England caused much annoyance to the German who was giving the 'running commentary'; the Germans started using a female commentator but this was promptly countered by a female voice from England ordering the German pilots to land because of fog at their bases. 'Spoof' fighter flares dropped by Mosquitos north of the bomber stream also caused some diversion of German effort. Bomber crews noticed that flak over the target was

unusually restrained, with the German fighters obviously being given priority. 20 aircraft - all Lancasters - were lost, 5.2% of the bomber force. The target was again cloud-covered and the Pathfinders carried out skymarking, but many of the Main Force crews aimed their bombs through the cloud at the glow of 11 major fires still burning from the previous night. Much further destruction was caused in Berlin. The huge flak tower at the Tiergarten took a direct hit, which merely shook the structure and put out the lights.

The day after their return from this third Berlin op in a row, Vic was approached by an excited Arthur Heap. Arthur had also carried out the op to Berlin the previous night.

"G'day Vic I just heard from a mate I trained with that there is a new RAAF squadron being formed out of 467 over at Waddington and they're looking for more Aussie crews to get the squadron up to strength. All my blokes are in, Tony and Ken are really keen on the idea and my Brit blokes are fine with it, how about you and your crew join us?" Vic did not take long to answer, his enthusiasm for the idea breaking through the slightly down feeling that often came the day after a raid.

"Gee, that sounds great Artie, flying with an all Aussie squadron would be great. We should stick together on this. Who's the CO?"

"A fella called Kingsford Smith, related to the famous Charles they reckon. No idea what he's like but one of the flight commanders is a fella I trained with back in Oz, Harry Locke. He's a good bloke and chewed my ear about it this morning. He's keen on getting some experienced crews in."

"It sounds good Artie, I'll go and have a chat with the boys and see what they think."

The Trimble crew were not listed for ops that night but Vic had already organised a time for yet another dinghy drill in mid-afternoon so he broached the subject as soon as the crew had assembled for the drill. The first response was a ribbing from Bill Aldworth.

"Come on Vic, we already have to put up with you and Jack, we'll be swamped with noisy Aussie buggers." After a bit of chiacking they all became serious and cheerfully agreed that if Heap's crew were going then they were in as well.

"Good, all agreed then, Artie and I will head off and see Wingco Jennings this afternoon, keep your fingers crossed." Wing Commander Jennings, the CO of 207 Squadron was not initially receptive to the idea, not wanting to lose two experienced crews who had completed 15 and 12 ops. He saw however that the two Aussie skippers were determined, had the support of their crews and deserved a transfer to 463 Squadron, so he graciously acquiesced. The Trimble crew subsequently carried out one or possibly two more trips to Berlin with 207 Squadron before heading off to Waddington where the two Australian squadrons were based.

26/27 November 1943
Berlin: 443 Lancasters and 7 Mosquitos to Berlin and Stuttgart (diversion). Both forces flew a common route over Northern France and on nearly to Frankfurt before diverging. The German controllers thought that Frankfurt was the main target until a late stage and several bombers were shot down as they flew past Frankfurt. Only a few fighters appeared over Berlin, where flak was the main danger, but the scattered condition of the bomber stream at Berlin meant that bombers were caught by fighters off track on the return flight and the casualties mounted. 28 Lancasters were lost, 6.2% of the force, and 15 more Lancasters crashed in England. The weather was clear over Berlin but, after their long approach flight from the south, the Pathfinders marked an area 6-7 miles north-west of the city centre and most aircraft bombed there. Because of Berlin's size, however, most of the bombing still fell within the city boundaries and particularly on the semi-industrial suburb of Reinickendorf; a smaller number of bombs fell in the centre and in the Siemensstadt (with many electrical factories) and Tegel districts. The Berlin Zoo was heavily bombed on this night. Many of the animals had been evacuated to zoos in other parts of Germany but the bombing killed most of the remainder. Several large and dangerous animals - leopards, panthers, jaguars, apes - escaped and had to be hunted and shot in the streets.

The losses do not include those aircraft lost on return. Fog covered most of the air bases and 30 aircraft force landed or crashed on return with 15 totally destroyed. 39 aircrew and 2 civilians were killed from these crashes.

RAF policy for Bomber Command was to grant aircrew a week of recreation leave between OTU and HCU and then again, approximately every six weeks until they had completed their tour. Their policy was also to grant further leave after particularly difficult ops and during extended periods of bad weather. With this scheme in place, they could ensure that the hard worked crews received rest and recuperation as well as time away from the stress of ops and the trauma of experiencing the continual losses of personnel on the bomber bases. During the short period between transferring from 207 Squadron and arriving at 463 Squadron the Trimble crew were granted a week of well earned leave, having just spent more than six weeks on ops.

These more extended periods of leave were generally the only times that Vic Trimble allowed his crew to drink, so before heading off to tackle the complex wartime arrangements to transport them to distant parts they always visited a pub together, a ritual that started when they left HCU for 207 Squadron. At their first airfield, Langar, where they enjoyed their first beers as a crew since commencing operational flying, the pub would have been one of the many local hangouts of 207 crews in the villages around the airfield (being The White Hart at Harby, The Plough at Stathern and The Unicorn at Langar). Most RAF bomber bases were surrounded by small villages, nearly all of which possessed a pub and despite moaning about the weak, warm beer, the Australian aircrew enjoyed the homely atmosphere and warmth of these country pubs. Their moaning about weak beer was warranted. Because of rationing of sugar and barley, the alcohol content of British beer during World War 2 was reduced by 20%. At Spilsby after their first six weeks on ops they headed for The Bell at Hatton Holegate, the favourite of the 207 crews and the pub itself is now a dedicated memorial to the 207 and 44 Squadron crews who inhabited Spilsby during World War 2.

Despite Vic's rule about drinking, for some of the crew it was certainly not their first beer for 6 weeks. Some occasionally joined in the free flowing beer consumption at riotous nights in the mess as a means of relaxing and forgetting about the horrors of ops and the common experience of waking up to empty beds in their rooms. Although they had grown accustomed to the presence of administration teams gathering up the belongings of missing or dead crews and the arrival of new faces in their 10 men accommodation units, they still needed to let off steam and find a way to put the consistent high losses out of their minds. In just over 12 months whilst based at Langar 207 Squadron lost 39 aircraft, with two of these destroyed on crash landings where the crews survived, one of these being the Trimble crew soon after their arrival at Langar. Of the 265 aircrew in the Lancasters that were lost, 19 became prisoners of war, five evaded capture and 241 died. Three other aircrew died on ops from flak and fighter attacks and three ground crew also died in ground accidents during this period. Flt Lt Denys Street, one of the few who managed to bail out and undergo captivity, was subsequently one of the 50 murdered by the Gestapo after the famous "Great Escape" from Sagan prisoner of war camp in 1944. Street's ashes lie in the Berlin war cemetery, the only one of the murdered escaper's remains not taken to Poznan, near Sagan after the war.

Apart from Vic, some of the others in the crew had also had an occasional ale prior to attending the whist nights or dances arranged at the villages around the Langar, Spilsby and Waddington airfields. The local people adopted the squadrons based at Langar and made sure that there was a constant social life available for both air and ground crews. Even the owners of the nearby Belvoir Castle looked after the RAF personal and the Duchess of Rutland could often be sighted on the airfield with her staff, distributing tea, buns and conversation. Along with social life on the base, which consisted of film evenings, theatre, music and mess events, the surrounding population ensured that when not operating, the aircrew had access to abundant social life and relaxation.

Upon leaving the other crew at The Bell the two gunners travelled by train to Darlington, enduring a slow journey on crowded and blacked out wartime trains, before spending five days relaxing and being feted by the locals. Bomber Command aircrew were admired by the majority of the population because they were the main offensive troops at this stage taking the war to the Germans and they rarely paid for a beer over the five days in Darlington. Jack in particular as an Aussie in his easily distinguished dark blue uniform, was something of a celebrity. A photograph shows the two gunners proudly in uniform in the back garden of the McNaughton house in Mallard Road. It was also an opportunity for Roy to get to know his future wife a little better. The British crews all had family and homes to go to whilst on leave so as usual the other four English crew all visited their homes and families. On this occasion, Vic journeyed to Nottingham and spent time at one of his "homes away from home" with the Bose and Cox families.

Both Vic and Jack visited the families of all their crew mates whilst on leave, with Vic travelling up to Darlington on one occasion and spending time with the families of Roy, Ron and Arthur, who all lived in close proximity. Roy's parents, Jack and Reeney were very impressed with his way of running the crew and his disciplined methods. They were relieved that their boy had ended up in such a crew and their worries about Roy flying operations were somewhat eased upon meeting Vic.

Fig. 7. Roy (Mac) and Jack Lawrence, Darlington 1943.

For the Australians and other Dominion aircrew, if there was no family to visit they were still well looked after. There were hospitality centres set up in Brighton, Sussex (the new home of the reception centre for overseas aircrew after it moved from Bournemouth) and in London. These centres were set up through an organization funded by Lady Frances Ryder, Miss MacDonald of the Isles, CBE and the Australian Comforts Fund. Early in the war, Lady Ryder and her friend Miss MacDonald opened up their houses in London to hundreds of Commonwealth servicemen, just as they had done in World War 1. They followed up on this initiative by arranging for hundreds of English upper and middle class families close to air bases to open up their houses to look after Commonwealth aircrew on leave and give them a sense of "home". It was through this scheme that Vic and Jack had homes and friends to go to in Nottingham. In addition to the hospitality centres, from 1943 all Bomber Command aircrew could take advantage of a scheme set up by Lord Nuffield. The Nuffield Foundation provided aircrew on leave with an extra five shillings a day and access to a number of subsidised hotels throughout the UK.

When crew were in London there was also the "Boomerang Club" set up by the Australian government in Australia House. This was a well-equipped club that took up the whole of one floor of the building and was available to all Australian servicemen from April 1942. It boasted facilities where one could snooze in an easy chair, enjoy a game of billiards, write a letter home, take in a movie, have a haircut, take a shower, and even get your uniform mended and was a home away from home for RAAF personnel and a place to meet up with friends and take guests. Vic and Jack, like others, also made firm friends with the families with whom they were billeted and consequently spent some of their leave with their new English friends.

Many Australian RAAF personnel also met British women and returned home as married men after the war. A number of these were WAAFs who they met on the airbases or women they met through billets or the hospitality system. Most Australian Bomber Command airmen spent up to four years in Britain at an age when relationships form, so it was not surprising that many went home to Australia with a partner. Thousands of British war brides were transported to Australia by the Australian government in 1945-1947, often in large numbers. The sister ships MV Stirling Castle, and the MV Athlone Castle, large passenger liners of the Union Castle company, transported 410 and 600 British brides to Australia in April and May 1946. The Stirling Castle made four journeys to Australia returning troops and war brides and the Athlone Castle two trips before both were converted from troop carriers to normal passenger ship duties in late 1946. In July 1946 the Atlantis, a World War 2 hospital ship, transported another 400 war brides. Approximately 90% of these war brides (and fiancées) were partners of RAAF personnel. A conservative estimate based on the rough numbers of UK war brides is that one in three RAAF aircrew returned to Australia with a British bride or fiancée.[2] For those that had trained in Canada, there were Canadian war brides who also made their way to Australia post war in quite large numbers.

Like most Australian aircrew in the UK, Vic and Jack would also keep in touch with friends made when they enlisted or those they made friends with in training. For Vic, there were a number of mates from his time in the 51st Militia Battalion who had also joined the RAAF. When opportunity arose, they would catch up by visiting each other's bases or

---

[2] Information gleaned from the records of these voyages available electronically at the Australian National Archives.

arranging to meet whilst on leave in London or in the cities close to the bomber bases.

Whilst on leave in London in early 1944 Vic wrote home[3] that he had met up with George Royes and had a somewhat raucous party one night before he entertained "Blue" Emslie the next day. Vic and Blue (William), who had been a clerk and a private in 51st Battalion, joined up on the same day and travelled together to Bournemouth via South Africa after initial pilot training. From the reception centre in Bournemouth they parted ways and by May 1943 Blue was flying Typhoons with 137 Squadron in Manston, Kent. Typhoons were extremely powerful high performance ground attack aircraft and in 1944 Blue had a few landing accidents. The first one occurred when he was low on fuel and returning from a shipping strike. He had to avoid a Spitfire on landing, bounced up and executed a go around. Unfortunately his engine then cut out and he crashed on the circuit. Both the aircraft and Blue were reparable. In July 1944 again low on fuel, he attempted a landing in a cross wind, trying this time to avoid a crashed Mosquito bomber. The result was a smash up worse than the first one and this time although Blue was partly reparable the aircraft was not. The crash resulted in the loss of an eye and hearing loss.

After recovering from this last accident, Blue was offered repatriation to Australia but by then he had an English girlfriend, so he re-mustered as a Warrant Officer Disciplinary rather than making his way home to Oz. When eventually discharged in 1946, he was followed home by his English wife, Phyllis, after getting married in June 1945. Phyllis travelled on the Stirling Castle in 1946. Blue and Phyllis settled back in Cairns and their children attended school with the children of Vic Trimble.

George Royes, with whom Vic had a "merry time", was also a North Queensland friend originally in the 51st Battalion. George was a draper's assistant in Mareeba and trained in Canada as a WOP/AG before being posted to 3OTU Coastal Command. From here, he seems to have had a most interesting war moving on to 7OTU (Fighter Command) then 1 Torpedo Training Unit before spending time with 303 Ferry Training Unit. From there he moved around as a training instructor and on ops with Coastal Command, RAF Limavady, Ireland, RAF Talbenny, Wales with Ferry Units and finally 105OTU (Transport Command), Warwickshire before heading home to Mareeba. Vic and George were photographed whilst having their "merry time" at "The Cogers", a pub near Fleet Street and close to Australia House. Cogers was a favourite

---

[3] Thanks to Vic's daughter Judy Nickles and the Trimble family for allowing me access to Vic Trimble's letters home and his logbook.

haunt of the Australian aircrew and the place where many drunken parties started[4].

Cogers was also treated as a home away from home by Australian aircrew and the occasional Australian navy and army personnel based in London. Between 1938 and 1946 a number of visitor's books record the well-oiled thoughts of almost every Australian visitor. On Vic's first visit (9 Sep 1943) whilst on his first leave since commencing ops, he wrote along the same vein as others, "I'll be back!" For Vic that turned out to be true and he visited Cogers a number of times. Many others were less definitive and added in brackets or parentheses "I hope" and of course many were killed on ops and never returned to Cogers or to home. Vic's September entry had an added comment signed by Blue Elmslie, "Let me

---

[4] Seven visitor books for Australians from Cogers' club now reside in the Australian War Memorial library. The first one is a volume inscribed with "THE KANGAROO CORNER – by Evie". Evie was the Cogers' club barmaid throughout the war who along with Mrs Collinson, the owner, warmly welcomed Australian servicemen and set up a special venue for them. An Australian badge is mounted on the cover of the second book and on later volumes an RAAF badge is added. The third book was presented by the clientele and inscribed: "This book has been presented to CODGERS FOR COBBERS". Another is inscribed: "This book is an appreciation to Mrs Collinson and Evie for the kindness extended to our Australian boys, who will always remember the many pleasant hours spent at the Cogers". The occasional Brit attempted to sign the books but all such entries were made illegible with comments such as "No Poms in Here". The occasional Canadian or New Zealand entries remain intact. The three Heap brothers from Brisbane all signed the books. Edmund on 27 November 1942, Arthur on 29 November 1942, just 11 days after arriving in England and probably in the company of his brother, and Kevin on 16 August 1943: "Mine's a Fourex" and 17 September 1943. Kevin's second entry was unusual in that most patrons of Cogers only signed on one occasion despite visiting often. In addition to signatures and comments there are photographs, currency notes, postcards and stamps in the visitor books. The comments range from comical to drunken to serious, examples being:

"The flaming beer's no good" "Beer is best" "Still grogin up" "This is home to every Australian" "First visit – but not the last (I hope)"
   "First visit – the closest to home I have yet sampled" "A home away from home" "Little bit of Australia" "Four years – almost a Pommy"
   "more beer" "very bedworthy" – signed by R Kingsford Smith, Mosman, NSW.

The bar is termed Codgers or Cogers in a variety of sources, with the latter being the spelling used by the owners and bar staff.

know when".

Vic wrote home after the day out with George that "Poor old George has too many girlfriends and I am afraid he'll be married before he gets out of the country" Sure enough in January 1945 George married an Irish WAAF radio operator named Veronica and she followed George to Australia in the Rangitiki, another war bride ship. George and Vic had yet another 51st Battalion friend who they joined up with, Gordon Ingram and they kept in touch with him throughout the war by mail. Gordon had been a knifeman in an abattoir before enlistment and he trained in Canada as WOP/AG with George. He spent most of the war flying in Ansons out of Reykjavik, Iceland with air sea rescue/meteorological 1407 flight and then 251 Squadron. Despite trying to arrange a posting to the UK, he spent the war in the cold north and returned to Australia as a Warrant Officer (WO) at the end of 1945. He married one of George Royes' sisters after the war.

Vic also met up in London with another 51st Battalion friend who had joined the RAAF a few months after he had enlisted. Bill Barbour (William Morgan Barbour) was a bank clerk and enlisted in the RAAF on 14 September 1941. He trained in both Australia and Canada and was eventually posted to 455 Sqn, RAF Langham, Coastal Command where he flew anti-shipping Beaufighters. Soon after spending a day in London with Vic and signing the Cogers' visitors book, Fl Off Barbour and his navigator Fl Off F G Dodd were attacking a convoy of 10 merchant ships and minesweeper escorts when their Beaufighter had its tail section blown off by flak. They crashed into the sea and about a month later the body of the navigator washed up on one of the many islands off the Dutch coast. In October another body washed ashore, but because it had been in the sea for three months identification was not possible and that body was buried as an unknown. Fl Off F G Dodd was interred along with many other airmen lost in the north west of Germany or the Frisian islands in Sage War Cemetery near Bremen, Germany. Bill's name is remembered on the Runnymede Memorial, although it is likely that the unknown body buried next to Dodd in Sage War Cemetery is in fact Bill Barbour.

Fig. 8. Trimble crew whilst with 207 Squadron Front row, left to right Jim Marles, Vic Trimble, Bill Aldworth, Back row, Jack Lawrence, Roy McNaughton, Ron Nixon, Arthur Herriott.

6   NOT SO LUCKY CREW

Within a few days of arriving at Waddington, where two of the three Australian Lancaster squadrons were based, the Trimble crew set off on their first op as part of the newly formed 463 Squadron RAAF.

16/17 December 1943
Berlin: 483 Lancasters and 10 Mosquitos on the main raid to Berlin and 5 further Mosquitos dropped decoy fighter flares south of Berlin. The bomber route again led directly to Berlin across Holland and Northern Germany and there were no major diversions. The German controllers plotted the course of the bombers with great accuracy; many German fighters were met at the coast of Holland and further fighters were guided on to the bomber stream throughout the approach to the target. More fighters were waiting at the target and there were many combats. The bombers shook off the opposition on the return flight by taking a northerly route over Denmark. 25 Lancasters, 5.2% of the Lancaster force, were lost. Many further aircraft were lost on returning to England. Berlin was cloud-covered but the Pathfinder skymarking was reasonably accurate and much of the bombing fell in the city. In the city centre, the National Theatre and the building housing Germany's military and political archives were both destroyed. The damage to the Berlin railway system and to rolling stock, and the large numbers of people still leaving the city, were having a cumulative effect upon the transportation of supplies to the Russian Front; 1,000 wagon-loads of war material were held up for six days. The sustained

bombing had now made more than a quarter of Berlin's total living accommodation unusable. On their return to England, many of the bombers encountered very low cloud at their bases. The squadrons of 1, 6 and No 8 Groups were particularly badly affected. 29 Lancasters (and a Stirling from the minelaying operation) either crashed or were abandoned when their crews parachuted. The group with heaviest losses was No 1 Group with 13 aircraft lost; the squadron with heaviest losses was 97 Squadron, No 8 Group, with 7 aircraft lost.

COMBAT REPORT *Trimble crew*
At 20.08 hrs, 19,000ft over target heading 062°N. Airspeed 165 IAS. Mid upper gunner sighted Ju88 astern 500 yards up. When sighted E/A was starting to attack. MU gave order to corkscrew port and rear and mid upper gunners opened fire. E/A followed through and opened fire giving 3 bursts but was unable to get guns to bear. Both mid upper and rear gunners gave several short bursts but could observe no hits. E/A using wing machine guns but no tracer was used. E/A held off at 500 yards throughout corkscrew and then broke away to starboard down and was not seen again.
There does not appear to have been any cooperation with ground defences. Weather 10/10 ths cloud about 10,000' clear above. Fighter flares in vicinity. No hits claimed. Visual MONICA fitted but WOP was in astro hatch. MONICA worked satisfactorily throughout. 1500 rounds expended. No Claim.

On this fourth altercation with German night fighters the crew escaped without any damage. The fighter was observed before it attacked and the corkscrew commenced to evade its attentions. Just after this op, on 19 December Vic had his logbook endorsed by the base commander Gp Cpt Elsworthy for "Gross Negligence when taxying".

20-21 December 1943
Frankfurt: 650 aircraft - 390 Lancasters, 257 Halifaxes, 3 Mosquitos. The German control rooms were able to plot the bomber force as soon as it left the English coast and were able to continue plotting it all the way to Frankfurt. There were many combats on the route to the target. The Mannheim diversion did not draw fighters away from the main attack until after the raid was over but the return flight was quieter. 41 aircraft - 27 Halifaxes, 14 Lancasters - lost, 6.3% of the force. The bombing at Frankfurt did not go according to plan. The Pathfinders had prepared a ground-marking plan on the basis of a forecast giving

clear weather but they found up to 8/10ths cloud. The Germans lit a decoy fire site five miles south east of the city and also used dummy TIs. Some of the bombing fell around the decoy but part of the creepback fell on Frankfurt causing more damage than Bomber Command realised at the time. Part of the bombing fell on Mainz, 17 m to the west, and many houses along the Rhine waterfront and in southern suburbs were hit.

Frankfurt am Main was a major target, first of the RAF and later of the USAAF. The largest medieval city centre in Europe was eventually totally destroyed. Like Hannover, there is a museum with a model of the city at the end of World War 2 showing the complete devastation and like Hannover a small medieval city centre was reconstructed from the remaining facades. In September 2017, a 4,000lb blockbuster bomb was found in Frankfurt. 60,000 people were evacuated and the bomb safely defused. One of many thousands found in Germany since World War 2.

23/24 December 1943
Berlin: 379 aircraft - 364 Lancasters, 8 Mosquitos, 7 Halifaxes. The bomber casualties were not as heavy as on recent raids, partly because German fighters encountered difficulty with the weather and partly because the German controller was temporarily deceived by the Mosquito diversion at Leipzig. The main force of fighters only appeared in the target area at the end of the raid and could not catch the main bomber stream. 16 Lancasters were lost, 4.2% of the force. The Berlin area was covered by cloud and more than half of the early Pathfinder aircraft had trouble with their H_2S sets. The markers were scattered and sparse.

By early 1944 the RAF were exploring new strategies to minimize losses and confuse the German defences. The first were Radio Counter Measure (RCM) sorties run by 100 Group where their aircraft were equipped with extra wireless operators and an array of state of the art equipment to jam and confuse the German communications and radar. They started operating in December 1943 using a range of aircraft and by early 1944 some were equipped with B17 Flying Fortresses. The second were termed Serrate patrols and these were undertaken by Beaufighters or Mosquitoes of 100 Group carrying equipment that locked on to the German night fighter radar frequencies. These aircraft flew amongst the bomber stream to try to intercept and shoot down German night fighters.

LUCKY POMMIE BASTARD

Two of the dozen 463 a/c sent to Berlin were flown by the Trimble and Heap crews. Arthur Heap, in ED420 JO-L took off 15 minutes after Vic Trimble. ED420 was shot down over the centre of Berlin and crashed at Kaulsdorf, with the loss of all seven crew[1]. Arthur Heap and four of his crew, Robert Gall, navigator, Daniel McCreadie, bomb aimer, Bill Carter, flight engineer and Leo Ryan, WOP were identified and are all interred in marked graves in the Berlin war cemetery. The two gunner mates of Roy and Jack, Fred Tunnicliff and Ken Glover, were not identified and so are remembered on the Runnymede memorial, although there are two graves of unknown airmen buried alongside the other five and these are highly likely the gunners. The Australian wireless operator, Tony Boultbee, who had transferred with them from 207 to 463, was hospitalised with jaundice so did not continue flying with the Heap crew and was grounded for a few weeks. His role was taken over by another Australian, Leo Ryan of Traralgon, Victoria.

Boultbee seemed to live a charmed life as upon his return to duties he joined the crew of Fl Off Fryer and flew three ops with him before transferring out with Sqn Ldr Harry Locke to 97 Squadron, a Pathfinder squadron. Soon after Boultbee's departure in early May, Fryer and his crew were shot down on approach to the target and crashed at Poivres (Aube), 20 km NNE of Arcis-sur-Aube. All seven crew members were killed. Boultbee continued his charmed life and went on to carry out numerous ops on 97 Squadron, was awarded a Distinguished Flying Cross (DFC) and returned to Australia as a Flying Officer. He drew the right cards in the lottery of life and was a "Lucky Australian Bastard". His pilot Harry Locke, who seems to have been responsible for ensuring that the Trimble and Heap crews transferred to 463 Squadron also led a charmed life, completed a Pathfinder tour with 97 Squadron, was awarded a DFC and a Distinguished Service Order (DSO) and returned to Australia as acting Wing Commander. Soon after the end of the war, he obtained an early release and transfer to the reserve airforce, joined Trans Australia Airlines (TAA) and flew constellation and Viscount aircraft with distinction.

One can only imagine the thoughts of the Trimble crew on their return

---

[1] Arthur Heap was shot down by either Andreas Hartl or Kurt Emler, both had victims over the correct area of Berlin that night. Hartl claimed a four engine a/c over Berlin at 0415 and Emler a Lancaster at 0420 over Berlin. Heap took off 15 min after Trimble, who bombed at 0402 so either are possible. It was Emler's ninth and last kill. He died on 3 Jan 1944 KIA. Hartl was KIA on 8 Apr 1944 by a Mustang in daylight after 11 kills.

to Waddington when they realised that the mates who had been with them for so long and were just as experienced, were missing on their 17th op. With the loss of the Welch crew on their third op soon after joining 207 Squadron the mates who had progressed through the system with them were now gone. The following morning there would have been empty beds in their shared rooms and the presence of men from the Committee of Adjustment bundling up belongings. For Roy the loss of fellow MUG Fred Tunnicliff, with whom he had trained, would have hit hard. The loss would have also had a major impact on Vic and Jack who also lost mates that they had trained, travelled and socialised with for over a year.

Talking to aircrew later in life they would say that the initial thought on learning of a crew not returning was "thank God it wasn't us" followed closely by a deep sadness when those who had "bought it"[2] were close friends. Many crews purposely isolated themselves from all other crews after seeing a number of close friends not return. Essentially cushioning themselves so that they would not be so badly affected by the constant loss of the crews around them. This action resulted in even tighter crew friendships that kept other crews at a distance and made for even stronger bonds between the seven men who relied so heavily on each other. There was though a certain black humour amongst the aircrew that showed an acceptance of the likelihood of death. Before an operation, aircrew would ask each other if they could have their egg and bacon at breakfast if they did not come back. Aircrew also kept in touch with the men who had trained with them and the attrition rate for them was much the same as those on the squadron. Chapter 13 outlines just how bad the death rate was in Bomber Command.

Arthur Heap was the youngest of three Queensland brothers who joined the RAAF in 1941/42 and were all posted to Bomber Command. Fate was kinder to both his brothers and they survived the war to return home, although both died in Australia at a relatively young age. Arthur's brother Edmund was 10 years older and trained as a WOP/AG before being posted operational on 21 July 1942 to 102 Squadron, RAF Pocklington flying four engine Halifax bombers, a full year before Arthur commenced operational flying. His first op was to Frankfurt on the night of 8 September 1942 as mid upper gunner in the crew of Flt Sgt Frances Farrell. The a/c W7677, DY-Q "Queenie" was hit by flak over Frankfurt immediately after releasing the bombload and turned for home badly damaged. Approaching Luxembourg Farrell realised that the a/c was losing height rapidly and becoming uncontrollable and ordered the crew

---

[2] RAF slang for being shot down and killed.

to bail out. Four of the crew including Edmund, the rear gunner, Sgt John Griffiths, the flight engineer, WO Frederick Whitfield, and the bomb aimer Sgt Kevin Wright, successfully bailed out. Wright and Whitfield were almost immediately captured and made prisoners of war, but Heap and Griffiths independently evaded capture. Pilot Frances Farrell, the navigator Sgt John Goodson Phillips and the radio operator Sgt Owen Barclay Kidd all went down with the a/c and were killed on impact. They lie together in a grave in the cemetery of the Church of Folschette (Rambrouch) in Luxembourg and are commemorated there as a CWGC site. WO Whitfield died as a POW of natural causes in 1945 and is buried in the Berlin war cemetery.

After descending to earth and hiding his parachute and flying kit, Edmund Heap lay hidden in the woods near the Belgian border for two days. Eventually he was discovered by a local farmer, who then contacted the "Comet" network, a Belgian resistance group formed specifically to help escapers[3]. Edmund's experience was typical of those who managed to evade capture after surviving being shot down. For almost five weeks he was passed through the hands of the famous network. He was delivered through a chain of Comet members to Brussels, where to maintain security he was constantly moved around a number of different houses before being accompanied by a guide to Paris.

In Paris, Edmund was again shuffled from house to house before departure for the unoccupied south of France with two guides and a group of three other allied airmen. On 6 October they were escorted over the Pyrenees into Spain by a Basque guide, this being the 26th Comet extraction of evaders over the Pyrenees. By 12 October 1942, he was in Gibraltar awaiting a flight to England and arrived back in London to be debriefed by MI9 on 1 November 1942, more than three months after he took off from Pocklington. A few weeks after this he was drinking in the Cogers' club and meeting up with his newly arrived brother Arthur.

The other evader, flight engineer Jack Griffiths, landed in a tree, released himself from his parachute and then injured himself by hitting the ground headfirst. Thinking he was still in Germany, he spent 10 days marching across Luxembourg towards France. After spending the first five days alone, he was then helped occasionally by farmers and villagers who fed him and sent him on his way. Eventually on 18 September, he arrived in France and was met by a young boy who arranged for him to cross the river Meuse and put him in touch with a resistance group. On 1

---

[3] Story available for French speakers at http://www.evasioncomete.org/fheapet.html - **accessed 24 Aug 2020.**

October, guided by the same teenage boy over a circuitous route, he was escorted across the border into Liege, Belgium. After a number of weeks spent being moved around Liege he was accompanied to Brussels. Like Edmund Heap, he was eventually taken to Paris and joined a group that were guided over the Pyrenees as the 29th Comet group of evaders a few days later. After making his way to Gibraltar, he was flown out to London on 6 December, arriving in Britain more than four months after taking off from Pocklington.

The Comet line was set up by a 24 year old Belgian woman, Andree de Jongh, and her father Frederic. In August 1941, she arrived unannounced at the British consulate in Bilbao with an escaped British soldier and two Belgians who wanted to join the allies, having travelled over the Pyrenees on foot. After overcoming initial doubts MI9 subsequently supported her, and she and her compatriots set up the Comet line with a number of alternate routes through Belgium and France to Spain. In 1941/42, the line succeeded in moving 400 evaders through the routes with de Jongh guiding 119 of these over the Pyrenees herself. During most of this period, the French Vichy government administered the south of France, so once over the demarcation line and away from the German occupied north the line could operate without the German military and Gestapo investigating.

In November 1942 whilst Edmund and Jack made their way through the organised escape routes, the allies invaded North Africa and the Germans subsequently occupied the south of France. From this time on, the Comet line was in great danger and the Germans soon broke it up and arrested many hundreds of people in France and Belgium. Most of the resistance groups based around Liege involved in assisting evaders were discovered and dismantled by the Germans and a great number of the people who helped the two airmen escape were sent to concentration camps (mainly Buchenwald), where like most of those arrested in the Comet system they were executed. The French and Belgian patriots paid a high price for their assistance to allied evaders with 156 Comet people killed. Andree de Jongh was arrested in January 1943 and incarcerated in Ravensbrück concentration camp. She survived the horrors of Ravensbrück and Mauthausen camps and was decorated by the British with the George Medal in 1946. Her father Frederic, who ran the line from Brussels, was arrested and shot by firing squad.

Both Edmund and Jack were awarded Distinguished Flying Medals (DFMs) with the citation for Edmund Heap reading:

'In various capacities as a member of an aircrew, this non-commissioned officer has displayed great gallantry and determination in attacks against targets in enemy

occupied territory."

Given that he was shot down on his first op, the DFM was obviously awarded for his escape and the citation was merely camouflage to ensure that the Germans did not receive information about the successful number of evaders. Edmund's DFM was officially awarded at Buckingham Palace on 10 Oct 1943 and the Australian War Memorial (AWM) has a photograph of Edmund Heap, by now a Plt Off, together with his brothers, Arthur and Kevin, taken immediately after the ceremony. It was the last time the three brothers were together and just over two months later Arthur was dead.

Edmund spent the next two years moving between the RAF gunnery school, Sutton Bridge, at Cranwell, RAF Uxbridge and a secretive location RAF Defford. Some of the time he was probably employed informing aircrew of his experiences as an evader. Eventually he retrained as a navigator and after a stint at 60OTU RAF High Ercall, was posted in September 1944 to 487 Squadron flying Mosquitoes on intruder operations. This was highly unusual, as most successful evaders were never returned to the same area of conflict in case they were captured and tortured to give away the names and addresses of resistance workers. Possibly everybody he knew had already been detained by the Gestapo or the policy had been changed as the allies freed more of Europe after the Normandy invasion. Just over a year later, Edmund was back in Australia and was discharged on 4 April 1945 as a Flt Lt. He reportedly died in 1959 from exhaustion whilst digging a well on his sheep farm in Queensland.

Kevin Andrew Heap, the middle brother, was born in 1914 and despite being married with two young children when war was declared, he also joined the RAAF and trained as a pilot. He followed his two brothers to England, arriving at Bournemouth a couple of months after his younger brother Arthur and cooling his heels there for the obligatory two months. After the usual advanced flying training on Oxfords, he trained as a night bomber pilot at 21OTU, Moreton in the Marsh, Gloucestershire. He and his crew were posted three weeks before Arthur's death to the Middle East and 40 Squadron flying Wellington bombers, where the losses were a little lower than in the UK.

Kevin Heap and crew joined 40 Squadron at RAF Oudna No. 1 in Tunisia and two weeks later the squadron moved to RAF Cerignola No. 2 in Italy before moving again to RAF Foggia main two weeks after that. Hence, their first month seemed to consist of moving base and most of their ops were carried out from Foggia against targets in Northern Italy, the Balkans and occasionally Austria and southern France. A tour of Bomber Command in the middle East/Italy sphere was 40 ops and he and his crew carried out 40 night bombing ops over a six month period before he became an instructor at 77OTU Qastina, an RAF base in Palestine which was subsequently used by the Israeli air force. In the time Kevin was flying ops, 40 Squadron lost 21 aircraft, so it was still an extremely dangerous occupation with losses close to those of squadrons operating out of Britain. During his operational duty, Kevin was commissioned and eventually repatriated from the Middle East directly to Australia He was demobilised (released from military service) on 18 Dec 1945 as a Fl Off.

Fig. 9. Graves of five of the Heap crew – Berlin CWGC, 2018.

7   LUCKY CREW

1/2 January 1944
Berlin: 421 Lancasters despatched to Berlin. Despite a Mosquito 'spoof' raid on Hamburg, German fighters were directed on to the bomber stream at an early stage and were particularly active en-route to Berlin. 28 Lancasters were lost, 6.7% of the force.

After this New Year's Day op, the Trimble crew were sent to RAF Syerston for a week of refresher training at the Lancaster Finishing School. They flew there with an experienced instructor Plt Off Cockschott, DFC who had finished a tour of ops on 61 Squadron. Cockshott went on to carry out a second tour of ops with 617 Dambuster Squadron as a squadron leader, where he was awarded a bar to his DFC, took part in a number of famous raids and dropped the huge armour and concrete piercing six ton Tallboy and ten ton Grand Slam bombs.

463 Squadron ORBs   RAF Waddington   14/15-1-1944,
Brunswick *HK535 JO-N Naughty Nancy*
Fl Off Trimble   Sgt Marles   Fl Off Herriott   Sgt Nixon
Sgt Aldworth   Sgt McNaughton   Sgt Lawrence

Fl Off Trimble, bombing BRUNSWICK. Sortie completed. Up 16.52 hours. Down 22.30 hours. 8-10/10 cloud, tops 10,000ft. Green TIs, 20,000ft. 19.50hrs. 1 x 4,000HC. 1500 x 4. 80 x 30 incendiaries. Red glow on port side under cloud. Attacked by fighter leaving target, causing much damage. R/G unconscious due to damaged oxygen M/U fired at E/A six sec burst, E/A temporarily lost to sight, but next seen through thin cloud layer to burst on ground.

A/B hit by splinter. Crew suffered from lack of oxygen. Landed at Wittering for long runway due to no brake pressure.

COMBAT REPORT – Trimble Crew.
1922 hrs course 299N Height 25,000ft speed 160 IAS position 52.05N 10.08E
First indication of fighter, crew saw tracer from port quarter down which smashed elevators and port rudder. Rear gunner then sighted FW190 breaking away to starboard up.
Enemy aircraft then positioned himself on port quarter level and turned to attack at 400 yards. Rear gunner gave dive port but was unable to fire due to lack of oxygen, pipe had been severed in first attack.
Mid upper gunner gave six sec burst at 300 yards and fighter was lost to sight starboard down for five secs and was then seen to dive to starboard in flames. E/A was seen by mid upper gunner to dive through layer of cloud and blew up on ground. 400 rounds ammo expended. Visual MONICA U/S (unserviceable) throughout trip. Rear gunner unconscious through lack of oxygen throughout second attack. No fighter flares or searchlight cooperation.
GROUP CAPT commanding: As the attacking aircraft was lost to sight for 5 secs after the six sec burst from the mid upper gunner, I do not consider that the aircraft seen going down in flames can definitely be established as the same aircraft. Claimed; probably destroyed.

Despite the probably destroyed claim the 5 Group newsletter of January 1944 declared the FW190 as "destroyed"[1]. This was one of three FW-190s claimed by 463 Squadron in January and a short description of these successes became part of RAAF bulletin No 324[2].

14/15 January 1944
Brunswick: 496 Lancasters and 2 Halifaxes on the first major raid to Brunswick of the war. 38 Lancasters lost, 7.6% of the force.

---

[1] "V Group News, January 1944," *IBCC Digital Archive*, accessed June 16 2020, https://ibccdigitalarchive.lincoln.ac.uk/omeka/collections/document/17248.
[2] The RAAF base at Kingsway, London provided bulletins for eventual release in Australia. When aircrew personnel were named in these bulletins, a copy was attached to their biographical file. These are available at the Australian War Memorial with some also on line – AWM65. Bulletin 324 thus appears in the biographical files of Jack Lawrence, Vic Trimble and Rollo Kingsford Smith. Being for the Australian media, the role of RAF personnel was somewhat down played. Apparently, on arrival in the UK, all aircrew filled out a proforma to form the basis of these biographical files.

The German running commentary was heard following the progress of the bomber force from a position only 40 miles from the English coast and many German fighters entered the bomber stream soon after the German frontier was crossed near Bremen. The German fighters scored steadily until the Dutch coast was crossed on the return flight. 11 of the lost aircraft were Pathfinders. Brunswick was smaller than Bomber Command's usual targets and this raid was not a success. The city report describes this only as a 'light' raid, with bombs in the south of the city which had only 10 houses destroyed and 14 people killed. Most of the attack fell either in the countryside or in Wolfenbüttel and other small towns and villages well to the south of Brunswick.

Vic was roused out of a deep and comfortable sleep to hear what after 18 completed bomber ops over Europe, was a well worked phrase, "Ops tonight Vic, you're on mate. And you have been promoted to Flying Officer." He and his crew had just returned to RAF Waddington late the previous evening, after an intense week of training at the newly named Lancaster Finishing School at RAF Syerston in Nottinghamshire[3]. In mid tour they had honed their skills in gunnery, fighter affiliation, evasive action and handling engine failure on Lancaster bombers. The training had provided a short but welcome break from operational flying over Germany as well as a chance to update the skills that had succeeded in keeping them alive so far and that might enable their continued survival through a full tour of 30 ops. During the week away they had also practised their dinghy drill, carried out numerous corkscrew evasion manoeuvres, successfully flown a four engine Lancaster bomber on three and then two engines only, practised landing go arounds and then landing with only three engines. After returning from such a break from routine crews were usually thrown back into the fray at the first opportunity, so he had been fully expecting to go straight back on to ops.

Vic slowly extracted himself from the warm blankets and grasped the hot milky tea that a WAAF batman had placed by his bed in both hands.

---

[3] This chapter is based on RAF operational record books and combat reports, Vic Trimble's logbook and a long conversation with flight engineer Jim Marles. The book "Piece of Cake" – Geoff Taylor was useful in informing some of the detail in this chapter along with "Lancaster: The Second World War's Greatest Bomber" – Leo McKinstry and "The Airborne years – a mid upper RCAF gunner's memoir" – JA Campbell.

Having somebody bring him a cup of tea in the morning, make his bed and clean his room was an advantage he had grown to appreciate since his recent promotion from flight sergeant to pilot officer. Tea finished, he was fully awake as he padded down the corridor in his bare feet to deliver the news to his English navigator, Arthur Herriott, a flying officer who was also housed in the luxuriant RAF Waddington Officers' mess. Arthur was already neatly dressed and ready for the day. Greeting Vic with a broad smile he said simply "We're on. Ready and raring to go Vic". Vic wandered back to his room wondering how his toffee nosed navigator managed to be so bloody cheerful all the time. He reluctantly pulled on thick warm socks, boots, gloves and greatcoat, ventured outside and trudged gingerly through the cold and icy winter morning over to the sergeants' quarters.

The pristine white snow of 10 days ago that had seen the Australians playfully fighting with snow balls had turned into a treacherous ice layer topped by a dirty brown slush. This was Vic's second English winter but he still found the biting cold of Lincolnshire hard to handle. Filtered by the fog of condensation from his breathing, Vic recognised the familiar signs pointing to an upcoming op. Bomb trains were gathering inside the sand bagged bomb dump, fitters were busily working on the engines of a number of aircraft, aircrew were collecting parachutes and readying for an early air-test and a number of air and ground crew pedalled bikes purposefully back and forth between the widely dispersed squadron sections.

RAF Waddington, the home of 463 and 467 Australian Lancaster Squadrons was already bustling with activity and working through the well practised routine leading up to an op over enemy occupied Europe. There seemed to be an extra air of purpose after almost two weeks of snow and fog had curtailed bombing operations and frustrated Bomber Command. 463 Squadron had been formed from one of 467's three flights the previous month and Vic and his crew were posted in mid tour from 207 Squadron to form part of B Flight. As he walked through the permanent RAF base, he still could not help noting thankfully that everything on this base seemed more organised and permanent than their previous airfield, Spilsby, where everything was temporary and rough and ready in comparison. The embarrassing memory of flipping his first 207 Squadron Lancaster by overshooting the RAF Langar runway resurfaced but with the comfortably long concrete runways, no slippery grass, a greater awareness and the calmness that he now felt in the air there was less prospect of a repeat performance. He was secure in knowing that after that frightening experience he would never again be thoughtless enough to land downwind. Waddington was the best equipped and most comfortable base they had so far operated from and Vic was now a much more experienced pilot after more than 180 flying hours on Lancaster bombers in training and ops out of numerous different airfields.

In the sergeants' mess, he hunted out the crew's flight engineer, English Flight Sergeant, Jim Marles, who was not long out of bed and lounging about in the cosy warmth of the mess anteroom reading a newspaper. "Well, we were right, we're on Jim. You had better get the rest of the boys moving. 10 o"clock in the crew room should do it."

"OK, skip." Jim would round up the rest of the crew, all sergeants and flight sergeants, and make sure they eventually made their way to the crew room. For Vic it was then another long walk from the massive concrete sergeant's quarters through the slush and ice to Squadron Leader Bill Brill's flight commander's office where many 463 B-flight pilots were already gathering to find out who was on tonight and which aircraft they were flying. There were a number of push bikes propped up on the bike stands, indicating most of the pilots were already present and Vic wondered briefly why he hadn't grabbed a bike rather than walking. The prospect of riding on ice was not appealing though and had deterred him from attempting a bike.

Chalked on the blackboard in the crew room against Vic's name was HK535 JO-N , "N" being the code for "Naughty Nancy", the Lancaster bomber they now considered their very own. It was a brand new aeroplane when they flew it to Berlin in December and as a senior experienced crew they could now rely on being allocated their "own aircraft" for their ops. Another advantage of having the same aircraft was having a dedicated ground crew with whom they had built a rapport and with whom they could iron out any aircraft serviceability issues. This would be their fourth trip in Nancy, and Vic and Jim had worked out most of her idiosyncrasies.

After a quick chat with some of the other pilots, all fellow Aussies, Vic strode purposefully out of the flight commander's office, still with no clue as to the target for the night, but headed for the sergeant fitter of N for Nancy to arrange the time for a pre operational air-test. It was two weeks since their last trip in Nancy and she would have been flown on training flights by other crews in their absence, so obtaining an update on its condition was essential. Vic's approach to the war was risk minimization in every aspect of their flying and training and he believed that forewarned was forearmed, so hearing from the sergeant fitter that Nancy was in fine fettle was welcome news.

By late morning, the complete crew of seven had assembled their flying kit, collected their parachutes and were sitting around in the crew room somewhat apprehensively waiting for a truck to take them to the aircraft dispersal area. The tension in the air never failed to affect them and they sat fidgeting trying to dissipate the nervous energy that would build up through the day as they went through the essential preparative routines. After just a short time waiting, a WAAF mechanic who they affectionately called Scotty pulled up in a crew truck and they all piled in, by now chattering and cracking the odd joke. Scotty, with her broad Glaswegian accent that amused the Aussies, always drove them to dispersal when she was on duty and waved them off for every op regardless of whether she was on duty. Her presence always enlivened them and drew them out of their nervous state so on the short trip to dispersal they brightened up and arrived in high spirits.

Nancy was ready and waiting, with the ground crew of three fitters and a rigger assembled under the nose after their busy morning of preparing the aeroplane for its fourth op. They, together with a host of specialist ground crew, would be required later to ensure that the aircraft was in full operational condition after successful completion of the air-test. Vic and his crew struggled into their positions through the confined space of Nancy and the pre-flight routine started. Each of the huge 12-cylinder Merlin engines were sequentially kicked into life using a battery saving accumulator mounted on a trolley. The procedure was to start from the starboard outer engine and finish with the port outer with each massive engine run up in turn by the flight engineer to maximum revs. Four times throughout this procedure, the intense roar of the Merlin engine and the vibrations as the aeroplane strained against the chocks assailed the ears and bodies of the aircrew and ground crew. Today all four Merlins worked perfectly and the magneto checks as they were run down resulted in a satisfying change in pitch. The chocks were pulled out from under the wheels by the ground staff and they rolled forward to join the other 463 and 467 aircraft waiting in line for take-off.

After around 20 minutes, they reached the head of the queue and Vic lined Nancy up with the runway, readjusted his seat so that he could more easily reach the rudder pedals and began the take-off routine in conjunction with Jim, the flight engineer. On completion of their final check list he released the brakes and pushed all four throttles forward, putting a little more power on the port engines to combat the natural swing of a Lancaster to port. Nancy, with a small load of fuel and no bomb-load accelerated quickly to take-off speed and they arced up into the winter sky, the now familiar shape of Lincoln cathedral with its tower pointing skywards in the crisp air to their left.

As soon as they had gained enough height, Vic worked the aircraft through its paces by climbing, weaving, banking and diving to test the main flight controls whilst the other aircraft flight systems were checked by Jim feathering/unfeathering the propeller blades, checking the engine temperatures and testing the fuel tank pumps, gauges and instrument panels. The redheaded English MUG, Roy McNaughton, the youngest in the crew and the laconic Brisbane based Australian Jack Lawrence in the rear turret, swung the gun turrets side to side, and went through their gunnery checks. Bomb aimer, Englishman Bill Aldworth checked the bomb-sights and bomb-doors, as well as the hatch in the floor of the front compartment, which was the escape route for him and most of the crew in an emergency. The English WOP, Ron Nixon, tested the radio and navigation aids and everyone checked the oxygen supplies and intercom. The navigator, Arthur Herriott, essentially came along for the ride with the spire of Lincoln cathedral providing an unmissable landmark in the flat Lincolnshire countryside for the short flight home. On night ops, in bad weather and cross-country training flights his role was stressful and constant and he more than earned his way, but on local test flights he was almost redundant.

After 30 minutes of air test Vic received landing permission from the tower, put Nancy down smoothly on the runway and after taxiing to the dispersal area handed the aeroplane back to the ground crew, complementing them on Nancy's excellent condition. The entire crew then headed off with Scotty in the crew bus to their respective messes for yet another early quick meal of spam and salad.

Immediately after lunch, Vic joined the other skippers for the Captains (pilots) briefing, where their curiosity would be satisfied and they would find out the target for the night. The briefing room was quiet, with the 29 Aussie skippers of 463 and 467 Squadrons waiting at their little tables mostly in silence as they stared at the giant map of Europe on the wall, played with pencils or rustled notepads and papers and tried to guess the target. The station commander Group Captain Elsworthy, DFC, DSO, AFC and the Intelligence Officer (I/O) entered the room, chairs scraped back noisily and the 29 skippers stood up. After a short introduction from Elsworthy the intelligence officer silently approached the map and pinned one end of a long red tape into a position on the Norfolk coast, extended it over the North Sea almost due east then over north Holland before stretching the final length of tape south east just short of Bremen into Germany. The last pin was jammed in on top of the German city of Brunswick (Braunschweig) and the silence was immediately broken.

There was firstly a gentle sigh of relief because it was not the "Big

City" Berlin, which being some 140 miles further into Germany and well defended by flak and fighters, was the more dangerous option and assumed by many before the briefing to be once again the target for the night. When the noise abated, the I/O outlined in detail how the squadrons would combine their aircraft with 496 other Lancasters and two Halifaxes to drop a mixed load of high explosives and incendiaries on Brunswick. At the start, he informed them of the other smaller ops over Germany that night that would hopefully draw off some of the German night fighters. Then, he outlined details of the route, timings, speeds, bombing heights and TI colours before showing detailed photos of the town to aid in target recognition. As soon as he started to outline the location of flak, searchlights and possible night fighters en route the tension level in the room rose and as he finished and started to unpin the red tape from the map a general hubbub of conversation broke out as the pilots compared notes and thoughts. Group Captain Elsworthy rose from his chair and as the noise abated, he looked over the assembled throng and simply said "Good luck gentlemen, have a good trip."

During the Captains' briefing, the other crew members were attending their own specific briefings run by the 463 and 467 Squadron specialist leading officers. The 463 Gunnery briefing was taken by the gunnery leader, Flt Lt Brian Moorehead, an experienced Australian on his second tour of ops and his deputy Fl Off DaiRaw-Rees, a red headed Welshman. Moorehead outlined the tactics for the operation, the choice of ammunition, the latest tactics of the enemy night fighters and stressed the constant need for turret rotation, a good lookout, communication and cooperation. With the experience of all their training and 18 previous ops Roy and Jack had their own system and set of rules, which they would once again go through later with the full Trimble crew. Good vision was essential and as the mid upper gunner, Roy had a clear view of the rear turret and was ready to support Jack in defending attacks from that quarter. Jack, like many other rear gunners, had removed some of the perspex panels that restricted his view and consequently would be subjected to even more extreme cold during the night. The twin .303 Brownings of the mid upper gunner were automated so that Roy could not shoot off the tail plane, a feature that allowed him much greater freedom of action. The other important routines were the rigorous checking of the intercom and of the oxygen supply that was essential at the altitudes flown.

One of the biggest problems for the gunners was icing up of the oxygen supply and if Roy observed the rear turret had not rotated for a while, Jack in his isolated position would be queried to ensure he had not passed out through lack of oxygen. The mid upper gunner had no one to check constantly on him, and a few MUGs had succumbed to lack of oxygen and returned home sitting dead in their turret. Usually an experienced pilot could feel through the controls the turret movements as the gunners rotated and watched for fighters but the constant weaving whilst over enemy territory often disguised the turret movements. The only crew member who could observe and check on the mid upper gunner was the navigator when taking star sights through the astrodome.

During the afternoon the ground crew were flat out readying Nancy for the night's work. Although most of the aircraft systems had been checked prior to and during the air test there was still much for them to achieve. The specialist armourers filled the ammunition tanks along the rear fuselage with 10,000 rounds for the four rear guns and racked up 2,000 rounds in each of the mid upper and forward twin gun turrets, cleaned and checked the guns and tested the belts and loading mechanisms. Roy and Jack watched over the process and assisted in getting everything ship shape. They had a good relationship with the armourers as well as faith in their standards and had already built a rapport with them during their six weeks on the squadron. All the aircraft fitters were then required for the complex refuelling task, the amount of fuel giving all concerned some clue as to the likely target. Today some 1500 gallons of high-octane fuel was pumped in at 40 gallons a minute, enough for a trip of 7.5 hours. Not enough for Berlin or any distant targets that required the full 2150 gallons but enough to indicate that the closer Ruhr region was probably not the target. Immediately after the fuel tanks were filled, the oil supply tanks for the 12 cylinder engines were topped up to 100 gallons each.

On completion of the fuelling operation the highly skilled WAAF drivers of the bomb trolley tractors delicately lined up the 4,000 lb high capacity Cookie, a blast bomb, under the bomb bay whilst the fitters hauled huge winches through the fuselage into place over the delicate Cookie. The back breaking task of manually getting the monster in place began and it wasn't until an hour later, having successfully loaded the Cookie along with 1500 × 4 lb and 80 × 30 lb incendiary devices, that the armourers moved on to the next aircraft. Bombing up was always a dangerous occupation and a month later at Waddington a WAAF driving a tractor pulling bomb trolleys was blown to pieces on the perimeter track. The fitters and the riggers spent the remaining time before take-off checking and perfecting the myriad of items that could contribute to mid-air problems. They checked tyre pressures again, cleaned all the visual surfaces with anti-icing fluid, polished out any problem areas in the

Perspex windows, filled oxygen bottles, checked the flares, the batteries, the dinghy, cleaned the control surfaces and instrument panels, loaded up the window (aluminium strips used to confuse the enemy radar) and ensured everything was locked securely in place. By the time the aircraft took off, they would have had an extremely long and exhausting day.

In the early afternoon, the Trimble crew gathered together and joined the throng of aircrew making their way to the huge Nissen hut where the final overall operational briefing was to take place. It was a noisy, mostly jocular walk as the crews bantered between themselves and with other crews in accents ranging through the whole Commonwealth of Nations. Despite being Australian squadrons with Australian pilots, at this stage of the war the majority of 463 and 467 aircrew consisted of English, Scots, Welsh and Irish with Canadians, Americans, New Zealanders, Rhodesians and South Africans scattered through the crowd. Some 30% of the aircrew were Australian and on 463 and 467 most of the ground crew were British. The 91 aircrew of 463 rostered on for tonight's op sat in front of a raised stage with a map of Europe as the backdrop.

In succession each of the leading specialists in signals, engineering, wireless, armament, flying control, navigation, meteorology, and intelligence hopped up on the stage and talked the crews through their area of expertise to support the earlier briefings given to the individual groups. By the end of the process the crews had a host of facts, figures and images in their brains: bomb and fuel loads, take-off times, turning points, timings over navigation points, heights, wind speeds and directions, maps, charts, skymarkers, target indicator colours. Finally the room was darkened and aerial photos of the city of Brunswick were projected on to the screen and landmarks pointed out. The briefing finished with Wg Cdr Rollo Kingsford Smith summarizing all the information and wishing everybody good luck. Despite his seniority he and his crew, as was often the case, were also carrying out this op. Immediately after the briefing, all crews headed off to their respective quarters and tried to relax until take-off. This was the time when nerves could get the better of the crews, as there was little to do other than pen what might be a final letter, read or smoke. Only the navigator was busy, plotting courses on his charts, checking whether the wind predictions had changed, recognizing navigational markers such as lakes, rivers or towns and working out how close they would get to flak hot spots.

Eventually, almost two hours before take-off and after the traditional ops night meal of bacon and eggs together, it was time to kit up, which for the gunners required a major effort to combat the freezing cold that they would have to endure for hours on end. Their inner layer consisted of silk stockings, and woollen kneecaps over coated with fleecy long johns. Over this was a long-sleeve, neck high shirt and trousers, normal socks under long thick woolly socks, followed by a thick white sweater and standard battle dress top. Over all of this came an electrically heated full-length suit and electrically heated slippers that would be plugged into the turret power supply. Fur lined flying boots, white silk gloves overtopped with heated black gloves and then leather gauntlets completed the outfit. Over all this went a parachute harness and a Mae West life jacket. Finally anti-freeze ointment was spread over faces to combat frostbite, parachutes were picked up and the gunners waddled out to the crew room to join the rest of the crew and wait for Scotty and her crew bus.

In the crew room, they synchronised their watches, made last minute adjustments to their gear and chatted to the medical officer handing out pills and the padre handing out cheer and good wishes. The pills were benzedrine sulphate, termed "Wakey Wakey pills" by aircrew, which by 1943 were issued under medical supervision to those crew who wanted them. Most didn't use them because many ops had been cancelled just before take-off and the prospect of lying awake for the night before a probable op the next day did not appeal. For the gunners there was also the cod liver oil pills, taken to combat the cold.

The trip out to the flight line was a quiet one as they tried to settle their nerves and joked with Scotty. On arrival at dispersal, they all greeted the ground crew whilst Bill Aldworth counted the bombs, checked them off against his list and signed for them. They then gathered up coffee flasks, sandwiches, chocolate bars, escape kits, chewing gum, parachutes and the homing pigeon in its cage and climbed into Nancy via the ventral door situated between the rear and mid upper turrets. After the formal pre-flight checks between pilot and engineer, the engines were run up and the crew checked bomb-sights, intercom, oxygen supply and gun turrets before Vic switched off and they all disembarked to stand around nervously chatting to the ground crew, telling a few jokes, horsing around and waiting for their take-off time. Around Waddington, the same procedure was being followed by 28 other crews, all of them in the same tense, reflective mood. Merlin engines spluttered to life intermittently across the airfield and then became silent. Vic and the Flt Sgt fitter, Jim Turrell had a last look around to ensure the covers were off the Pitot tubes, there were no glycol (engine coolant) leaks, the tyres looked in good condition and everything was ship shape before signing off the aircraft as serviceable.

Eventually after a last smoke by some and a nervous pee on the tail wheel by all, a peculiar ritual that the ground crew did not appreciate (it rusted the gear) they climbed into N-Nancy for the third and final time that day. Firstly Jack, who turned to the back, climbed over the rear spar and worked his way into the rear turret after hooking his parachute up on the inner fuselage. He closed the turret doors behind him and was then cocooned in his metal and Perspex box for his lonely six hours aloft. Bill squeezed his way forward into the bomb aimer's compartment where he would spend his night either standing up behind the twin front guns or lying prone on the floor over the locked escape hatch lining up for the bomb run. Vic and Jim next made their way into the front cockpit with Arthur and Ron the next to board and take up their positions in the rear of the heated part of the aircraft, where both of them needed lights and were curtained off from the others. Then Roy, who clambered over the high main spar, hoisted himself into the mid upper turret and flipped the seat into place under his backside. He too would be isolated from the rest of the crew for the night and would be their main pair of eyes. A Lancaster was not a spacious aircraft like the American Flying Fortress or even the Halifax and required at least the front five to board in sequence. The cramped space was also a problem if they needed to bail out, with the hatch under the bomb aimer's position the major exit point. From now until they landed, most of the crew would only leave their stations in an emergency and would be isolated apart from the intercom system.

The final dispersal checklist was efficiently carried out and the engines started in sequence before the ground crew pulled out the wheel chocks, gave them the thumbs up and they rolled into their place in the snaking take-off line to await their turn. Ten to fifteen minutes later at the head of the queue, Ron used the Aldis lamp to signal a request for take-off. The green light winked on the top of the control caravan, triggering the next checklist drill, which when completed resulted in 63,000 lbs of Lancaster bomber powering down the runway to take-off speed. Vic adjusted the throttles to combat the torque and at 1642 hours, the heavily loaded Lancaster staggered up into the darkening sky. Then after a final gentle touch of the rudder bar, the aircraft was re-trimmed, turned on a heading to the rendezvous and slowly and steadily gained height at 175mph cruising speed. The usual crowd of senior officers, WAAFs, the padre and a few of the aircrew not on tonight's op waved them and their fellow crews off from around the control caravan and the ground crews made their way to a well-earned supper while Vic and his crew settled into their positions and adjusted their eyes to the fading light. Now, they were transformed into a calm team, efficient, focussed and ready for their latest dice with flak, fighters and possible death.

As they gained height over Waddington Jim's voice crackled over the intercom, "9,000 feet, oxygen on" and they all clipped on the masks. After a relatively short time they joined a multitude of other aircraft, still gaining height and watchfully keeping an eye out as they loosely formed up into what would be a stream of bombers heading for Germany. Vic listened into the beam that was transmitted to keep them in place over the rendezvous and corrected his course as they stooged around the sky waiting for the next timing. They were bumped around continuously as they hit the slipstreams of the aircraft forming a loose gaggle. As the sky fully darkened and the allocated departure time clicked over, they set course out over the North Sea for Holland, happy that now some 500 Lancasters were all heading in one direction at similar speeds and the prospect of collision diminished considerably. Shortly after they had crossed the English coastline and set out over the ocean a red flash on the sea was reported over the intercom by Jack in the tail. Somebody was in trouble and had already jettisoned their Cookie into the water. They would be going home early and hopefully they would get down in one piece and survive their wing commander's interrogation as to why they had turned back.

Before they approached the enemy coast, Vic gave the gunners permission to test their guns and he could feel the aircraft yawing slightly as Roy and Jack traversed their turrets, tested the guns with short bursts and then settled into their watchful routine. The navigator, Arthur, was hunched over his table behind his curtain checking and rechecking position and making use of the GEE navigational aid before it became useless through jamming by the Germans. This was his best opportunity to obtain an accurate check of the wind speed and direction whilst Ron was listening in and starting to obtain bearings to feed to Arthur during the long night. In the nose, bomb aimer Bill reported the Dutch coast ahead and warned of flak coming up from the island of Texel where the Germans had set up a large number of flak guns. The Texel flak was soon left behind as the bomber stream moved on towards Germany.

Everybody except the navigator and wireless operator was now on the lookout for enemy fighters and other bombers and Vic occasionally rolled the aircraft from side to side so that Roy in the MUG position could see into the blind spot below. They zigzagged along their path to Brunswick with the engines droning loudly and harmoniously. The view of Vic and most of his fellow Lancaster pilots was that flying on a straight line course was far too dangerous, hence the random few degree course changes. These evasive manoeuvres made precise navigation more difficult and timing the flight to the aiming point at the right time a little trickier, but kept the whole crew happier and safer. Their squadron commander, Rollo Kingsford Smith, had an opposite view and he always flew straight to and from the target, believing that the extra complication of zigzags put too much pressure on the crew. He did not compel the other crews to follow his method however and left the decision on how to best get to the target to the individual captains. Ron was fiddling unsuccessfully with the MONICA system. It refused to operate at all, so was powered down. Given that at this time the Germans were aware of the frequencies used and were beginning to test systems designed to use MONICA's beam against the bombers, it was in retrospect not a problem but possibly a blessing. Ron's other task was to drop bundles of the radar confusing strips of aluminium window from the flare chute, which he did every minute when required.

Nancy and the other Lancasters droned on over Holland and then the North Sea into the night, before turning south into Germany just short of Bremen and its protective flak screen. Already the sky would light up occasionally as they saw other Lancs in trouble and they witnessed two aircraft head earthwards in flames. The German night fighters were in amongst the bomber stream long before the target and it looked like being another hot night for Bomber Command. From Bremen onwards the bomber stream left a trail of crashed and burning bombers, a trail that continued until they recrossed the Dutch coast on their way home. Thirty eight Lancasters were destroyed that night, mostly by night fighters. Time seemed to drag as they flew south over Germany until after what seemed an eternity, Arthur announced over the intercom that the last turn towards the target was two minutes away and they all settled down to prepare for the most dangerous part of the op, the bombing run. It was now whilst they were flying straight and level, that they were most vulnerable to fighter attacks or being coned in searchlights. They had been coned by searchlights before and were lucky to escape after Vic threw their Lancaster all over the sky. It had been a frightening experience that they hoped would not be repeated. Below they could see only cloud that topped out around 10,000ft so thankfully tonight there were no searchlights probing the bomber stream, just night fighters prowling the sky.

Other Lancasters ghosted through the sky around them, one slightly above them to the left and another even higher just off in front. There was almost no flak over the target, a sure sign that many night fighters were active over Brunswick and the German gunners did not want to hit their own aircraft. As if to confirm the presence of night fighters there was a blinding flash off to the right as a Lancaster and its crew blew up, leaving trailing streams of burning petrol and flaming debris lighting up the scene. Vic reminded his gunners to keep a keen lookout for fighters and settled into the bombing run, heading steadily and inexorably towards the cascading TIs ahead and the dull red glow under the cloud. The aircraft was now under the control of Bill in the front compartment.

"All yours bomb aimer."

Bill had already calibrated the bomb sight using the information on wind speeds, wind direction, altitude and air speed from the primitive computer system with it's array of sixteen switches and dials. The bombs were fused and organised for release in the correct order, with the high explosive Cookie to arrive first and the incendiaries last. Bill started giving Vic instructions so as to line up on the TIs.

"left, left,   r-i-i-i-ght, steady,   steady, bomb doors open."

Time seemed to stand still as they approached the centre of Brunswick, still aiming for the green TIs that the Pathfinders had set up. Bill peered through the Mark XIV bomb-sight waiting agonizingly for the moment that they could drop their load. He once again reminded himself of the final comment of every bomb aimer's briefing: "avoid creepback – count to three after you reach the aiming point", saw the green TIs in the bombsight, counted to three and pressed the release. An upwards jerk of the aircraft and "bombs gone, bombs gone" over the intercom signified that they had another 20 or more seconds to count off before the aiming point photos were taken and they could extract themselves from the extreme danger of the target area. These always seemed to be the longest seconds of their existence and Bill mentally counted off as the crew held their breath and the gunners caught sight of another flash of an aircraft starting to burn up. After what seemed an eternity the photoflash went off and he handed control back to the pilot.

"Bomb doors closed, Ok, Skipper – your aircraft."

Almost simultaneously with Bill uttering his final instruction, a line of green tracer arced up from below the port quarter and cannon shells smashed into the elevators, the port rudder, both port engines and the rear turret. The rear turret was disabled as shells and jagged metal fragments flew violently and randomly through the aircraft, injuring the bomb aimer and rear gunner and leaving jagged holes in Nancy's fuselage and wings. The prolonged minutes of steady flight over Brunswick had provided an excellent opportunity for a night fighter to locate them, position itself in their shadow and surprise the gunners. From the shattered rear turret, the injured Jack saw the attacking FW190 swing up over the starboard quarter and watched as it set itself for another attack by moving to their port quarter. His turret was useless and as he shouted

"Corkscrew port" into the intercom, his brain faded out and he vaguely felt the vibration as the mid upper turret open up as he passed out. His oxygen line had been hit, his turret immobilised and he was out of the fight.

Roy looked through his gun sights and estimated the deflection as Vic corkscrewed violently to port. The recent refresher training had ensured his reactions were almost automatic and he gave a six second burst at 300 yards as the fighter approached and readied to fire again. With a feeling of surprise and great relief, he saw the fighter dive underneath Nancy and head off downwards to starboard without firing. Either the fighter was out of ammunition or he had managed to hit it. Seconds later far below him he sighted a FW190 diving in flames through a thin layer of cloud before being lost to sight. After a long pause there was a brief but violent flashing explosion on the ground below, not big enough for a Lancaster falling to its death, but just what might be expected from a small fighter.

Nancy was now losing height rapidly with Vic struggling to get the aircraft under some sort of control after his violent evasive manoeuvres. The battle with the flight controls was exhausting, but eventually Vic managed to pull the Lancaster out of the diving corkscrew manoeuvre, achieved almost level flight at around 14,000 feet and began to assess the damage as Nancy continued to slowly lose height. Both port engines had been knocked out. "Engineer, feather port engines and then check the damage". The rudder and elevators were not responding well. Vic rapidly did a check of the crew on the intercom and everyone apart from Jack answered, although Bill the bomb aimer reported that he had been injured. From the mid upper turret, Roy reported that the rear turret was a mess and there was no obvious sign of life.

"Should I check on the rear gunner, skipper?"

"No way wireless op, we'll check him out when we are under control."

Even under the stress of action, the crew maintained the discipline of calling every other member of the crew by their roles rather than names, a routine that was instilled into them. Roy continued to rotate his turret and keep a lookout for fighters but he was now getting colder and felt a stickiness in his right boot. His heated flying suit was no longer functioning. It was going to be a cold trip home and his were the only set of eyes now searching the night sky for fighters.

Vic pushed the throttles forward on the starboard engines and manhandled the controls to try and keep the aircraft straight and level and halt the constant loss of height. With his foot hard over on the left rudder pedal to counteract the effect of having only starboard engine power he managed to straighten Nancy up. Jim successfully feathered the port inner but the port outer continued to windmill out of control despite the feathering procedure so he worked steadily through the feathering procedure three more times without success and the propeller on the port inner windmilled on. It was only afterwards that they remembered that the mid upper turret was powered by the port outer engine, so without the rotating prop Roy would have been of little use as a lookout or gunner. After some ten minutes of experimentation, Vic had worked out how to keep the aircraft more or less under control and was heading west towards home.

"Navigator give me a route home, as direct as possible and no flak."

"OK, skipper, we'll stay north of the Ruhr and then head straight home along the Rhine valley."

They flew on, losing height slowly as their two remaining engines strained on full power to keep Nancy aloft. The training of the previous week that saw them practising flying on two engines was coming into its own. Vic set the course for home aware that they were highly vulnerable if sighted by another fighter. Given the state of their aircraft there was little else they could do. Jim, the flight engineer, eventually made his way back through the cramped and damaged fuselage and after using an axe to break into the wrecked rear turret, managed to extract the unconscious Jack and drag him forward into the warmer part of the aircraft. He quickly strapped an oxygen bottle to the unconscious rear gunner and went back to his flight engineer's role. A scan of the gauges revealed that the levels in the port fuel tanks were dropping more rapidly than the starboard ones even though no port engines were operating. The port tanks despite being self sealing, were leaking badly so he set to, laboriously transferring the remaining fuel in the port tanks to the starboard tanks in the hope that Nancy would have enough fuel to stagger home. With the two good engines operating at full power they were burning through their fuel supply rapidly as they laboured on over Germany.

By the time they were overflying the Ruhr, Nancy had lost enough height to allow them to dispense with the oxygen masks and soon they were down to 4,000 feet where Nancy was holding her own. Jack, covered in oil and blood had regained consciousness. To the rest of the crew he had looked just about gone and they were worried he would not survive the trip home. On closer examination though, they found that his main wounds were from shrapnel in his lower legs. He had lost a lot of blood, but been lucky given that the shattered rear turret was an absolute mess of oily bent metal and smashed Perspex. As they struggled their way on two engines and flew steadily out over the sea towards England and home, the hydraulic pressure gauges displayed progressively lower pressure readings. The number of problems for the crew to deal with were mounting as the night went on and maybe all that damned dinghy training would also come in handy.

"Looks like we will have trouble with the landing gear, and the flaps skipper, and the fuel is getting very low."

"OK engineer, we will try for a landing at Wittering."

Wittering was situated much closer than Waddington and it had an extremely long runway that was often used by aircraft in emergencies[4]. Consequently, it was always at the back of the mind of any aircraft captain in a damaged aircraft.

"Wireless operator, put out a mayday when we get close to Wittering, that will get the flare path turned on. Navigator, give me a course for Wittering."

They staggered on through the sky with Jim carefully watching the dials, Vic concentrating on keeping Nancy flying and the rest of the crew hoping for a good outcome. Eventually as they turned on to the approach to Wittering the flare path lights came on and Vic asked for the landing gear to be lowered, hoped for the best, and concentrated on lining the badly damaged aircraft up with the lit up runway ahead. The landing gear refused to come down using what remained of the hydraulic system so they made use of a pneumatic bottle, supplied for that purpose, to get it lowered. After struggling for a while, Jim managed to get the port wheel down and probably locked in, but the starboard wheel would not lock. He pressed the intercom button and relayed the bad news.

"Ok, skipper, the port wheel is locked in but the starboard isn't."

---

[4] Embry had taken over a night fighter wing and was concerned because of a large number of accidents caused by a combination of a short, wet, grassy runway and the high landing speed of a Beaufighter. He could not extend the runway so thought of a solution by simply linking the Wittering runway with a satellite airfield close by. The powers above declared it was too expensive, would take months to complete and would ruin a potato crop for the farmer running the land so they canned the idea. Embry was not to be thwarted. He talked to the landowner and got the OK, presented a bottle of scotch and payment for the potatoes to the farmer, arranged for machinery to remove hundreds of trees and got his airmen to do the physical work on top of their normal duties. Within three weeks they had a three mile long runway and reduced the accident rate considerably. Within weeks it was also in use as an emergency landing ground for heavy bombers with problems. If Embry thought he had a good idea he was not one to let the bureaucrats get in the way and this is just one example of his many achievements whilst in the RAF. He retired as an Air Marshall. See "Mission Completed" – Basil Embry.

Vic, by now somewhat fatalistic about their chances replied.

"Righto crew, crash positions and brace yourselves."

Vic had to fight the controls as they lost their remaining height and he managed to align Nancy just about perfectly with the longest runway in Britain. They were a little too low though and as they reached the airfield perimeter, they ploughed straight through a hedge. This advantageously ripped off the landing gear, although they didn't know that at the time. Nancy touched down remarkably easily but before Vic could congratulate himself on a near perfect landing, he felt and heard the contact of metal on concrete as they belly-landed on the bomb bay. He took his feet off the now useless brakes and they careered down the runway accompanied by the screeching noise of metal on concrete. After about 300 yards, Nancy finally skidded to a grinding halt just off the runway and luckily out of the path of any other aircraft trying to land. They all clambered out of the aircraft as rapidly as possible, assisting the injured Jack and Bill to get as far away as possible in case Nancy caught fire.

As they extracted themselves from the mess of metal that was Nancy, a fog descended on Wittering and it was sometime before an ambulance and tender pulled up nearby. A Southern American drawl broke the silence.

"Waall, ye'all sure made a mess of that plane. Are you guys OK?"

"Blood oath we did Yank, you're a sight for a sore eyes. A couple of our blokes need an ambulance."

Vic and the others ensured Bill and Jack were stretchered off in the ambulance and then he and the remaining crew turned around and took a long look at the third Lancaster they had pranged. At least this prang was not down to his flying! Nancy had brought them home to England and she even looked salvageable. Maybe she would fly again. Eventually a crew truck arrived and they drove off to the crew room in a quiet reflective mood as the adrenaline slowly drained away, Roy shivering with cold and trying to get his circulation going again after hours in the turret without heating. They were not debriefed, that would have to wait until their return to Waddington, but they were taken to the USAAF mess and treated like lords with coffee, cake and cookies laid on. Before too long though they were stripping their flying gear off and clambering into comfortable beds. During this process, Roy discovered a hole in his flying boot, a spent shell and congealing blood down his leg. The shell had shorted his electric suit and glanced off his leg, leaving a gash that he had not felt until now.

It was usually relatively easy to sleep after a raid because they were exhausted after up to 18 hours of preparation, actual flying and stress, and could wind down through drinking a cup of tea during the intelligence debriefing and by comparing notes with other crews over the post op meal. This night though they all slept fitfully. In the dreary winter morning light next morning they were given a huge breakfast and told that with luck they would be collected by a 463 Squadron driver. It seemed odd marking time on an unfamiliar air base so they went off to have a look at Nancy in the daylight. The rear turret was a mess, there were jagged holes in the metal along the port wing and the fuselage and a dipstick showed that they had only 40 gallons of fuel left in the tanks, so less than eight minutes flying time. They definitely would not have made it to Waddington.

The USAAF were the main occupants of Wittering at this time and they were given an escorted tour of the P38's and P51's of the 55th fighter squadron before Scotty eventually showed up late in the morning to collect "her" crew. They gave her an enthusiastic and relieved greeting, threw all their gear in the back of the truck and then drove back to Waddington mostly in silence, quietly pondering their lucky escape from a fiery death. Scotty seemed to know that they had no desire to talk about their experiences and that the near disaster of the previous evening had left them somewhat the worse for wear. Shortly after arrival at Waddington, they were debriefed by the deputy Intelligence Officer, delivered their raid and combat reports for the squadron ORBs and then headed off for a well-deserved meal and a drink in the mess.

Later that same afternoon Vic was called into Rollo Kingsford Smith's office, where he was first congratulated for bringing the damaged aircraft back to England and then told he and his crew would be having a three-week rest from flying. So the next day, after visiting Jack and ascertaining that his injury wasn't as bad as they had first thought, the crew went their various ways on leave, happy to be alive and kicking, with 19 ops now down but wondering anew about their chances of surviving the remaining 11 ops of their tour. Jack was to spend almost four weeks in hospital recovering from his wounds, which were described in the records as "light". Both Bill Aldworth and Roy McNaughton were recorded as having light wounds as well, but both were out and about very quickly[5].

---

[5] The wound descriptions are contained in the casualty report for Jack Lawrence. NAA: A705, 166/24/262.

Fig. 10. Naughty Nancy over Brunswick.
Commissioned by Barry Hope and painted by Geoff Bell[6].

---

[6] Barry Hope still has some copies of the limited edition print – contact can be made through his facebook page "and in the morning".

8   THE LAST OPS

15/16 February 1944
<u>Berlin</u>: After a rest of more than two weeks for the regular bomber squadrons, 891 aircraft - 561 Lancasters, 314 Halifaxes, 16 Mosquitos - were dispatched to Berlin. This was the largest force sent to Berlin and the largest non-1,000 bomber force sent to any target, exceeding the previous record of 826 aircraft (which included Stirlings and Wellingtons) sent to Dortmund on the night of 23/24 May 1943. It was also the first time that more than 500 Lancasters and more than 300 Halifaxes were dispatched. The German controllers were able to plot the bomber stream soon after it left the English coast but the swing north over Denmark for the approach flight proved too distant for many of the German fighters. The German controller ordered the fighters not to fly over Berlin, leaving the target area free for the flak, but many fighters ignored him and attacked bombers over the city. The diversion to Frankfurt-on-Oder failed to draw any fighters. 43 aircraft - 26 Lancasters, 17 Halifaxes -were lost, 4.8% of the force.

Berlin was covered by cloud for most of the raid. Heavy bombing fell on the centre and south western districts and some of Berlin's most important war industries were hit, including the large Siemensstadt area. This was really the end of the true 'Battle of Berlin' with only one more raid on the city in this period and that was not for more than a month. For the Trimble crew this was their eighth and final trip to Berlin and their first op since the near disaster over Brunswick a month earlier. Apart from Jack Lawrence, who was in hospital for the month, they had all had a period of leave. Jack was not discharged from hospital until 17 February, so his rear gunner position was taken by an experienced New Zealander, Flt Sgt Jack Childs.

19/20 February 1944
Leipzig: 823 aircraft - 561 Lancasters, 255 Halifaxes, 7 Mosquitos. 78 aircraft - 44 Lancasters and 34 Halifaxes - lost, 9.5% of the force. The Halifax loss rate was 13.3% of those dispatched and 14.9% of those Halifaxes which reached the enemy coast after 'early returns' had turned back. The Halifax IIs and Vs were permanently withdrawn from operations to Germany after this raid.

This was an unhappy raid for Bomber Command. The German controllers only sent part of their force of fighters to the Kiel minelaying diversion. When the main bomber force crossed the Dutch coast, they were met by a further part of the German fighter force and those German fighters, which had been sent north to Kiel hurriedly returned. The bomber stream was thus under attack all the way to the target. There were further difficulties at the target because winds were not as forecast and many aircraft reached the Leipzig area too early and had to orbit and await the Pathfinders. Four aircraft were lost by collision and approximately 20 were shot down by flak. Leipzig was cloud-covered and the Pathfinders had to use skymarking. The raid appeared to be concentrated in its early stages but scattered later.

This was the heaviest Bomber Command loss of the war so far, easily exceeding the 58 aircraft lost on 21/22 January 1943 when Magdeburg was the main target. Almost 100 of the aircraft sent to Leipzig turned back before the target. Arthur Herriott was unavailable so the navigator on this op was Flt Lt Williams. Fl Off Pettit fulfilled the navigator role on the next op.

20/21 February 1944
Stuttgart: 598 aircraft - 460 Lancasters, 126 Halifaxes, 12 Mosquitos - to Stuttgart. The North Sea sweep and the Munich diversion successfully drew the German fighters up two hours before the main bomber force flew inland and only 9 aircraft - 7 Lancasters and 2 Halifaxes - were lost, 1.5% of the force. Four further Lancasters and one Halifax crashed in England.

Fig. 11. Trimble crew under Uncle Joe Stalin after the Leipzig raid, Waddington, Feb 1944.

24/25 February 1944
<u>Schweinfurt</u>: 734 aircraft - 554 Lancasters, 169 Halifaxes, 11 Mosquitos - carried out the first Bomber Command raid on Schweinfurt, home of Germany's main ball bearing factories. 266 American B-17s raided the factories the previous day. The first wave of 392 bombers encountered the fighters and losses were 5.6%. The second wave two hours later were better off, losses were 3.2%. An overall loss of 4.5%.

Schweinfurt was one of the most famous bomber targets of World War 2. The ball bearing factory there supplied 50% of the German needs through four factories and so the city was targeted 22 times – particularly by the USAAF. The USAAF, flying in daylight, could more easily target specific sites and so employed a strategic bombing strategy that differed from that of the RAF. This strategy resulted from the much stronger defensive armament of the B17, the lack of navigational training to allow night bombing and later in the war the availability of long-range fighters like the P51 Mustang to accompany the bombers. The heavy armament and design of the B17 meant that the bomb loads were almost half that of the Lancaster. Thus, the USAAF often attempted to knock out critical components of German industry like ball bearing plants or oil facilities. The RAF concentrated more on area bombing but some raids were directed at specific sites. The Germans combatted the bombing offensive by decentralizing their ball bearing manufacturing plants (and other industries) and by importing supplies from neutral countries. Bomber Command introduced a novel tactic on this night. The Schweinfurt force was split into two waves - 392 aircraft and 342 aircraft, separated by a two hour interval. Part of the German fighter force was drawn up by earlier diversions. The first wave of the Schweinfurt bombers lost 22 aircraft, 5.6%; the second wave lost only 11 aircraft, 3.2%%, and it is believed that night fighters shot down only four bombers from the second wave.

25/26 February 1944
Augsburg: 594 aircraft - 461 Lancasters, 123 Halifaxes, 10 Mosquitos - on the first large raid to Augsburg. The various diversions and the splitting of the main bomber force into 2 waves again reduced casualties still further with the second wave arriving when most of the night fighters were refuelling. 21 aircraft - 16 Lancasters, 5 Halifaxes - lost, 3.6% of the force; at least four of these casualties were due to collision.

The bombing at Augsburg was outstandingly successful in clear weather conditions and against this 'virgin' target with only weak flak defences. The Pathfinder ground-marking was accurate and the raid became controversial because of the effects of its outstanding accuracy. The beautiful old centre of Augsburg was completely destroyed by high explosive and fire, with much less than the usual spread of bombing to the more modern outer areas, where some industry was located. There were 246 large or medium fires and 820 small ones; the temperature was so cold (-18° C) that the River Lech was frozen over and many of the water hoses also froze. The Germans publicised it as an extreme example of 'terror bombing'.

1/2 March 1944
Stuttgart: 463 Squadron sent 13 aircraft to join the 557 bombers attacking Stuttgart. The weather was still freezing and heavy cloud all the way prevented the fighters from getting into the bomber stream. Cloud over the target covered the markers. Pathfinders could not keep the target marked, and crews could

not assess the results. Post-war German records say the city was heavily hit, with the Bosch and Daimler-Benz works badly damaged. Losses were 0.7%, none from Waddington.

This was the third trip to Stuttgart for the Trimble crew and they had to land because of a fuel shortage before getting home. Because of the southerly position of Stuttgart they must have been returning home through France and they landed at Tangmere in west Sussex, an airfield famous as a fighter station. As soon as they arrived back at Waddington, the crew quickly packed and went on leave.

This period of leave was certainly out of the ordinary. HK535 Naughty Nancy, the aircraft that they brought back from the Brunswick raid on two engines, was the first Lancaster produced by the Vickers Armstrong Castle Bromwich factory, which was originally setup in Birmingham in 1938 as a Spitfire production plant. In 1943, the factory commenced production of Lancaster bombers and eventually produced 300 Lancasters in addition to 12,000 Spitfires. The factory were proud of their achievement and the initial Lancaster aircraft, HK535, which first flew on 22 October 1943, was paraded extensively for publicity purposes when completed and again when delivered to 463 Squadron at Waddington in November 1943. When the badly damaged aircraft was returned to Castle Bromwich for repair just two months after its completion, they again considered the publicity and morale angle and asked Wg Cdr Kingsford Smith to arrange a visit by the Trimble crew to the Birmingham factory.

The crew duly arrived after recovering from their long trip to Stuttgart in the homes of their Nottingham friends and were feted over three days as the crew who brought the damaged aircraft back and shot down the first German night fighter from a Castle Bromwich built Lancaster. The factory laid on a huge party at a local hotel with copious amounts of food and drink and a dance band. Large numbers of the employees attended in order to celebrate and meet the aircrew and Vic had to deliver a number of warmly applauded speeches. He also had to sign up on the dance cards of numerous young women swooning around the flyboys. The crew were adopted by the factory essentially as a "pinup crew" for their Lancaster production facility. Roy, as the gunner responsible for shooting down the fighter, was presented with a photograph of a Lancaster in flight signed on the back by the factory managing director J. V. Morton.

"With Congratulations and Best Wishes to the gunner who registered the first "Kill" for our factory".

The fact that the "kill' was in the squadron records as "probable" and unconfirmed didn't stop what might now be referred to as "spin". The crew were also all presented with copies of a photograph taken of them with the factory bigwigs under the wings of a brand new Spitfire.

Apart from the factory shindig, the remaining seven days of leave were typical of how the crew made use of their time away from ops. From the Castle Bromwich factory in Birmingham the whole crew travelled to Broughton, Banbury, the home of flight engineer Jim Marles where they were entertained by his extended family for a few days. Vic wrote a letter home expounding how welcoming everybody was and how in the family homes everyone had a great time making their own entertainment.[1] After the few days together in Banbury, they returned to Waddington to complete their tour of ops.

Fig. 12. The Trimble crew photographed at Castle Bromwich Aircraft factory. Front row Left right Jack Lawrence, Ron Nixon, Roy McNaughton, Jim Marles, Vic Trimble, Bill Aldworth, Arthur Herriott. Back row Mr. Leach, production manager, Mr. Cook, general manager, Mr. Davis, technical manager. February 1944.

---

[1] From Vic Trimble's letters home.

THE LAST OPS

Fig. 13. HK535 – First Lancaster from the Castle Bromwich Factory. Photo presented to MUG Roy McNaughton.

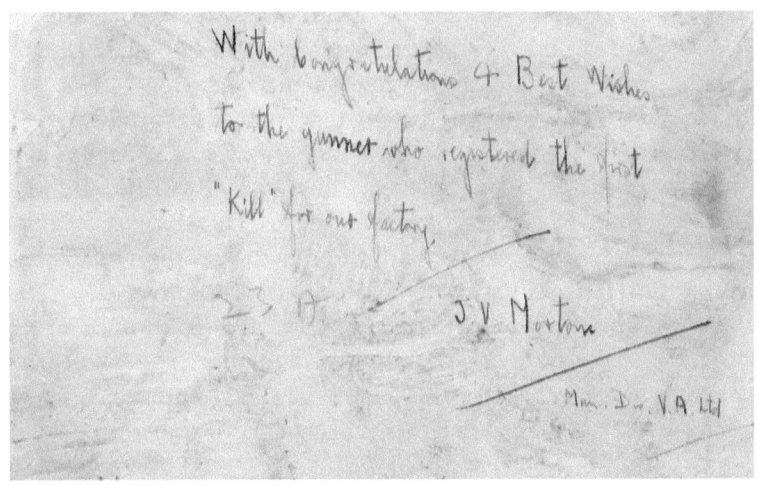

Fig. 14. Inscription on the back of the factory photo of HK535 presented to Roy McNaughton.

15/16 March 1944
Stuttgart: 863 aircraft - 617 Lancasters, 230 Halifaxes, 16 Mosquitos - ordered to attack Stuttgart. The German fighter controller split his forces into two parts. The bomber force flew

over France nearly as far as the Swiss frontier before turning north east to approach Stuttgart. This delayed the German fighters contacting the bomber stream but, when the German fighters did arrive, just before the target was reached, the usual fierce combats ensued. 37 aircraft - 27 Lancasters, 10 Halifaxes - were lost, 4.3% of the force. Two of the Lancasters force-landed in Switzerland. Adverse winds delayed the opening of the attack and the same winds may have been the cause of the Pathfinder marking falling back well short of the target, despite the clear weather conditions. Some of the early bombing fell in the centre of Stuttgart but most of it fell in open country south west of the city. The Akademie was damaged in the centre of Stuttgart and some housing was destroyed in the south western suburbs.

This was the Trimble crew's fourth and final trip to Stuttgart. By this stage of the bombing offensive, the tactics employed by Bomber Command included a number of smaller raids to split the German fighter force, attacks on German fighter airfields, RAF fighters to attack the night fighters and electronic countermeasures. Despite the new weapons and approaches, the losses continued to be high. The experienced Trimble crew also recognised the dummy enemy markers and bombed on the city centre unlike many crews who bombed open country.

On the afternoon following the Stuttgart raid, the Trimble crew were gathered together to attend the final briefing for yet another op when it was announced that ops were cancelled due to bad weather. Because of the long stretch of extreme winter weather, cancellation was happening regularly and the news was greeted by a loud cheer and the departure of most crews for Lincoln and a night on the town. With such a reprieve most aircrew would head for the movies, go drinking in pubs or search out company, anything to keep the nerves and apprehension at bay and to celebrate another night that they would be alive. Vic and his crew were sauntering back from the briefing room when the adjutant approached him.

"G'day Vic, the wingco would like to see you in his office straight away." Vic replied with an OK and muttered to himself, "Strewth, I wonder what we've done now? I had better go and see what's up." Kingsford Smith was renowned as a disciplinarian and could be a martinet so in some trepidation he made his way to the squadron commander's office and took a seat outside Kingsford Smith's office.

After cooling his heels for some ten minutes, he was called in, expecting to stand in front of the desk for a bollocking about some misdemeanour or crew failing. Surprisingly, Kingsford Smith looked at him and smiled.

"Flying Officer Trimble take a seat." Somewhat relieved Vic gingerly sat down and tried to relax. "Well Trimble you and your crew have almost completed a tour and I have an issue to sort out. Group have a problem filling instructor positions in the training schools at present, apparently there are not enough time-expired crews coming through. They have requested that I release any crews who have done 25 ops or more and declare them tour expired so tonight was going to be your last op. With tonight scrubbed I have had to put things on hold. The word on this new instruction would probably have got out so I thought I should tell you now that your next op will be your last." Vic immediately wondered, having personally done more than the 25 ops, why they needed to do another one but resisted asking the question, merely saying

"That's great news Sir, the boys will be happy." Kingsford Smith looked at him for a while and eventually answered the unspoken question.

"I need to put up a full complement of aircraft on the next shindig to keep Group happy so I am afraid I need you and your crew one last time. Just make sure you get back in one piece."

Vic left the Wing Commander's office in something of a daze and searched out the rest of his crew. When they were all together he told them the news and as they took it in, he declared

"We had better be on our toes and make it a safe one. Shit, it better not be Berlin." Later in the day, they discovered that the crew of Flt Lt Wilson would also be flying on their last op that night.

Some six weeks earlier, another 463 crew had also been informed that they were on their last op. Flt Lt Ivan Durston DFC (RAAF) and his crew took off in Lancaster ED687 to attack Berlin on their 27th op. They did not return and the aircraft crashed near Oranienburg, about 30 km north of Berlin. At the time, only one of the crew (Flt Sgt Griffiths) was identified and his body was eventually interred in the Berlin CWGC site. Some 57 years later the crash site was rediscovered by a German "Fliegerschicksale" group, and the remains they discovered allowed the identification of the other crew members. In July 2003 the whole crew were interred together in Berlin and a memorial was placed at the crash site.

Kingsford Smith did indeed have a problem on his hands with crew numbers because new crews were not coming through at the same rate as the loss rate and now with two prematurely tour expired crews this was exacerbated. Soon after this period, after a phone conversation to the Air Officer Commanding RAAF in London he placed in writing a "complaint" about the lack of crews reaching 463 Squadron and declaring the squadron would be non-operational if some of the many Australians coming through the training scheme were not sent to 463[2]. This approach was eventually successful and all the Australian squadrons began to receive more replacement crews.

Vic woke early the next morning and after his morning cuppa quickly made his way over to the flight commander's office to check out the list of crews on ops. Sure enough his name was chalked up there on the board against "Uncle Joe" along with 17 other listed crews and their aircraft. Eighteen aircraft was a full complement for 463 with only two flights, so the Wing Commander had been true to his word. Knowing this was the last time they would have to face an op over Europe he breathed slowly and tried to stem the mounting apprehension. He knew he would have to keep the crew busy all day to minimize the time they had to dwell on the coming op and its possible outcomes. Gathering his thoughts, he walked briskly back to the mess to begin the usual routine in preparation for an op.

In late morning, Vic and his crew were sitting pensively in the crew room waiting for Scotty to bring the crew bus and transport them to dispersal for the air test. The other crews, most of whom they hardly knew, kept their distance. Nobody wanted to jinx them for their last op and the whole squadron desperately wanted them and the Wilson crew to get through the night and show that it was actually possible to finish a tour on 463. Jack Lawrence was the first to break the silence.

"Gees tomorrow we are going to have one big piss up, what do you reckon skipper, we all put a pound on the bar and drink till it's gone?"

"No worries Jack, if we finish this op my drinking days start tomorrow." A couple of minutes later Scotty appeared at the door and they all brightened as they hopped in the crew bus and started to chatter nonsense with her. The well-practised routine continued with an uneventful late morning air test with the only minor issue, as usual with Uncle Joe Stalin, being getting the engines synchronised. Once again, Jim could not quite get them synched and gave up.

After lunch, they all sat attentively and nervously through their individual briefings before gathering together as a crew for the final briefing. For hopefully the last time they leant forward from their ops table as the Intelligence officer displayed the map of Europe and started to pin up the route to the target for tonight. The tape was extended out

---

[2] The letter written by Kingsford Smith is available at the National Archives of Australia and at https://www.ordinarycrew.co.uk/463-squadron.

over the North Sea once again and then over Holland and into Germany before turning due south below Bremen and terminating at Frankfurt. Not an "easy" target like one in France or Italy but at least not Berlin. The I/O stuck in a second tape indicating that a stream of some 90 aircraft would split off and head to the Heligoland Bight to lay mines and act as a diversion to the main force of some 850 aircraft. Other smaller forces would be sent to Kassel, whilst Mosquitos would raid the German airfields in Holland, France and Belgium to disrupt night fighters. In total, 1046 aircraft would be active over Europe.

To distract his crew and prevent them from thinking too much about the coming op, Vic took them off once again to practise dinghy drill and emergency landing procedures. After this they all headed into their respective messes for a final pre-ops meal, keeping fingers crossed that the op was not scrubbed at the last minute. By late afternoon, they were all kitted out in their flying gear, had collected parachutes, escape gear, wakey wakey pills, coffee flasks and the homing pigeon and were waiting nervously in the crew room. Scotty appeared at the door, smiled broadly and beckoned them to come out and hop in the crew bus. At dispersal the ground crew were gathered around Uncle Joe to farewell them and fix any last minute issues. They all clambered aboard in the usual order and ran the engines up, checked the radio, radar, bombsights, intercom, oxygen supply and gun turrets before Vic switched off and they all disembarked to await final take-off time. Vic did his usual walk around checking that the pitot tube covers were off, tyres were pressurised, there were no fluid leaks and the control surfaces were all normal before signing off with Chiefy Powell, the ground crew boss. All the ground crew came up and instead of the usual chit chat shook hands with the aircrew and heartily wished them a safe return.

As their allotted take-off time approached they started to board for their final flight together and Jim, the flight engineer peed ritually on the rear wheel, ostensibly to help discharge any static electricity. The ground crew and Scotty gave them a final wave as the chocks were pulled out and Uncle Joe rolled forward to take its place in the snaking line of Lancasters. With eighteen 463 and twenty two 467 aircraft to take-off it was a long procedure, but at 1905 they were given a green light, ran the engines up to full power, accelerated down the runway and slowly climbed away over the outskirts of Lincoln and set course for their allocated start point and Holland. All the nerves that had built up through the day were now gone and they settled into their familiar roles for the more than six hours that it would take to complete the op and their tour of operational duty.

18/19 March 1944

<u>Frankfurt:</u> 846 aircraft - 620 Lancasters, 209 Halifaxes, 17 Mosquitos - to Frankfurt. The German fighter force was again split. One part was lured north by the Heligoland mining operation but the second part waited in Germany and met the bomber stream just before the target was reached, although cloud made it difficult for these fighters to achieve much success. 22 aircraft - 12 Halifaxes, 10 Lancasters - were lost, 2.6% of the force. The Pathfinders marked the target accurately and this led to heavy bombing of eastern, central and western districts of Frankfurt. The later phases of the bombing were scattered but this was almost inevitable with such a large force; new crews were usually allocated to the final waves.

463 Squadron ORBs RAF Waddington 18/19.3.44
Frankfurt   ED611 JO.U
Crew: Fl Off Trimble   Flt Sgt Marles   Fl Off Herriott Sgt Nixon
*   Sgt Aldworth   Sgt McNaughton Sgt Lawrence*
Fl Off Trimble, bombing FRANKFURT. Sortie completed. Up 1906 down 0121. Thin cloud at almost own height. (22,000ft). Numbers of red TIs burning on ground. 20,000ft, 2203½ hrs, 1x4,000HC, 1200x4, 150x4 XIB 58x30 Inc. Target consisted of pattern of red TIs and incendiaries which were reasonably well placed in relation to the TIs. There was some evidence of creep back. Route good. Considering there were far too many aircraft over the target at one time. This was a real nuisance on making bombing run with other aircraft close at either side it was necessary to bomb the western most markers missing chance of aiming point.

Apart from some flak when the bomber stream came close to flak concentrations, the trip for the majority of the way to Frankfurt was undisturbed by the German defence. The gunners occasionally reported bombers close by as they weaved their way over Holland and Germany and Vic twice had to evade bombers that were too close. Approaching Frankfurt, they saw one Lancaster well ahead of them light up and go down in flames but with cloud up to 22,000 ft, the fighters were not having a lot of success. Vic took in the sight of the bombers all around, saw the red TIs off to the east a little and assessed the situation as too dangerous to aim directly at the main markers. That would require crossing the paths of other bombers.

"OK, bomb aimer we will head for the western markers. The aircraft is yours."

Vic followed Jim's instructions, heard "bombs gone" as the aircraft leapt up and flew steadily on waiting for the camera to take its aiming point pictures. At the "All yours skipper" statement from Jim he turned the aircraft west and headed for Luxembourg, Belgium and home.

The fighters would be ready for them by now.

"Keep your eyes peeled gunners, there's plenty of cloud about but the fighters will still be around and there are lots of Lancs and Hallies around." "Navigator give me a course for Blighty." The trip home was uneventful and time seemed to stretch out endlessly but eventually, almost three hours after releasing the bombs, they were approaching the English coast and soon after that settling into the crowded sky for a landing at Waddington. At 0121hr on 19 March 1944, their wheels kissed English earth and Vic touched the rudder to align Uncle Joe with the runway. They had completed their 28th op and Uncle Joe was well on its way to completing 100 ops. As they rolled to a stop at dispersal, they saw their ground crew and Scotty waving animatedly from close by the crew van. They had all stayed up and come out in the hope that their boys would be back and felt just as relieved as the aircrew that they had arrived home safely.

A grinning Scotty greeted them one by one as they descended from Uncle Joe and after shaking hands with all the ground crew they piled noisily into the crew van for the short trip to the debriefing room. A number of crews were ahead of them in the room but Kingsford Smith, who had also been to Frankfurt that night and had landed twenty minutes before them, beckoned them over ahead of the other crews, shook each of them by the hand and congratulated them before handing them over to the I/O for their debriefing. An hour later they were all still hyped up but trying to settle down to sleep, knowing that they now had an excellent chance of actually surviving the war. The next morning though Roy and Jack woke to find the adjustment team were at work in their quarters. Despite relatively few Bomber Command losses on the previous night's raid Gardner's crew had failed to return and they were removing the possessions of Jim McGrath, his 21 year old rear gunner from Western Australia. Gardner and his crew had all died the previous night.

True to their word, early on the evening of the 19 March the crew were ensconced at the Horse and Jockey, starting to drink their way through seven pounds worth of drinks. Earlier that day Vic had been approached by a senior squadron leader and asked if they were interested in joining 617, the Dam Buster Squadron for a tour, and he was now telling his crew about the offer.

"I hope you told him to bugger off Vic, we're all looking forward to a bit of leave and an easy life."

They could now start to think realistically about life after the war and by the end of the year at least three of the Englishmen in the crew would be joining Bill Aldworth as married men. Roy, Jim and Bill Nixon would be married and starting families. The crew of Sq/L Wilson also completed their tour on the Frankfurt raid and they too were asked to sign up for 617 Squadron. They too all declined apart from their flight engineer Sgt Felton, who joined 617 and was subsequently killed in action (KIA). The remainder of the Wilson crew survived the war. Soon afterwards, Vic Trimble was awarded a DFC with the citation:

"Flying Officer Trimble has completed many sorties including eight attacks on the German capital. This officer is a gallant and efficient captain and pilot and his determination to complete his missions successfully has been highly commendable. One night in January, 1944, he piloted an aircraft detailed to attack Brunswick. Whilst over the target area the aircraft was engaged by a fighter and sustained much damage. Nevertheless, Flying officer Trimble flew the aircraft back to base although on the homeward flight he suffered from lack of oxygen. This officer has set a fine example of courage and devotion to duty".

Kingsford Smith sent a congratulatory telegram on behalf of the whole of 463 Squadron to Vic, who was then enjoying a couple of weeks leave in London staying with Ginger Aldworth and his wife prior to embarking on an instructor's course.

9   AFTER OPS

Eventually finishing their incident packed tour of ops in late March 1944 the Trimble crew were posted out to a range of OTUs and HCUs scattered over the southern parts of England. They were the first of two crews who appeared that month in the 463 Squadron ORBs as posted out to units rather than being nominally posted to the War Casualty N/E Accounts Dept Air Ministry unit after being shot down or killed in accidents. With a week of leave before reporting for instructor duties, both Roy and Jim Marles went home to their girlfriends and proposed marriage. Both were accepted, although Nancy had to agree to a pre-nup agreement that maybe one day she would end up in Australia.

Vic Trimble, with his pilot's logbook now containing the grading of above average, spent five weeks at No. 3 Flying instructor's school at Lulsgate Bottom (now Bristol airport) and after graduating on Airspeed Oxfords became an instructor on Wellingtons at 27OTU's satellite airfield at Church Broughton, Derbyshire. Vic spent 18 months instructing on Wellingtons before being posted back to Australia, arriving in Sydney in August 1945 and having more than 600 hours of flying experience. After release from the RAAF with the rank of Flight Lieutenant on 9 September 1945, he returned to Cairns and was engaged to Margaret (Meg) Griffiths just before Christmas 1945. The Griffiths family were good friends of the Trimble family and Meg had been a quartermaster in the VAD (Voluntary Aid Detachments) during the war. After a stint selling insurance, Vic became involved in the family business, built a home and supplemented his income through purchasing land with partners and growing crops. Vic and Meg raised a number of children and were successful enough to ensure that all of them were well supported and provided for. Vic's major regret was that he did not go to university after the war so he ensured his children had that opportunity. Vic died on 29 November 1977.

Jack Lawrence was posted to 12OTU (RAF Benson, Oxfordshire) and became a gunnery instructor after a course at 7AGS RAF Stormy Downs in Wales. After eight months of instructing gunnery and now a commissioned officer, he was posted home to Australia, arriving April 1945 and discharged on 10 July 1945 as a Flying Officer. He returned to Brisbane and started a family with Merle. He spent the rest of his life constructing rather than destroying buildings. He died 11 August 1977.

The two Aussie members of the crew, Vic and Jack, died within months of each other at the relatively early age of 56 and spoke very little about their air force days in Bomber Command. This silence was much the same for most returned servicemen after the war in that their experiences were bottled up and unspoken. RAAF aircrew who served in Europe had extra difficulties because, unlike those who served in all Australian units in the army or navy who spent the majority of the war with a group of comrades, they did not generally end up with the strong support of mates when back home. During their service, they were transferred between many different units spread all over England, mostly with few other Australians. Even a close knit crew, and there were virtually no all-Australian crews, were together for about one year and then went their separate ways. The Australian squadrons were in 1943/44 at most 50% Australian and many of the men that they either joined up with or became mates with on the squadrons were killed. On returning home, they were often also geographically isolated from other returning aircrew. Vic having joined the RAAF with his local militia mates, some of whom survived, was an exception in having a few good mates with similar experiences around him.

Jim Marles was posted out to 1654 Conversion Unit as an instructor. He married his sweetheart Joyce soon after and later in the war after a stint in Ireland, was sent to India as a flight engineer on Liberator aircraft that had been converted to freighters. He joined a crew who ferried equipment around India, Ceylon, Cocos Keeling Islands and Australia. He flew more than 1,000 hrs in total and visited every Australian city apart from Brisbane. Upon discharge, he returned to Broughton near Oxford, worked as an electrician with a number of companies and raised a family of four. Like many English crew members on the Australian squadrons, he developed a warm feeling for Australia and Australians and until his death in August 2012 he assiduously attended the annual Anzac Day commemoration in London.

Roy and Bill Aldworth were posted to 14OTU, their original

operational training unit, which had been relocated to Market Harborough, Leicestershire. Bill Aldworth after demobilization returned to London and his wife and died in Lincolnshire in early 2004, aged 83. Ron Nixon was transferred to 11OTU (RAF Westcott, Buckinghamshire) and Arthur Herriott to 1654HCU (RAF Wigsley, Lincolnshire). In November 1944 Arthur was promoted to Flight Lieutenant. All of the crew continued flying and there were significant accident and death rates at all these units, but in comparison to operational flying, they were safe. By the end of their tour of ops all the sergeants, except Roy, who had joined up later than all the others, had been promoted to flight sergeant. Aircrew promotions in both the RAFVR and RAAF for non commissioned personnel were made simply on a yearly basis, unless someone was commissioned. Roy was promoted to flight sergeant (Temporary) exactly 12 months after his promotion to sergeant (Temporary) on finishing the MUGs course and 12 months exactly to the day after that was promoted to Warrant officer (Temporary). All his promotions were temporary ones and he was "demoted" to sergeant on discharge as were all RAF Bomber Command non-commissioned aircrew. This "demotion" always rankled with him and other aircrew and they believed they had been badly treated by a government that wanted to sweep the bomber war under the carpet and save on the amount of money that aircrew would receive on discharge.

In contrast to their RAF brothers in arms, it seems that virtually all the Australian Bomber command aircrew who survived a tour of ops were promoted to officer rank before their return to Australia. Out of more than 30 RAAF returning Bomber Command aircrew investigated for this book, all returned to Australia as officers, whereas of a similar number of British aircrew very few were commissioned. The only Australian aircrew who remained non-commissioned seem to be those who flew in other theatres of war or who finished the war in non aircrew roles. Vic's 51st Battalion mate Blue Emslie, although operational as a typhoon pilot, was discharged as a warrant officer after converting to the role of Warrant Officer Disciplinary in order to remain in England with his sweetheart. One of Vic's other 51st Battalion mates, Gordon Ingram, who had spent the active part of his war as a Warrant Officer gunner flying Hudson and Flying Fortress meteorological aircraft out of Iceland was not successful in being commissioned despite two applications. It appears that the seemingly automatic commissioning in Bomber Command was not the case for coastal command crew. The promotion of surviving Bomber Command RAAF aircrew to officer rank was partly a consequence of them joining the RAAF directly rather than though a reserve system as existed in Britain. The commissioning of aircrew must have been a policy of the RAAF and seems to have been an expectation of RAAF aircrew when they joined up. Unlike their Aussie mates, most of the British bomber aircrew remained as temporary non-commissioned officers and even if rising to higher ranks were discharged as sergeants with commensurate pay and prospects. They had joined the RAF volunteer reserve with its separate rules and regulations. One can only conclude that RAAF aircrew were much better treated by their government after service than their RAF comrades in arms.

As an operationally experienced air gunner Roy, still only 19 years old at the completion of his tour of ops, joined others who had survived their tour of ops as an instructor and enjoyed the opportunity to impart his knowledge, play football, socialize with other aircrew and start to think about a normal life post war. The ORBs of 14OTU for the months he was there provide an insight into the way such a base operated and the social structure that existed. The records contain bare statistics on training, together with detailed sports results where the base enjoyed success in football and cross-country running and the airmen participated in numerous other sports on a weekly basis. Keeping up morale and fitness was an obvious focus of the unit and the records include a description of the efforts to look after the WAAFs by providing flowers in their quarters and sprucing up the decor, and comments on WAAF dances, airmens' dances and a myriad of social events. Wellington Xs were still the major training aircraft but the base also had a complement of Miles Martinets for towing targets, Airspeed Oxfords for general training and Hurricanes for fighter affiliation. During April of 1944, there were six air raid warnings, constant problems with radio communications, dances twice a week and visits by music, theatre and comedy companies. In May, the chaplain distributed "Australian comforts" to the Aussies and tried to reinvigorate the religious discussion group. The "Australian comforts" were provided by an extensive women's volunteer organization back in Australia, "The Australian Comforts Fund", and were generally items that were not provided to Australian servicemen by the military such as socks, underwear, pyjamas, cigarettes, razor blades, soap, toothbrushes, toothpaste and books. At times the distributed packages also contained fruit cake, chocolate and other sweet items. Many of the food items ended up in the homes of the families who hosted the Aussies.

There were often visits by senior RAF staff, such as the visit by Group Capt D.J. Eayrs, DFC on 25 May who arrived in his own aircraft from RAF Driffield. Having read his logbook, it is apparent that Eayrs was a prolific visitor to air bases all over the world and flew numerous aircraft types (more than 100). He has the distinction of being the subject of questions asked in the British Parliament of the Air Minister as to what Eayrs was doing flying all over Australia over a period of months in 1942. The rapid expansion of the RAAF required the import of senior RAF personnel in the early years of the war. Eayrs was a permanent RAF officer who was sent to Australia as CO of the RAAF's Camden Central Flying School in 1941. After completion of that assignment, he seems to have spent many months simply visiting bases around Australia before eventually returning to Commanding Officer roles in Britain. Soon after his visit to Market Harborough, he was appointed CO of 640 Halifax Squadron and carried out a number of ops over Europe.

From the statistical records, gunnery practise consumed 429300 rounds of ammunition in June whilst 1273 bombs were dropped by day and 1174 by night. In this month (like every month) numerous movies were shown with the main features being My Friend Flicka, Alexander's Ragtime Band, Slightly Dangerous, Thank Your Lucky Stars, Reveille with Beverley and Assignment in Brittany, so mainly musicals, comedies and light relief with the odd propaganda/morale boosting war movie. In May, the single war movie shown was "In Which We Serve", starring Noel Coward as the dashing Louis Mountbatten and John Mills in one of his first film roles.

Around this time at 14OTU, an intelligence library was set up on the base and the ORBs noted that the resource was increasingly used by trainee aircrew, who mainly accessed the MI9 bulletin. MI9 were responsible for ensuring as many downed airmen as possible returned to Britain and the bulletin contained information on how best to escape capture after being shot down. The base also had a "German room" which was "well attended" so it seems the crews took escape seriously and worked on acquiring the necessary knowledge to improve their chances of escaping imprisonment if they survived being shot down. In August, there were more aircraft crashes with two fatal Wellington incidents and 10 deaths. The ORBs briefly mention gunnery infrared trials, which were aimed at testing out infrared telescopes aligned with the rear turret guns to identify friendly aircraft equipped with IR emitters. Infrared signals were flashed from a lamp located in front of the bomb aimer of friendly aircraft and the rear gunner identified friendly aircraft as he traversed the turret with the co-aligned IR telescope. In this manner, he was rapidly capable of identifying the flashes as "friends" to prevent the shooting down of bombers.

Roy remained at 14OTU for three months, until admission to the RAF hospital at Cosford suffering from the mumps. Because of this he was the only one of the Trimble crew to miss the July wedding of Jim Marles in Banbury. Upon discharge from the hospital, it seems the RAF didn't quite know what to do with him and he was posted to the aircrew allocation centre at Brackla, Inverness shire in Scotland. There he spent 9 weeks sitting aptitude tests and exams and enduring interviews to determine how the RAF could make best use of his skills. Surprisingly the RAF eventually concluded he would be best employed as a fully qualified gunnery instructor and he was posted to 12AGS, RAF Bishop's Court in County Down, Ireland as a gunnery instructor. After attending a seven week air gunner instructor's course (60AGI), he passed with an A and immediately proceeded on leave to Darlington.

Roy and Anne married on the first day of this leave at the 12th century St Andrew's church in the little town of Haughton-Le-Skerne, just outside Darlington, with Roy's sister Eva the bridesmaid and Jim Marles the best man. It was a typical wartime wedding, with the men in uniform and the women dressed in whatever they could put together from the limited materials available and the number of clothing ration coupons they had saved up for the occasion. Soon after marriage, Roy relocated his new wife from the wartime dangers of mainland Britain to Ireland for a short honeymoon. A reminder of this time, a painting of the harbour at Ardglass, a pretty coastal village close to Bishop's Court where they lived for a while, accompanied our family movements for a number of years. At 12AGS, he carried out senior instructor duties in the quiet backwater of Northern Ireland for nine months. According to my movie-mad mum, two of his trainees were the actors Richard Attenborough and Jack Watling, who had joined the RAF and trained as air gunner cameramen. On finding out there were two young actors in training she declared of Richard Attenborough – "with a name like that he won't go far". When Attenborough became famous, the comment became a family joke. Attenborough subsequently flew a number of ops over Europe in the rear turret of Lancasters and apparently damaged his hearing permanently whilst at 12AGS as a consequence of the instructor not bringing ear muffs to the firing range one day[1]. That instructor was not Roy!

---

[1] See "Entirely up to you darling" – Richard Attenborough and Diana Hawkins, Random House 2014.

Fig. 15. Wedding of Roy and Anne, 18 November 1944. Left to right Eva McNaughton, Roy and Anne, Jim Marles.

In May 1945 with the end of the war and no further need for new gunners, 12AGS closed down and Roy was posted to the No 2 aircrew holding unit (2ACHU) in Penhros, Wales. In typical armed forces fashion, at Penhros he was kept busy doing nothing until, in September 1945, long after the end of the war and with little need for gunnery instructors, he was re-mustered as a clerk and posted to the RAF records office in Gloucester. At Gloucester he further developed skills in organization and record keeping until some months later in May 1946 he was re-assigned to the postings branch. Here he quickly twigged to the fact that all the previous incumbents in his role had remained in the job for a very short time. Realising that he was in a position to send himself wherever he wanted, he rapidly arranged a posting to 13OTU, RAF Middleton St George, the former Canadian bomber base just outside Darlington and very close to home. At Middleton St George he was employed as a senior clerk with the rank of Warrant Officer, living in Mallard Road until his eventual discharge on almost the last day of 1946, more than 18 months after the end of the war and four years after joining the RAFVR.

The war had a profound effect on Roy's life. In addition to his operational experience, he had travelled and lived in numerous places in England, Scotland, Wales and Ireland, been allocated senior office roles, flown and worked with men from all over the world and faced death a number of times. The major influences were his Australian crew mates and his time with an Australian squadron. The seeds for immigration had been planted during the most stressful time of his life. Roy had started the war as an 18 year old labourer with little formal education and finished it a 22 year old veteran with a lifetime of experiences, organizational abilities and a knowledge that there could be better places to live than England. He also had a wife and my brother Alan (born late 1945) to care for so thoughts of immigration were placed on the back-burner.

Soon after his release from the RAF Roy set up in Darlington as a "Man from the Prudential" convincing people to invest in life insurance and then collecting the weekly commitments by travelling door to door, either on foot or on a pushbike. In the cash environment of the time it was the common approach to insurance, it kept him fit and with his chatty personality, it suited him in the short term. By 1949, Roy and Anne had a second child (my brother Steve, born mid 1949) and Roy had moved out of insurance and was working in the newly built Paton and Baldwin's factory close to home where Australian merino wool was turned into fine yarn. After seven years living in two different "temporary" war service houses in Mallard road my parents, older brothers, Alan and Steve and myself, a new baby (born 1951), moved closer to Darlington town centre and into a larger house. This was the first of a number of moves as Roy and Anne seemed to suffer from a seven year itch which required a change in environment in order to scratch it. We initially shared the "larger" house with my maternal grandparents, who helped with the mortgage and I imagine, also with child minding.

By the mid 1950s, war rationing was at last over but there was little food choice in the shops and children were still provided with free orange juice concentrate and cod liver oil to make up for the nutritional limitations of the available diet. Britain was still in the throes of recovering from winning a war, rebuilding damaged towns and cities, divesting itself of an empire and starting to pay back £21 billion it owed to Canada and the USA in war loans. The loan to the USA was paid in 50 instalments starting in 1950 and finishing in 2006 with a final payment of $US 83 million. Thrift was prevalent and wartime experiences were constant topics of conversation.

All of the adults involved in our lives had experienced the war firsthand, so even in the eyes of a child, the dark cloud of World War 2 still hung over the British landscape. So much so that as a child growing up in Darlington in the mid to late 1950s, for some time I was convinced that the ruined area around the railway station was a bombsite and a product of World War 2 destruction. In my family every adult had been directly involved in war work of one sort or another. My uncle Eddy (the eventual husband of Roy's sister Eva) had joined the British army before the start of the war and as a gunner in the British Expeditionary Force, fought in the retreat through France and Belgium and was stretchered on to a hospital ship at Dunkirk with a bullet wound to the foot. He was left with residual metal fragments in his foot, which prevented him from marching and curtailed his general mobility. Because of this injury, he was allocated to the more sedentary role of a gunner in the merchant navy where he manned the deck pop guns provided to merchantmen as defence against surface raiders and U-boats. He was based for most of the rest of the war in Simonstown in South Africa and survived the torpedo sinking of two ships. Despite these experiences he showed no signs of post traumatic stress, was imperturbable and known by all the family as "Steady Eddy".

In 2018, at the age of 96, Eddy died as an indirect result of his war wound. An ulcer developed precisely at the spot where the bullet had entered his foot and where metal fragments remained. He went downhill from that point after losing his mobility and independence. My Uncle Arthur (two years younger than Roy) was also in the army by the end of the war whilst Uncle Fred was young enough not to be involved. Uncle Jack, my Dad's older brother, spent the war in the RAF in a ground crew role. My two grandfathers, John William and William John, both served in the volunteer fire service for the duration of the war. In the 1950's, as a result of most males and females having been directly involved in war work of one sort or another, the war was still a constant topic of conversation and a thread that bound everybody's lives together.

Darlington, as a railway and marketing town provided us with a playground. When not standing on the railway bridge near our house experiencing the vibrations and sounds of the Flying Scotsman rocketing underneath us in a cloud of smoke, cinders and steam, we kids were often found admiring the massive, seemingly alive steam engines under the enormous Victorian triple arched Darlington Bank Top station roof. Around the station precinct our other occupation was exploring the ruins of old houses and sheds, finding discarded tins, cutlery, crockery, toys and artifacts that a modern archeologist would probably find fascinating. Occupational Health and Safety was not as pervasive in those days and a host of little boys and girls roaming over demolition sights raised no eyebrows. Between our house and Bank Top station there was also the strategically located stockyard, where livestock auctions took place a few times a week and we could often be found there annoying the farmers and admiring the cattle, sheep, chooks and particularly the pigs. It was a hive of activity but again little boys and girls were accepted as just part of the scene and we were often gainfully employed by being provided with sticks with which to help herd the animals.

At that time one of the Bank Top station platforms was also home to George Stephenson's "Locomotion No. 1". This was the world's first steam railway engine to serve a passenger train, built in 1825 for the Stockton and Darlington line, the first commercial passenger railway in the world, which subsequently became part of the LNER (London and North Eastern Railways). The "Derwent", another historic engine built in Darlington in 1845 was also displayed on the platform, so for young boys the area was heaven and the exposure led to a lifelong interest in railways. Both of these engines are now displayed at the Darlington North Road railway museum, located at the long defunct workshops where my Uncle Fred helped construct rolling stock until it closed down in the 1960s. The closure of the 100-year-old workshops, the largest employer in town and the backbone of the town's life, set Darlington on a different path, one that led to mass unemployment and the destruction of much of the town's infrastructure. Modern Darlington doesn't have a great deal to commend it to a visitor but the majestic listed Victorian Bank Top station with its triple arched roof and classic columns is worth a visit along with the railway museum.

In one section of the park close to our house, which was situated not far from Darlington station, there was a disused air raid shelter or bunker, essentially a long concrete tube half buried in the earth with steps at each end right angled to reduce blast. We would play in there, making siren noises and imagining aeroplanes overhead with anti-aircraft guns blasting away. It was of course fantasy because Darlington escaped the attentions of the Luftwaffe by being located in a low lying valley where the mist and fog often hid most of the features that could be used for aerial identification. The ruins around the station that I had imagined to be bomb damage were actually the result of a 1950s slum clearance that was taking an inordinate amount of time to clear.

Returning to Darlington in the winter of 1978, the winter of discontent, when Arthur Scargill and the unions were fighting a losing battle to retain the last British coal mines and the industry of the North, the town was depressed, downtrodden and on its last legs. The heavy industries were all gone, the station's role as a transport hub much reduced and Darlington's role as a market town diminished, though the stock yards were still operating (and in 2020 are also still operating, although close to moving out of town). Over the years, Darlington steadily declined and each time I return I thank my father for taking us to Australia at the right time. The Darlington soccer team, the Quakers, provides an excellent proxy for the town's decline. In the 1950s, 60s and 70s it bounced around between the third and fourth divisions after earlier being a second division team, but now languishes in the National league North after a number of years in even lower divisions of soccer. Despite the town going steadily downhill, my memories of the time I spent there as a child paint a more positive picture and without the incumbent worries of an adult or the knowledge of brighter more positive places to live it was a happy childhood. There was however no perceivable future for us in 1960s Darlington, a factor that contributed eventually to propelling us to the other side of the world.

Despite the town deteriorating slowly, as an important railway junction Darlington still provided easy routes into many surrounding towns and in summer we would have a week's holiday in the close by coastal town of South Shields. This required a short train journey to Newcastle and then a journey south on the electric train that ran both north and south of the city. By 1963, soon after our departure, these electric trains were gone and replaced by diesels. The diesels themselves were replaced by a metro system in the 1980s connecting the major towns of the Tyne and Wear. The attractions for us were the wide beaches (usually cold and windy), donkey rides, bandstands, parks, fish and chips, bingo halls and lots of other kids to play with. We stayed at the Beachams of 106 Beach Road where we three boys usually slept in an attic room in the roof space and where the act of sitting up in the middle of the night resulted in a sore head. The breakfasts were of the "Full English" variety and a highlight for us boys, who would normally have just toast and cereal at home. The house was close to the long sandy beach and the Marine Park with its lifeboat memorial and a tiny steam train that chugged around the park perimeter.

There was an extensive train network around Darlington so in the days prior to the decimation of the railways by the Beeching cuts there were many places to choose from for day trips. On the long days of summer weekends, we would often head off as a family by rail to Saltburn by the sea, Seaton Carew or Redcar for more of the same sort of beachside attractions. Sometimes we would head off to the market town of Richmond in Yorkshire, where a massive ruined but child accessible Norman castle built centuries before to keep the northern rabble under control towered over the river Swale and protected the gateway to the Yorkshire Dales. The view from the castle ramparts over the looping bend in the river is a picturesque and memorable sight. Here of course we played at being Robin Hood or knights of the round table and protected the castle keep against all comers.

As seven to ten year olds we could often be found playing in Darlington's South Park just a few minutes' walk from our house where we enjoyed football and cricket, climbed and fell out of trees, flew kites, caught sticklebacks, redbellies and newts in the lake and slid down what we perceived to be the world's highest and steepest slide. Some 30 years later I checked the slide out and it scared the daylights out of me – just a narrow metal polished surface with small lips set at an immense angle and a simple almost vertical iron step ladder leading some 30 foot up. No safety features at all. No wonder there were broken arms and cuts and bruises galore.

In autumn we would venture down into the lower area of the park by the River Skerne where the towering horse chestnut trees created a vast dark, dank vale to collect "conkers", the chestnuts we would skewer and mount on string to generate hopefully a weapon-like "conqueror" capable of destroying everybody else's conkers. It was essential to take a friend or an older brother to ensure the imaginary gremlins or the more dangerous real perverts didn't get you. It was not an area frequented by the girls, who probably didn't appreciate the strange male inhabitants exposing themselves! It was bad enough for us boys. On the way home in summer we would often detour via the luscious gardens backing on to the park and relieve the owners of strawberries, blackberries, gooseberries and whatever else was in season. I don't think they minded too much as there always seemed to be an excess of produce and we judiciously distributed our thievery over a number of gardens to disguise the damage. Our parents also kept us out of mischief by joining us up with the "Life Boys", a Christian based organization similar to the cubs and we would attend once a week, take part in parades on some Sundays and gain badges for various mental and physical pursuits.

With Darlington being close to Yorkshire, just a couple of miles from home the River Tees formed the county border and we would often walk through South Park, skirt around the dark vale and venture cross-country to the pretty, picture postcard village of Croft, where the Tees cascaded vigorously over the rocks below an old stone bridge. Once there we would ford the shallow river below the bridge to Yorkshire and in summer it was a beautiful calm place to while away the school holidays. Mum would pack my brother Steve and me a lunch and send us off with John and Peter the boys next door. I guess it was safety in numbers. On the walk home we would often unthinkingly collect birds' eggs from the hedgerows, which would be blown to add to our collections.

Another favourite place was the Middleton St George RAF base (now the Tees Valley airport) some four miles in the opposite direction to Croft, where we could sit above the small town and watch the RAF planes taking off and landing. The unfulfilled desire to be a fighter pilot was probably a product of the day I was covered in goose bumps watching English Electric Lightnings powering vertically up from the end of the runway like rockets. A trip to the RAF base involved a long day with eight miles to walk and on one particularly hot day some adults in a car took pity on us and gave all four of us a lift home. It didn't seem unusual at the time, just a natural kindness. In this day and age they would need a police check I imagine before they could stop and pick up four young kids.

Every Sunday, as a family, we would either walk or hop on the bus and travel across Darlington to my paternal grandparents' house. Grandma Mac would cook up a storm and the tea table would be covered in homemade cakes, sandwiches, scones and biscuits, often including ingredients from Granda Mac's garden where he had a large greenhouse as well as a prolific garden bed. Usually our local cousins, aunts and uncles would be in attendance, and occasionally aunts and uncles from more distant parts with a tribe of cousins in tow would turn up for a get together. I never really became familiar with the tribe of cousins, although I do vaguely recall playing with some of the girls of around my age and collecting ice-cream with them from the van playing Greensleaves that somehow seemed to know that there were lots of kids ready to nag their parents. These family gatherings were usually quite subdued from the adult viewpoint, with card games being the main occupation of the adults and older kids although I learnt some 30 years later that my Aunt Maureen was something of a party animal when not in the company of my paternal grandparents.

My mother's side of the family, the Browns, were a different kettle of fish and although she was an only child, my mother seemed to have large numbers of uncles and aunts and a hoard of mostly female cousins who were always in for a party. Her parents had 13 siblings between them. When my maternal grandparents lived with us there would often be visits from these relatives and I remember a number of times creeping down the steps late at night to find a party in full swing with my mum playing the piano and a large number of well lubricated adults singing and dancing in a fug of smoke. My mum was the quiet one of the crowd, but she was an excellent piano player who could be coerced away from playing classics and jazz into bashing out popular tunes. If mum wasn't playing the piano then Granda would have his accordion on his lap, rolling from side to side as he squeezed life into it. My brother Steve and I would observe the festivities through the railings from a vantage point at the top of the steps until spotted by a parent or relative. If it was a parent, it was straight off to bed but the relatives usually encouraged us down to the party for a while and we would be allowed to join in a rendition of "Roll out the Barrel" or "We'll meet Again" or dance the "Hokey Cokey" before being taken off up to the bedroom that we shared.

My Aunt Maureen's propensity for partying became explainable when I learnt that she was actually one of Mother's many cousins, so consequently a Brown and genetically programmed to party. She had met Dad's younger brother Arthur when visiting my mum in Darlington and the two young lovers at ages 17 and 19 eloped. They lived happily together with four daughters until my uncle's premature death from mesothelioma in 1981. He had worked most of his life as an engineer on ships containing lethal asbestos engine lagging.

Whilst my older brother Alan had moved up to attend the prestigious Queen Elizabeth Grammar School, set up by Queen Elizabeth the first, my brother Steve and I, attended the Dodmire school and walked to and from school daily, crossing under the main London to Edinburgh train line just outside the station. After my maternal grandparents moved out of our shared home, the walk home after school was often past their corner shop where we would usually be presented with a treat and could watch them smoke the proceeds of their endeavours. I had a particular soft spot for my Granda Brown, who owned a 1940s motorbike and sidecar. A trip in the sidecar being thrown from side to side as we hurtled down country lanes was a rare treat.

Memories of Dodmire are somewhat limited, because I didn't particularly enjoy school at that stage. I was a slow starter and my earliest memory of school is of standing on the steps in front of the imposing school doors bawling my eyes out as my mother walked away whilst a teacher did her best to entice me inside. I was extremely shy, four years and two weeks old and not exactly keen to begin school life. I suspect in these more enlightened days I would have been granted another 12 months grace before starting school, or attended a kindergarten prior to school. Two other early school memories are vivid. I was selected for personalised reading lessons with what seemed to me to be an ancient female teacher, which must have been reading recovery with somebody over 40. The sessions worked and I became an avid reader, possibly because it allowed me to put my head in a book and ignore the real world. At the age of eight, I was presented with an Enid Blyton famous five book at the Paton and Baldwin's children's Christmas party and was extremely disappointed with such a "babyish" offering. My books of choice at the time were Captain Marryat's "Children of the New Forest" and any Biggles book, which I felt were much more appropriate reading matter for me. The former underpinned my interest in history and the latter encouraged boyhood dreams of being a pilot.

The other major memory was one that helped form my initial reluctance to undertake sports. One of the popular winter lunch time outdoor activities was to determine how far it was possible to slide over the ice on the playground. After a while, the ice surface became highly polished so with a decent run up a gloriously long slide was achievable. Such a slide required excellent balance and familiarity with the movement. I lacked both, so overconfidence led to an extremely long slide which, although in my mind created a record, finished in a dramatic fall that knocked all the wind out of me. Upon standing, I was incapable of breathing and passed out from my short lived vertical stance. I can still hear the sound of my skull hitting the icy concrete, although there was no sensation of pain until I came back to my senses a minute or two later with a concerned teacher bending over me. The consolation prize was an afternoon at home.

The school dinners that were provided by the government to all students are also memorable. Memory doesn't stretch to the main courses, apart from the lumpy mashed potato, but I vividly remember the desserts. Spotted dick with its currants in a suet bed, sticky treacle tart, spicy bread and butter pudding, apple pie or pudding covered in lashings of custard, apple crumble and a revolting sago pudding which consisted of clear ball bearing like objects in a milky slop of nondescript flavour.

After the seven year itch had been scratched and we moved to the new house, Dad continued to work at Paton and Baldwins, the massive modern yarn factory on the outskirts of Darlington that employed 4,000 people. In addition to its own railway sidings the factory grounds contained a number of playing fields and a large social centre so was a hub that we occasionally attended on the weekends. Sometimes we watched from the sidelines as Dad played football for the works team or loosed arrows on the archery field, no doubt employing his knowledge of gunnery. My older brother Alan always made sure we were not behind the goals because about the time I was born, when he was six and despite being told not to, he stood by the goal and collected a full blooded drive from the centre forward, Monty Buckley, directly in the face and went over like a ninepin. Whether it was the ball in the face, or the bollocking from my father after he eventually got up that made him so diligent I don't know.

Dad lost another one of his cat's lives when in 1958 he was admitted to hospital to have his appendix removed. With his normal luck, the surgeon left a pair of scissors and a few other bits and pieces inside him before sewing him up and after discharge he became sicker and sicker until he had to be rushed back to hospital by ambulance sometime later. The surgeons discovered the problem and fixed him up but he spent an extended period in hospital recovering. He was still in hospital over Easter 1959 and I remember a giant chocolate Easter egg that was broken up during one of our hospital visits. We all proceeded home with large bags of chocolate pieces that were so big that they had to be gnawed rather than bitten. The chocolate sticks in my memory because for us the normal Easter eggs were hard boiled hen's eggs, decorated by us with paint and consumed on Easter Sunday. These eggs were also used in a traditional game where they were rolled down a hill with the winner being the child whose egg rolled the furthest. Chocolate was definitely a luxury item in short supply in our family.

1959/60 was not the worst post war winter by any stretch of the imagination, that distinction goes to 1962/63, but in Darlington there were a number of days when the roads were iced up and we had lived in the same house for approaching seven years. Dad at that stage was riding a bike to and from work at Patons and Baldwins' mill where he was a union man and the secretary of the Dyers, Bleachers and Textile Workers' union. The subject of emigrating to Australia occasionally came up, especially when the Australian government ramped up the advertising in the late 1950s. With three kids to look after, moving to Australia was still placed in the "Too Hard" basket.

Sometime in January 1960 Roy limped in the door a little later than normal, having fallen off his bike five times on the way home and expressed a deep and long felt feeling:

"Booger this we're goin' to 'stralia!".

My mother glanced up and calmly said

"OK Pet, sit down and have your tea first".

Dad was calling in the pre-nuptial agreement where Mum had consented to marriage fore-warned that one day she would probably emigrate to the far side of the world. As an only child, it was not a decision for her to take lightly, but the concept had been brewing for about 16 years since Dad's 463 Squadron days, so her casual reaction was not unexpected. The wheels were quickly set in motion on the emigration train, with one letter posted off to Australia House and another one to an old address for Jack Lawrence, the Aussie rear gunner, in Brisbane. The letter to Brisbane returned some three months later with multiple post marks and a large overstamp "not known at this address".

The letter to Australia House had more luck and it seemed that the Australian government was very much in favour of receiving a family of five willing Brits. After a few false starts, some 18 months later in early August 1961, we had sold the house and packed up. Our possessions were reduced to the contents of two trunks and three suitcases, and now we three kids and our two 10 pound Pom parents leant out the window of the soot covered carriages of a steam train heading for London and the "holiday" of a lifetime. That holiday was a wish come true for my mum. During the immigration application process, we had watched a TV program on the maiden voyage of the gleaming luxurious new Orient liner on the Australia run, the Oriana. "Ooo, be lovely to travel on that" she had cooed.

The move was an excellent one for me. I was to sit the 11+ exam the following year at the tender age of 10 so it would have been an 11- exam for me. The exam result dictated whether you attended further education at an academic grammar school or a secondary modern school aimed at producing trades people and I was highly likely at that stage to end up on the trade route. Roy's usual luck had also surfaced once the decision to emigrate had been made. A weekly flutter on the English "football pools" where you had to pick the highest number of draws where goals were scored had produced a win of some £2500, a considerable sum of money that converted to £AU3750 and helped set us up in our own house not too long after our arrival in Brisbane.

Fig. 16. Packing for Oz August 1961. Photograph by The Northern Echo.

10   TEN POUND POMS

At Darlington's Bank Top station, we gathered as a family of five beside Stephenson's Locomotion with three suitcases and our Darlington relatives. All present were stoic northerners so I do not remember any tears but despite my excitement I did pick up a feeling of apprehension and our grandparents were decidedly glum and not their normal selves. Given that both sets of grandparents later declared that they thought they might never see any of us again, there were probably stronger indicators that I did not pick up on. In 1961 international travel was still an expensive and time consuming occupation, so migration to the other end of the world was often considered a "Life Sentence" much as it was for the transported convicts of the 18th and 19th century. A few memories of the weeks before our departure still inhabit my brain. The clearest memory is of Granda McNaughton taking my brother Steve and me on a trip to the old Durham mining village of Cornsay to experience the area where our father was born and raised. It was a glorious summer day and in retrospect, it is clear that our Granda wanted to instil in us some feeling for our roots and a family memory before we headed off to distant lands.

Like most Englishmen of the time, Granda did not possess a car, so the journey was by train and then local bus via Durham. At Cornsay, where the colliery closed in 1953, there was one remaining mine entrance to the pit where both he and our Dad had worked and we entered a dark and forbidding opening to explore the musty insides. Luckily, after 20 metres it became apparent that it was too dangerous, and we withdrew to the pleasant summer's day outside and walked down the main street of the village where the house of my father's birth still stood. A number of the people in the street recognised Granda, even after the 20 years since leaving, and a number of chats ensued. The day finished with a walk through leafy glades to a large swimming hole on the River Browney where the McNaughton kids of Cornsay had played and learnt to swim. The deep pool was inhabited by large numbers of good-sized trout that mainly lurked in the dapple shaded sides under the overhanging riverbanks. Granda gave us a lesson in trout tickling, a banned fishing technique that saw the mesmerised trout scooped up on to the grass. The surprised trout flopped around on the grass for a while and then went back into the river to continue their normally quiet existence.

Having sold the house, for the four weeks before our departure we stayed with Dad's youngest brother Fred, who possessed a billiard table and temporarily became our favourite Uncle. He and his wife Margaret had no children at the time so we were totally spoilt. On our last day in Darlington, we met a chatty West Indian bus conductor, the first of many Brits of West Indian origin I have encountered on visits to Britain. He was extremely friendly and seemed perfect for a job that required interaction with the public. His beaming smile and strange accent stood out amongst the usually dour North Country English. The West Indians, Indians and Pakistanis were slowly taking over such service roles and he may have been the first one I had come across. Dad of course had a good chat with him and as a new immigrant himself, on learning that we would soon be heading off to Australia he told us of his recent arrival and expressed the view that he would prefer the sun and heat of Australia to the dank weather of the north of England. At that time, Australia still had the "White Australia" policy in place, so for him such a move would not have been possible[1].

The rest of our worldly possessions were already on their way to Australia in two large trunks that had already seen a large section of the world. The trunks were plastered with P&O, Cunard and Sitmar stickers from the past journeys of their original owner(s) and one of them was to have an extended life as a dog kennel for our Ozzie mutt Sandy and serve as a constant reminder of our immigrant origins. As the massive Gresley Pacific steam locomotive, with its classic smoke deflectors, screeched to a halt at the Bank Top platform, there were hugs and kisses all around and then a dive through the carriage doors so that we could snaffle good seats for the journey to Kings Cross. None of us three children had been more than 30 miles from Darlington before and we had only observed the

---

[1] The White Australia policy ended in 1966 under the government of Harold Holt but continued on by default until 1973 when the Whitlam government introduced the policy of Multiculturalism.

impressive main line locomotives when they were sitting on the platform or thundering through as expresses. The experience of occupying a seat in a mainline train and starting out on a long journey was the thrill of our young lives and a not to be repeated experience.

By the mid 1960s, most of the steam locos had been replaced with diesel electric systems and just seven years later the romantic days of steam were well and truly over in Britain. The romance of steam rail travel was accompanied by soot and cinders so by the time of our arrival in Kings Cross, where we could use the monopoly board knowledge we had already acquired to explore London, we had grimy faces and cinders in our hair from the many sessions sticking our heads out the window. The journey to Australia was essentially an extended holiday, so we began by spending a day exploring the sights of London prior to watching a cowboy movie in a huge Leicester Square theatre with a massive screen. Apparently, London could not totally hold the attention of my 12 year old brother and we attended the movie to stem a revolt. The clean air act of 1954 ensured we could actually see the London sights, but the grandeur of the buildings was heavily disguised by the blackening effect of years of coal fires. Consequently, despite the size of the city and the classic lines of Buckingham Palace, Westminster, the Tower of London and its accompanying swing bridge, it was by no means love at first sight.

On the afternoon of 6 August 1961, we peered up from the Southampton docks below the towering SS Oriana. The ship was too massive for the Tilbury docks near London and was the first vessel on the England-Australia run to leave from Southampton. The Oriana had been recently built for the Orient line primarily as an immigrant ship and was about to undertake its third voyage. We were in tourist class, the up market name for second class, which for us was the equivalent of first class, along with some 1200 other immigrants, a few tourists and a small number of Australians returning home. With a top speed of 30 knots, the journey time on the last and fastest Orient Liner, and later P&O liner, to Sydney would be a short 23 days via Gibraltar, Naples, Port Said, the Suez Canal, Aden, Colombo, Fremantle and Melbourne. Just like the steam trains, these liners were close to replacement as a major form of passenger transport. The Boeing 707 was already in service and was transforming air into the main travel mode for long distances, even for Ten Pound Poms. With some six hops from London to Australia the airplane travel time was a mere 34-36 hours , a time which shortened even further in the next decade with the advent of the 747 Jumbo jet, so by the 1970s ships like the Oriana were converted to cruise ships or scrapped. The Oriana's cruise ship life continued until 1986 when I was lucky enough to witness it glide majestically along Sydney Harbour through a summer nightfall and past the Sydney Opera house on its final cruise as my wife and I sipped champagne during the interval of "The Magic Flute".

The Oriana's departure from Southampton was accompanied by the sounds of a brass band, the sight of 100s of coloured streamers destined to break the bonds between people as the ship left the dock, the toots and whistles of other vessels and the increasing throb and vibration of the Oriana's huge set of turbines. The departure of an ocean liner was a major event with its own formalities and rituals and many family members of the immigrants on board had travelled to Southampton to farewell their relatives from the dockside. Exploration of the massive ship took hours, although we quickly discovered the games deck, pool deck and stern deck as the optimum places for kids, together with the promenade decks on either side where ice cream distribution points were set up twice a day. The trick we learnt over the next three weeks was to time a run to collect three serves of ice cream per session. The meals for children were served separately to those of the adults, who "dressed" for dinner, and we had the joy and privilege of being served by stewards for three weeks. After the austere meals of England, the food and its presentation was a highlight and we usually had second helpings.

In the weeks aboard ship, we rarely saw our parents, apart from my father who shared a cabin with us three boys at night. The promenade deck was the venue on the first day out in the Bay of Biscay where I learnt one of my first practical lessons in physics and relative motion. A sudden bout of seasickness prompted a regurgitation over the side but into the wind and a quick, but not quick enough, reaction from the adults downwind. Two weeks later in the Indian Ocean, after a birthday party held at the start of a massive tropical storm, I bounced from one side of the ships alleyway to the other as the ship rolled from side to side and felt absolutely fine. The initial experiences in the Bay of Biscay had given me "sea legs", and I have never been seasick to the point of throwing up again.

Despite all the excellent entertainment on board, my favourite occupation at sea was gazing out either over the stern from one of the upper stern decks, or from the promenade deck. There were often flying fish scudding over the waves, dolphins playing in the wash, seagulls on the lookout for food, passing liners and freight ships, or dhows and fishing boats to be seen. After two days at sea the first port of call was Gibraltar, the impressive rock. We all stayed on board because of the short turnaround time and simply admired the sights and sounds of our first foreign port. There was a hive of activity whilst the ship was being resupplied and on the ocean side, small boats attached themselves to the ship whilst their owners enthusiastically and noisily attempted to sell merchandise to the passengers.

After a further two days at sea, we berthed in Naples and disembarked as a family for a walk around the city, a trip to the fascinating ruins of Pompeii and to purchase one of Naples' renowned cameo brooches for mum. The history lessons imbibed at Pompeii, a "living" museum of the Roman world, were the best education I had experienced to date. Direct visual evidence of quick deaths in the gas cloud produced by Vesuvius, in the shape of bodies frozen in time was also a valuable lesson for a nine year old in the inherent uncertainty of life. Our walk around the city became a guided one when a self-appointed guide attached himself to us. He was paid off with a ten-shilling note and some cigarettes, still a valid currency in Naples at that time. The noise, poverty and dirt of 1960s Naples was overwhelming and provided a temporary baseline for comparing our home town of Darlington with the world. Darlington at this point came out tops!

On arrival at Port Said at the north end of the Suez Canal, we again remained on the ship, which was moored in the roads rather than docked. The port area was alive with bumboats and lighters buzzing like busy bees around the harbour. Within minutes of the anchor dropping, the water by the ship's sides was decorated with small colourful boats manned by strangely attired salesman who bantered with the passengers and displayed a huge variety of gaudy and sometimes strange items. The deck was soon covered in carpets, pouffes, straw hats, sandals, leather goods of all kinds, stuffed camels, postcards, jewellery, packs of playing cards and hookah pipes. Goods were trustingly roped up to the decks for inspection and then a price negotiated in whatever currency the buyer possessed. We became proud owners of a leather pouffe that bounced around our lounge room for years, a stuffed leather camel that slowly deteriorated as the years went by and a brass pot.

After a group of ships had congregated around the entrance of the Canal and a northbound convoy had funnelled out to complete the journey from the Bitter Lakes, we set off south in baking, harsh sunshine with the convoy of ships line astern along the canal. In some places, the canal appeared to be hardly wide enough for the width of the ship and on the top deck far above the sand, the views extended seemingly forever as they trailed off into the shimmering heat-haze. Occasionally camels topped with riders in loose robes could be seen loping beside the canal, and an occasional settlement with the minaret of its mosque visible for miles appeared. The Bitter Lakes, situated between the two halves of the canal, were reached around nightfall and the convoy spread out and anchored to await the next leg of the passage. Numerous freight ships with twinkling lights and one ocean liner lit up like a Christmas tree, were gathering in the gloom for the trip north. The following morning we proceeded through the southern part of the canal and out into the Gulf of Suez and the Red Sea bound for Aden, now part of Yemen. At that time Aden was still a British mandate and a common stop off point for shipping on the sea route to Asia. It seemed much like Port Said and we kids watched the activities of the bumboat traders and the busy port activities whilst our parents explored the delights of Aden.

From Aden, it was a four-day crossing of the Arabian Sea to Colombo in Ceylon, where the particular smell of Asia assailed the nostrils as we approached the harbour. It was the smell of tropical heat, spices, rotting vegetation, fish and a touch of sewage that is much the same today. As we emerged from the customs hall, we were harangued and pawed by a throng of touts, rickshaw drivers and beggars, with a one armed women dangling a naked and deformed child in front of us as we tried to make our way through the heaving crowd to a taxi. It was close to impossible to escape the mayhem but we eventually made our way to Mt. Lavinia Beach and after exploring the beach and cliffs had a sumptuous afternoon tea at the Mt Lavinia Hotel, which had once been the Governor General's residence. The hotel, still rather grand at that time, provided a temporary haven from the mayhem of Colombo port, which I for one was not keen on revisiting. In the late afternoon, we again pushed our way through the massed humanity outside customs and hopped on a boat to take us back to the haven of the Oriana.

From Colombo, the final and longest leg of the voyage was a six-day passage to Fremantle through the Indian Ocean and it was on this leg that we experienced extremely rough seas during a violent tropical storm. Before the storm truncated all outside activities we crossed the equator, with King Neptune appearing on the pool deck with his trident and a posse of assistants to celebrate the crossing. A number of willing adults and children were ceremoniously dunked in the pool and there were dress ups and numerous deck quoit and deck tennis competitions. As the storm brewed there was a large birthday party for all the kids celebrating a birthday during the voyage and a few days later I was invited, along with the other birthday kids and six orphans travelling to Australia as part of the child migration scheme, on a tour of the bridge and a meeting with the Captain.

By this stage of the voyage, many of the kids on board knew each other well and something of a gang like social structure had arisen. Being a loner,

LUCKY POMMIE BASTARD

I was more of an observer and rather liked to observe a young blonde girl some two years older than me. Maria was part of an extremely handsome family of immigrants who were also on their way to Queensland, and whom we had befriended during the voyage. In addition to being older, she was also out of bounds for all but the most daring of the boys on board. Her father was a rather forbidding character with a fierce disposition. He was heading for a job in a youth detention centre in Toowoomba and I felt sorry for the Toowoomba youth who ended up in his care. He had I think been in the military police and his icy look and general demeanour could kill at 10 paces.

We arrived in Fremantle, Australia on 25 August 1961 with me a shy 10 year old but with excellent sea legs, an addiction to ice cream, a strong Geordie accent, a developing sense of the joys of travel and a newly found appreciation for the female of the species.

11   NEW ARRIVALS

The Oriana cruised into Perth's port of Fremantle only 19 days after leaving Southampton and despite being at sea continuously for the previous five days, the ship was rapidly turned around to sail on to Melbourne. Our parents had a quick trip into Perth whilst we lads stayed on board and observed as a number of immigrants bound for Perth disembarked, amongst them the orphans and a few other shipboard friends. After a quick trip through the Great Australian Bight, our entry on the 27th into Port Phillip Bay through the extremely narrow channel known as "The Heads" or "The Rip" was memorable and a costly one for the Orient line. I have often wondered since whether "The Heads" was named after the two low headlands through which it runs, or after the name for ship's toilets because of the dramatic flush of water. Either way, the 42,000 ton Oriana bounced through the Heads like a roller coaster car with the noise of crashing glassware and crockery accompanying the most dramatic bounce.

In Port Melbourne, the ship docked at Station Pier and whilst we Sydney bound passengers caught a train into Melbourne city, many more immigrants disembarked for their new homes in either Melbourne or Adelaide. Melbourne at that time was a low rise city and my only memories are of leaving a somewhat rundown pier, travelling by a "red rattler" train to Flinders Street Station and looking at the windows of Myers, "the biggest department store in the Southern Hemisphere". The claim to be the biggest in the Southern hemisphere was to become a constant refrain over the next 30 or 40 years until Australia became more comfortable with its place in the world. Flinders Street Station itself was an unusually dramatic structure that would be more at home in an Indian city[1]. Unknown to me only nine years in the future I would become a Melburnian and "meet under the clocks" at the station entrance.

Later that night a much depleted cohort of passengers departed through the now subdued Heads on the final short leg to Sydney. The dining rooms were quiet, the crew more relaxed and everybody was looking forward to journey's end. The decks were still crowded though for the entry through Sydney Heads and the trip up one of the world's most famous harbours. The towering heads of Sydney Harbour and the width of the entrance channel left no doubt this time where the name "The Heads" had come from. The journey and approach into Circular Quay, framed by the famous coat-hanger bridge, where Sydney Harbour ferries busily moved in and out did not disappoint. Now this was a place that made the town of Darlington pale into insignificance. It was 29 August and late enough in the day that we spent one last night aboard before proceeding through customs and immigration the next day and then exploring Sydney as we waited for the night train to take us north to our final destination, Brisbane.

After a tiring day, we clambered aboard the Brisbane Limited just before 8.30pm and took our seats for the 14 hour trip to Brisbane. After three weeks enjoying the luxury of the Oriana it would have been a nice touch to have been provided with sleepers, but it was apparent that from this point the Australian Government was making sure we were not pampered and we were now in training for the process of getting on to our own feet in our new country. The Brisbane Limited was one of two train services to Brisbane, the other being the strangely named Brisbane Express, which took four hours longer than the Limited.

The lengthy train trip through a moonlit night was a magical introduction to the Australian landscape. We slowly made our way up through what we would learn to call "bush" where the ghost gums showed up eerily in the moonlight and an occasional set of eyes sparkled in the night. In the early morning, as the sun approached the horizon, foreign bird sounds created a symphony with a mixture of raucous calls, musical tweets, warbles, songs and the laughter of kookaburras. Occasional kookaburras could be seen perched up in the trees as the sun rose and provided a colourful backdrop to the landscape. There was also an introduction to the Australian Bushie with a number of rough looking,

---

[1] The structure of Flinders Street Station resulted in an urban myth that declared that the plans for the Melbourne station and Mumbai's station were mixed up so that Melbourne ended up with an Indian style building with Mumbai receiving a Victorian style.

sun hardened blokes playing cards and drinking beer through the long night. They were a friendly lot and one of them offered me an orange, which he proceeded to peel in one go with his tobacco and work stained hands. He was proud of the resultant single long peel and the now black coated naked orange. Despite my misgivings and the look on my mother's face that was somewhere between horror and gratitude, I managed to eat it whilst looking I hope sufficiently grateful. It was actually a treat because oranges were still expensive in England when we left and had been part of the treats, along with an apple, almonds, walnuts and hazelnuts that came along in our Christmas stocking each year. If not for their availability on the Oriana, it may have been my first orange since the previous Christmas.

Around 10.00am on the morning of 31 August, the train ground to a screeching halt in our new hometown at the unprepossessing South Brisbane station. It was 17 years before the Queensland government eventually managed to span the river with a railway bridge, so we detrained in the somewhat derelict looking suburb of South Brisbane and were taken by taxi to the Wacol migrant hostel. The taxi driver had a strong strine accent and was wearing shorts and long socks, a form of dress we had seen further south as well. The taxi trip was a little disconcerting, as we drove through what seemed to be bush before arriving at a largely deserted area an awful long way out of town. We had expected to be transported to the Yungaba hostel near the city centre, so the outer suburban bush venue came as a surprise.

The Wacol hostel was situated well on the way to Ipswich and had been built as a US military camp in 1942. Its military origins were apparent in the semicircular cross section World War 2 corrugated iron Nissen huts and long rectangular wooden huts that decorated the grounds. For Poms used to compact towns, we seemed to have been transported to the middle of nowhere. The Wacol hostel looked very much like the army camp that was located directly over the road, but without the security fences and boom gates and was sandwiched between the Brisbane to Ipswich rail line and the highway. On first impressions, the sight that greeted five newly arrived Brits was somewhat akin to a prison. Maybe the Australians still believed that arrivals from Britain were convicts?

We were soon ensconced in one longitudinal half of a Nissen hut, with a thin wall down the centre of the hut truncated a couple of inches short of the ceiling. Privacy was obviously not a priority and the separating wall turned out to be the home of many cockroaches. The cockies would often pop up to the top and peer over the edge to determine which side of the hut housed the most interesting source of food. Our less than palatial residence consisted of a small central "living" area with a couple of chairs and a small table and two tiny bedrooms, one equipped with two double bunks and the other with a double bed. Meals were served in a communal dining hall and we carried our supplied eating utensils to the hall, washed them afterwards and placed them on our little table until the next meal. The shower and washing blocks were communal and the camp had games and recreation rooms, so our Nissen hut was essentially only for sleeping. A great deal of time was spent sitting on the front steps as a consequence of there being so little room inside.

The communal meals were much appreciated by my mother, who had just had a month off from feeding the family. In addition to being free of cooking duties she did not have to prepare the school lunches, which could be picked up from the meal hall after breakfast. The meals were only just acceptable after three weeks on the Oriana but classed as "good" when compared with the dinners we suffered in our English schools, so we boys did not mind either. The pre-prepared lunches were usually peanut butter sandwiches, a carbohydrate hit of baked bean sandwiches, or a bread roll with a banana. Vegemite was not on the menu, perhaps as a sop to kids brought up on marmite, so it was only when we moved into our own house that we were converted from marmite eating Poms to proto-Aussie vegemites. Despite the lack of food preparation in the hut, the resident cockroachs did not starve but seemed to multiply. Even though we arrived in what was supposed to be winter the outdoor life prevailed for the 10 weeks we spent in the camp.

Although it was officially termed a hostel, everybody referred to Wacol as a camp and given the conditions, it was an apt description. About half the occupants were Poms (or Scots, Welsh, Irish who were often labelled as Poms) but there were a number of Dutch, Yugoslavs, Greeks, Italians and a few Poles in our neighbourhood. The Dutch seemed very similar to us and most spoke excellent English, but I quickly realised that the majority of the other residents were very different in background and attitude and an education in how socially different people can be was about to start in earnest.

Generally, the different nationality groups kept to themselves, played together and ate together, partly because of language and partly through it simply making for an easier existence. Soon after our arrival, we noticed that the toilets in the communal block had no seats and thought this was a little crude and unpleasant. Long term residents explained to us that the seats had been replaced recently but had rapidly disappeared again. My father solved the mystery for all. Being up for a chat with anybody, he became friendly with a nearby Yugoslav family who ended up inviting him and my mum around to their hut for a drink one night. Their hosts had settled in for the long haul and had brightened up their austere hut by displaying photographs of the relatives they had left behind in Croatia on the walls. These portraits were proudly framed in the toilet seats, a practical use that seemed unusual to us but not to a family who back in Yugoslavia had not had a need for toilet seats and thought the oval structures nicely framed a portrait.

We also became very quickly aware of the "Whingeing Pom" phenomenon. Unlike many of the other nationalities, many of the Brits had enjoyed comfortable conditions in Britain and had come to Australia after being drawn in by advertising that seemed to promise jobs and housing on arrival with a golden life in the sun and conditions much better than those in Britain. The advertising was so good that my brother Steve was convinced he would have a horse to ride to and from school. Spartan migrant camps like Wacol definitely did not live up to these expectations and the sound of "whingeing Poms" was often heard in the dining hall and throughout the camp whenever the Brits got together.

A number of families at Wacol had been there for years, often because for some the conditions were so much better than what they were brought up with, and sometimes simply to allow a family to build funds for a fresh start in Australia. In our case, the first major discussion I overheard between my parents after arrival contained the words

"The sooner we're out of here the better, I had better get any old job quickly."

The downside of employment was the requirement that the camp management had to be notified, and those families with a working member had to start paying rent. A number of families kept secret the fact that a family member (or members) had a paying job because this enabled them to build capital more quickly to get ahead in their new country. Roy, with his independent streak, lined up a job a couple of days after arrival at the Darra cement works further out of Brisbane towards Ipswich. He lasted two days carting cement bags around before his strength gave out and he had to admit that back breaking manual labour was not for him. Many of the migrants transiting through Wacol started their Australian working careers at Darra cement or the nearby Redbank Woollen mills.

Soon after our arrival, we protestant boys were sent off to the Darra primary school, whilst the Micks went off to the Sacred Heart. Big brother Alan had an academic record suitable enough for enrolment into Brisbane State High School, a somewhat selective State High school with an excellent reputation. It had the advantage of being close to the city so that no matter where we eventually settled Alan would be able to attend easily.

In order to get to Darra school we walked a couple of kilometres through the bush along the track by Bullock Head creek until we met the railway line and headed into the "town", often alongside a steam train belching smoke. This was a glorious daily adventure compared with the staid walk along Darlington's urban streets to my first primary school. There was always the intense aroma of eucalypts, and usually the sounds of kookaburras and magpies, the sight of a blue tongue or frilly lizard and the odd snake when the weather got warmer. We learnt how to distinguish the droppings of wallabies, rabbits and wombats, an apparently useful skill when I became a bushwalker.

Because of the adventurous surroundings and the large troop of kids on the track, the journey home usually took a lot longer than the morning journey to school. With three hours after school to get back for dinner, we could meander home through the bush. Unlike the kids, many of the adults, and particularly my mother, had a horror of the crawling insects, lizards, snakes and the wildlife in general so we of course regularly introduced newly discovered creatures into the Nissen hut in order to observe the effect. A dead snake some four foot long pushed slowly through the doorway with the aid of a stick had by far the greatest effect on my mother and the resultant screams could be heard throughout the camp.

With nothing of note near the migrant camp, many weekends were spent exploring Brisbane by walking to Wacol or Darra station and catching the train into Central. The train carriages were red wooden compartmentalised units that were built in the early part of the 20th century and had seen better days. They were beautiful in their way, with Victorian brass fittings and leather seats and were eventually replaced in the 1970s. Keeping them for so long in harness worked out well for the tourist attraction of the Zig-Zag railway in the Blue Mountains of New South Wales where some of these carriages were renovated and had a new lease of life. Coming from a railway centre where the passenger railway system was born, the stations on the line and their names fascinated us all. In the 1960s they were mostly of wooden construction, wide open and a number of them were prettied up with flower beds and hanging baskets. Auchenflower had a nice ring to it and the names of Aboriginal origin, Indooroopilly, Toowong, Taringa sounded exotic to our Pommie ears.

Just before Indooroopilly, the train crossed the Brisbane River on one of its few bridge crossings at that time. The railway bridge ran beside a delightful white suspension road bridge with towers at each end, like a mini Sydney Harbour Bridge. The towers were living quarters for the original toll collector and his family and proof of current occupation of the towers was the washing that sometimes hung from the windows. The Queensland trains are narrow gauge (3'6") and the bridge at that time was a bit rickety so the train trundled slowly over the river, resulting in a prolonged view of the bridge and the usually fast flowing Brisbane River. One of the other unusual sights that attracted our attention was the back gardens of the houses along the rail line, which all had neat little garden sheds. The aspect ratio of the sheds did not look quite right. Just what did the Aussies put in them? It was not long before we learnt to call the back gardens backyards, the sheds "dunnies" and that they contained not tools but a "thunderbox", the local name for the outside toilet where the canned contents of the box were collected once a week by the "night cart" for disposal.

In 1961, Brisbane essentially had the size and character of a small country town and exploration didn't take long. Those first few weekends introduced us to a number of places that became our favourite haunts. The Botanic Gardens, which were situated in a majestic loop of the mangrove lined river; the Treasury Building with its statues and cannons; Anzac Square and the nearby Victorian period post office, the historic customs house and the only tall building, the Town Hall. Further down river we discovered New Farm Park and its beautiful Jacaranda trees that blossomed not long after our arrival. Up river, we visited the Lone Pine animal sanctuary and discovered kangaroos, wallabies, wombats and koalas for the first time. Our broad northern English accents and terminology caused the occasional difficulty and we required rapid lessons in the Aussie vernacular. Two tubs of ice cream had to become two buckets, although the size was the same, sweets became lollies, tea became dinner, crisps became chips, ice pops had to become icy poles and pop became soft drink, a name that didn't make sense to me until I tried a beer on my 18th birthday. It wasn't just the different words that caused us problems. It took Roy three attempts to obtain an ice cream for us even after he gave away "tub". The ice cream vendor could not understand his pronunciation of "bucket".

Our other major discovery was that pedestrians could be fined for walking on the wrong side of the footpath. A few days after arrival, we were pulled over by two tough looking leather jacketed police and warned that we were transgressing the local footpath by-laws. Over the first couple of years in Australia our language adapted and even the Northern England expression "Our Mam" became plain "Mum".

After around 10 weeks Dad had found a more suitable and less physically demanding job in the head office of Chandlers, an electrical and white goods store chain and he and Mum had also located a suitable house in the outskirts of Brisbane at Carina. His clerking duties in the RAF towards the end of the war apparently qualified him for a position in the office at Chandlers. We were a little shy of having enough money for the purchase of the house, but Dad was reluctant to involve a bank in any transaction. On a handshake, the outstanding sum was paid to the previous owner, a Dutchman, in weekly instalments over two years. The house was 10 km to the east of the city, less than half as far as Wacol to the north. Number 109 was at the bottom of a hill close to an old creek gully and our road, Adelaide Street, was unpaved, had huge overgrown gutters and was not sewered. The only saving grace as far as Mum was concerned was the presence of a septic tank and a flushing toilet situated at the top of the back steps which she could term, "indoor". The majority of our neighbours had "Dunnies" and these were serviced by a night-cart that inexplicably traversed the streets of Carina on a Thursday afternoon, exchanging full cans in the thunderbox for empty cans.

At the time, we thought of our street as essentially the last residential street of Brisbane because it was the last stop on the trolley bus line before the terminus and beyond was bush. The trolley bus route to town traversed through the five ways intersection at the Gabba (Woolloongabba) which at that time was bisected by a train line leading in and out of the goods terminal. To our astonishment, all the traffic stopped when a goods train moved and the trains were led across the intersection by a railwayman on foot with two red warning flags. We had all been taught in history about the red flag act of 1865 in the UK where trains (and later cars) were kept to walking pace by flag waving guides, but to see it in action almost 100 years later made us wonder just how backward Brisbane was.

Our house was a typical Queensland house with high wooden stumps that provided a cool area underneath for a garage, playing, hanging washing and the dog kennel. A family of swallows resided just above the garage doorway for many years and they provided entertainment, particularly when they arrived back after summer down south. In the violent summer storms the old creek bed that had been covered by the road became a torrent and we often peered from our heights down on three or four foot deep raging water that almost came up to our fence and blocked the road for hours.

To make our way to our new school, Carina State School, we had to cross a set of paddocks and a rough football pitch, then tramp though the bush and over Creek Road, a major paved road with the school on the opposite side. We carried on our backs a school port, port being the peculiar Queensland expression for a pack or suitcase. The paddocks would have been termed fields back in England, where the term paddock referred to the small garden area at the back of a house. There were longer routes to school via the roads but the daily walk through the bush was by far the best of the alternative routes. Darra State School had been close to the migrant camp so everybody there was familiar with the large number of migrant kids from all parts of the world, so neither my brother nor I had any issues whilst attending school there. We weren't "wogs" or "clogs" so were almost acceptable.

Carina though was a pure "Aussie school" so a rather different prospect for a couple of kids still with broad Geordie accents. We were the only oddities in the whole school and were immediately labelled "Pommies" or "little Pommie bastards", depending on the context and it took some time before we became acceptable. The kids took their attitude from their parents, many of whom were bitter about being let down by Britain when the Japanese were on the rampage in World War 2. From the Australian perspective, Britain had left Australia to its own devices, actively trying to retain Australian troops in the European/Africa arena and breaking a promise to look after Australia. It was a view of the situation that contained some truth and was heavily politicised by the government through the war to bolster the population and increase support for the US presence in Australia. The propaganda had been very effective and years later I learned that many of the Australians serving overseas in Africa or Europe after Japan entered the war were sent white feathers of shame from Australian women. Amongst these were the RAAF boys in Europe and the Rats of Tobruk. This rejection continued when the RAAF airmen returned after World War 2 and for many years they kept a low profile and felt unappreciated in their own country. So much so that many, including my Dad, would not get involved in Anzac Day until much later in life. The other result was a degree of bitterness towards England and the English and in 1961 the feelings were still a little raw in Queensland. The kids had picked up on it, so we Poms had to learn to live with it. Combined with the Australian predilection for "taking the piss" it made life interesting for a while.

My older brother Steve immediately took on a Queensland accent broader than anybody at the school and within days sounded like Chips Rafferty on steroids. After a few weeks he had learnt the names of all the Aussie cricketers of the day and could be heard chanting "all Pommies are bastards" with the best of them. He hated being different and adopted the principle of "if you can't beat 'em, join 'em". Having talked with other Poms who migrated to Victoria and South Australia it seems this active and easily perceived dislike of Poms was most prevalent in the deep north of Australia where I presume the Japanese invasion threat had been more real and maybe the politics and propaganda driven a little harder. We were warmly welcomed though by a number of Aussie families, many of them with family or social links to Britain so the real "Pommie bashers" were essentially a minority, albeit quite a vociferous minority so they had a significant presence in the eyes of us new arrivals. After some time and after becoming more accepted in the community "Pommie bastard" became almost an honorific title, although my mother could never see it like that. I felt I had been fully accepted when I joined the RAAF at the age of 18 and was labelled a "Pommie Queenslander" without the addition of "Bastard". Maybe it was simply that it was just too many syllables for most Aussies!

My reaction to the baiting was somewhat polar to that of my brother Steve. I already had an independent, rather bloody-minded streak and could isolate myself from most situations. The derisive comments were close to water off a duck's back and the best form of defence was deflect and attack so I quickly took on the "take the piss" part of the Australian persona and set to in my own sweet way. It took longer but eventually on my own terms I became an accepted, albeit different, member of the Grade five mob the following year. The head teacher at Carina had recognised I was a somewhat quiet, shy individual with a record of being towards the bottom of the class and given my young age it was decided I would step back a year. I hence became one of the older kids in my class in contrast to being the youngest in my English school class and quickly realised that the reading, writing and maths were familiar and easily handled. After one term at Carina, I was in the mix towards the top of the class and never looked back. The move to Australia with its school year six months out of phase with England was a blessing.

The subject that I really enjoyed at Carina was history, which was mostly Australian history and vastly different to the constant stream of English monarchs that made up the history lessons at Dodmire. The Aussie kids had had their fill of Australian history over a number of years and there was a distinct torpor amongst the rest of my class during history classes. To me it was fascinating to hear about Captain Cook's voyages, convicts, the first fleet, Blaxland, Wentworth and Lawson finding a route over the Blue Mountains, Captain Bligh and the Rum rebellion, Hume, Hovell, Sturt and Stuart wandering all over the country and the ill-fated expeditions of Burke and Wills and the German Leichhardt. The cast of colonial characters got longer through the next few years of schooling with the appearance of Macarthur and his sheep, Frances Greenway, the first Government architect, the appealing Lachlan Macquarie, Matthew

Flinders and Batman of Melbourne, who was neither a cricketer nor a cartoon character. The names do not fade from memory because there are so many geographic features and streets named after these people around Australia.

In 1960s history lessons, the Aboriginals were allocated bit parts only as they appeared on the scene to spear the odd explorer or pastoralist or as observers of the white expansion. The only positive mentions of Indigenous Australians were that, firstly they rescued Burke and Wills' off-sider King and would have saved the main protagonists if they had only taken notice of their advice. Secondly, a bloke called Buckley, who was an escaped convict down south in Port Phillip Bay, lived with the local tribes for a number of years and consequently survived. It was hearing about Buckley that allowed me to interpret at a later date a favourite expression of my father in law's, often quoted when asked what chance St. Kilda had of beating Collingwood in the Aussie rules football: "Buckley's or none"!

For my parents, settling into Australia presented a few problems. They were both determined to make a success of our new life and we were soon in contact with Jack Lawrence, the rear gunner of the Trimble crew. Jack and his wife Merle had two daughters and soon after our arrival, they rolled up in their Holden station wagon to take us down to the Gold Coast and Surfer's Paradise for the day. Dad was greeted by Jack with the following words

"G'day Mac, what are you doing in blackfella country?"

The expression was not one that would be acceptable these days but did in its way acknowledge the original inhabitants. It was also well before the days of compulsory seat belts, so all nine of us piled into the vehicle with the three smallest kids in the very back of the wagon. In those days, Holden cars had a bench seat in the front and a column shift that allowed for three passengers in the front. The trip to the Gold Coast was along a single lane, pot holed road but that did not deter Jack from hurtling along at or above the speed limit as we bounced around in the back. "Surfers" was a small, low key village with many wooden beach houses on large blocks, but with a magnificent beach where the waves pounded in relentlessly. By then summer was upon us and that day we learnt about the power of the Australian sun and came back from the beach as five Pommie lobsters. It was my first experience of returning home from a day at the beach with painful salty skin pumping out heat, a raging thirst, a splitting headache and with a sand papered crotch. I was not destined to be a beach lover after that experience.

A couple from a nearby church who had a connection to Darlington also made contact, so Mavis and Roy and their friend Ivor provided another important social connection for us. Dad used up another one of his many lives when Ivor rolled his VW beetle one day. Ivor ended up in hospital for quite a long time whilst Dad of course walked away with just a couple of bruises and a stiff neck. My father's luck always ran both ways. He never drove a car in his life but was involved in three serious car accidents over the years. One notable one being in a taxi where the driver managed to write off the vehicle in a quiet suburban street of Brisbane. It was before the introduction of breathalyser tests!

Most of our original neighbours were Australian born of British/Irish heritage with the exception being our direct neighbours at 111, the Kehanes, who were recent Irish immigrants who lived in a rundown house that seriously needed a lick of paint. They were friendly and soon after our arrival they invited us all in for afternoon tea. As we started to sip our tea, we visitors noticed a number of large cockroaches wandering over the top of the TV and over the back of the lounge. My mother went rigid and her attempt at levitation to minimize contact with the surroundings failed. The Kehanes seemed oblivious to the wandering hoards but we extracted ourselves from the house as quickly as possible and always seemed to be committed to other activities whenever asked around for a cuppa. Within a year of our arrival, the house was knocked down and I mentally pictured thousands of cockroaches abandoning the house and radiating out as the wreckers started on it. My mum hated the cockroaches and despite explanations that there were two types, the dark brown/black ones who thrived in a home environment and detritus and the flying jet black ones who came in on a whim and then soon left, she always reacted as though it was a personal affront to her cleanliness when either variety was sighted. We would employ the pest controllers or "exterminators" at least once a year and they would fill our house with chemicals designed to kill or deter insects of all sorts.

On the opposite side to the Kehanes were two shops, a small supermarket come "corner shop" and a butcher. The supermarket changed hands rapidly and I think there were four different owners there in the next five years. The owners lived behind the shops so we usually knew them well before they had had enough of working 16 hours a day as grocers and moved on. Other living creatures in addition to cockroaches gained our attention. In the 1960s, Brisbane was inundated with cane toads, introduced originally to eat sugarcane destroying beetles, and they came out at night to fulfil their role as balls in cricket or golf practise. They were ugly and seemed to be indestructible apart from when they wandered on to the roads and under the wheels of cars. Each morning there were many more flattened toads drying in the harsh Queensland sun. A number of drivers went out of their way to run them over and many cars careered down our road at night weaving from side to side as though it was a slalom course. The roads were always decorated with numerous flattened toads in various stages of desiccation. Our own road was unsealed so we also had to contend with clouds of dust until the proactive lord mayor of Brisbane, Clem Jones, needed to drive down our road to access the bowls club. It was then sealed and the flattened toads stood out even more starkly on the dark asphalt.

The local amphibians were much more appealing and numerous frog species thrived in the subtropical setting. Bright green, luminous shiny ones were often found in the damp areas around the house. Since the 1960s the toads have moved on and only the occasional flattened toad can now be observed on Brisbane's roads. Hopefully, it will also mean a gradual return of the local species that all but disappeared through the long Brisbane reign of the cane toads.

We settled into our house in November 1961 and soon afterwards the Christmas beetles arrived. They were beautiful creatures that ranged in colour from golden yellow through bright green into blueish and some had the appearance of large flying opals. They would fly across the town in droves, clattering into windows or doors when they were disorientated, and then wandering around on the ground where we could marvel at the colours that would change depending on the angle of the light. Accompanying them were dark brown beetles locally known as stink bugs. These were useful for tennis practise with the downsides being the smell when struck by a good forehand and the necessity of cleaning the racket afterwards. All in all Brisbane was an exotic environment for new arrivals.

With the bush out the back separated from our house only by a rough football oval, snakes would also often appear in the backyard. Dad tried to maintain the lawn with consistent mowing and this sometimes resulted in snakes, often red bellied blacks, being ejected out the side of the mower in pieces, along with bits of the ubiquitous cane toads. Despite our house being so far off the ground, snakes occasionally managed to make their way inside. These were usually carpet snakes, one of the few harmless varieties around and one day I arrived home from school to find my mother very excited. She had walked into our lounge room to find our dog Sandy transfixed by a very large snake coiled upwards in the other corner of the room. Rather than panic as she might have done soon after our arrival in Australia or if somebody else was present, she extracted Sandy from the room and walked down to the shops, where she was sure Bob the butcher, a big burly bloke would handle it. He was not having a bar of it and sent his offsider, a young apprentice, to deal with the situation. The butcher's boy didn't know much about snakes and to be on the safe side assumed it was poisonous, so after an hour of chasing the poor carpet snake around the room he managed to kill it and remove it. The event had livened up my Mum's day and the neighbours all had fun asking the butcher what was in his sausages for the next week.

The very thought of snakes was one element of Australia that really succeeded in agitating new arrivals and we learnt the art of telling porkies and simply informing them that snakes were hardly ever sighted in the suburbs. This lie was caught out one day when a pair of Brits who had arrived in Australia the previous week went for a walk with us and a big black snake trundled across the path in front of us. We quickly learned to just give any snake space and they would stay away from you, although one day whilst returning from school a dark green fella about three feet long came skidding quickly across Creek Road, slithered over my bare foot and dived into the creek. It just kept on going and was way up the creek swimming with the same undulatory motion before I really knew what was going on.

Having been a keen gardener as a teenager in Cornsay, before long Dad had managed to generate a thriving vegetable garden as well as planting mandarin trees, pawpaws and lady finger banana trees. He did however have to spend a couple of years learning about the appropriate vegetables for the different seasons. In the wet, hot summers the insects, moulds, yeast, fungus and diseases thrived as well, ruining many a crop until Roy had learnt the ropes of a Queensland garden. One of his early bloopers was the planting of a tulip tree in the belief that it was a small flowery plant. A couple of years later he had a 30 foot tree in the back garden.

In the 1960s, one of the best ways of making social connections for both adults and kids was through the church and although my parents were not practising Christians, they decided "religion" was a good way forward for all of us. We all trooped up to the Carina Methodist Church soon after our arrival. Mum, being an excellent singer, took part in choir and played the piano when compelled to do so, whilst we attended church and Sunday School. The piano was a big part of my mother's life. She was an excellent player and a "beautiful piano" had been part of the furniture back in Darlington. The piano had not made the trip to Australia but when my parents discovered the price of pianos in Brisbane, they regretted the decision to leave it behind. Soon after we settled in Carina my father, after promising my mother a piano in Australia as part of the emigration deal, purchased at great expense a second hand piano. Mum declared it to be "quite a good piano" but not as good quality as the one back in Darlington. Music, along with movies remained as her major form of relaxation. She did find it hard to fit into Brisbane life and her main friends seemed to be fellow migrants that she met up with by connecting through mutual recognition that their different accents set them apart from the crowd. From these connections she and Dad ended up with a range of Scots, English and Dutch friends. They could all compare notes about previous lives, the strange Australian ways, the lack of decent pubs and social clubs and the dearth of cultural outlets. Dad of course had a working environment to form new friendships and social relationships and he had his garden.

One of the major problems for my father was the lack of soccer, or "football" as he always called it. Soccer in 1960s Australia was low grade and essentially local. It was played by "Poms, Wogs and Clogs" and was not up to the standard of even the fourth division Darlington Quakers and far from the standard of Sunderland. For a number of years on Sundays we would tune into the BBC world service and listen to the football results from all four English divisions and the two Scottish divisions intoned like a weather forecast. Dad would check his football pools, which he religiously submitted from Australia for a number of years, and then moan about Darlington or Sunderland losing once again.

The major Brisbane sport was rugby league, which despite being only a local Brisbane competition, was much more competitive. Although rugby league was a major sport in Yorkshire and Lancashire it was not big in Durham and it took many years before any of us could take it half seriously. The rough oval just beyond our back fence was the home of the Easts Carina Rugby League club, a feeder club for the larger Easts club and we often watched matches in an attempt to work the game out. Eventually we all decided that rugby union was a better option and that became the default "family sport" for most of us. Brother Steve was the exception having embraced the local culture and he became a rugby league supporter. He maintained this until he moved south into Aussie rules territory and became a "rules man". There was a local Australian rules competition which, being a minor sport at the time in Brisbane was also low grade. It was a distinctive Aussie sport, so Dad would often go along to watch the Coorparoo Roos in an attempt to assimilate and better understand the Aussies.

Big brother Alan quickly slotted into the church and before long was the drummer in a church based band, the Sonics, who started to practise in our front room. He and his mates laboured away on a small repertoire of songs and became good enough to get a few paying gigs around

Brisbane and earn some pocket money. My primary memory is of them repeatedly playing "Shaking all over", a Johnny and the Pirates number that was popular in the 60s. I was glad when after many weeks they eventually perfected it because it was disconcerting when the rhythm suddenly stopped as they made one of their numerous mistakes. The main aim of some members of the band seemed however to be to attract girls, for Alan a particularly gorgeous girl over the road called Penny. She had a similarly gorgeous younger sister Maria, a few years older than me. Alan did go out with Penny a few times but never got past first base and she was best described as a friend.

The band were also set the task by the minister of modernizing the church so they played at Sunday services and took part in music nights. Alan ended up meeting his first girlfriend through the band and church, but whether the attraction was to the rock drummer pose is open to question. Some older members of the church did not like the idea of a rock band in the church and I remember one particular elder of the church dragging his daughter out one Sunday claiming that we would all be damned. We soon learnt from the other kids that they were "wowsers", an Australian expression that quickly became part of our developing Aussie lexicon. It was certainly a social church and a bunch of kids would regularly be piled into the back of a few utes and taken for a day out to the beach at Wynnum or Manly, muddy bay beaches where the activities were usually cricket or other sports rather than swimming. The best part of the trip was charging down the road whilst being thrown around in the open tray of the ute, with the wind ripping through our hair. This exciting activity was soon to be banned of course. After a while, I noticed that my parents never attended church other than for social events and recognised the con that had been played on us. Our attendance at church on Sundays gave them a morning to themselves. Not being a very social animal and being a non-believer I decided at the age of 12 that I could do without church if it required actually attending Sunday school and church services. My parents had developed some friends through the church connection so their original aim had been achieved, and they slowly slotted into their new life in Australia.

The process of settling into an Australian life was set back occasionally by Poms, often of the whingeing variety, appearing on our doorstep. First to arrive was one of mother's many cousins, Mary, with her husband Jim and two kids, fresh from Sunderland. Their presence reminded my mum of the family we had left behind in England and particularly of the fact that her parents were across the other side of the world and missing her. These new arrivals also did their share of moaning to upset the apple cart, although Mary, being a Brown, was very much into partying. Their arrival was quickly followed by that of another Sunderland family who I discovered a few days after their arrival whingeing, wailing and crying in our lounge when I came home one Saturday afternoon. Mother, father and kids were all in tears sobbing loudly and declaring loudly that they had made the biggest mistake of their lives. I had never seen a man crying before so it made quite an impression. My parents were consoling them and trying to convince them to look on the positive side and were unsettled and emotional themselves for weeks afterwards.

This family were living in Yungaba, the original migrant hostel in Brisbane located almost under the Story Bridge, so in a position close to the city and superior to Wacol. They had arrived in Brisbane by aeroplane directly from London so had not experienced the joys of a three to four week cruising holiday to start adjusting to life away from the familiarity of England and their families. They stayed in Australia for 2 years and then returned to England where I am sure they whinged just as much about England. After two years in Australia they would have grown into the lifestyle and found that they missed certain aspects of Australian life. Assisted migrants were required to stay for two years or pay back the fares for their passage to Australia, a considerable cost that most could not afford. Mary and Jim stayed for quite some time but eventually also went back to England leaving their kids in Australia. The pull of an extended family and the social life of English pubs was greater than that of sunshine and suburban Brisbane for Mary, who was divorced by the time she returned to England. Around 25% of the one million British immigrants who came on the assisted passage scheme returned to Britain, although close to half of these became "Boomerang Poms" and returned to Australia, so the "success" rate of the 10 pound Pom scheme was a healthy seven out of eight.

My parents did slowly settle into Australia, although my mother never quite got used to the Australian way and would take offence at the most innocuous comments by Aussies, which she would invariably take as criticism. She did tend to live in her own little bubble and personalize every comment that came out of the mouths of others. In the late 1970s, my parents ventured back to England and lived there for two years after my maternal grandmother had died and my grandfather was slowly dying of cancer alone in Sunderland. My mother had already travelled back by herself for a five month stay after her mother had died, but this time Roy gave away his managing director position and moved back with her. Granda, a very proud and independent man, would not hear of them returning to look after him, so they settled in Churchdown near

Gloucester, where Dad obtained a position at Dowty engineering and they visited Granda as often as they could. Eventually, close to the end of his life, Mum was allowed to move in and take care of Granda. Upon his death they quickly sold everything up, returned home to Australia and settled back into Brisbane. Their summary of the experience was that in England everybody picked up their Aussie accents and they were looked upon as Aussies and did not fit in. In Brisbane people picked up their English accents and they were looked upon as Poms and did not quite fit in. They did however also rediscover all the reasons that had contributed to their decision to leave England in the first place and recognised that they had become more Australian than British and felt much more at home in Brisbane. Besides, it was a lot warmer than England and long johns were required for only a short period of the year!

12 WE WILL CALL AUSTRALIA HOME

Both of my brothers had managed to fit into Australia, Steve by taking on the role of a dinky-di Aussie sports person and Alan through friendships at school, church and the local neighbourhood. In Carina, I slowly made friends myself through school and casual cricket matches on the oval over the back fence. I was shy and withdrawn but known by the local mothers as "a good influence." This meant that I had a few crazy friends through various mothers arranging for me to be mates with their wayward boys. The one of these I remember best is Kim Ferguson, a red headed, freckled kid who lived in the next street and was into mischief in a major way. Rather than me being a good influence on him the reverse happened, although I think I did temper some of his wilder schemes and curtailed some of his more dangerous spur of the moment antics.

Armed with cane knives and fireworks we managed to chop down numerous trees, blow a few things up, almost burnt down a house and would often be hurtling through the bush after being chased out of some activity by one of the residents of our two streets. With the bush so close, we at least had numerous escape routes and hideaways at hand. One of our favourite activities when bored was to sit at my bedroom window, which overlooked the entrance to the store next door, and armed with peashooters harass the shoppers coming in and out of the store.

At the time our family didn't have a TV, so Kim and I would often be around his place after school watching "The Lone Ranger", "Superman", "Rin Tin Tin" or cartoons until directed to "go outside and play" when his mother got sick of us. The Fergusons had a little terrier with the same colouring and temperament as Kim and one Thursday we were mooching around the backyard when the "night-cart" arrived. As the dunny-man trotted past with the fresh empty can over his shoulder, the terrier started looking interested and on the return journey with the full can now on the dunny-man's shoulder, Kim made a few low growls. The terrier was immediately activated, pounced within seconds and vigorously worried the dunny-man's ankles whilst growling ever more loudly. The dunny-man panicked, with the result being a falling can and the dunny-man, dog and path covered in a week's worth of pee and poo. Kim and I hastily departed the scene. Kim was officially grounded for two weeks over that episode, his mother assuming rightly, but without any real evidence, that it was his fault. She soon forgot though and within a week, Kim and I were back together outside and scheming.

Carina State School was a very different environment to Dodmire in Darlington, partly due to weather but also due to the space available for outside activity. Sports in English schools were a minor component with indoor gym a major feature, whilst in Australia, a major part of school life revolved around outdoor sports and the school had a large oval for rugby league, cricket and baseball with separate tennis and basketball courts. The school buildings were high off the ground with cool space underneath for games and the tuck shop. Tuck shops were non-existent in English government schools because a school dinner was provided for all in a canteen. The items for sale in the tuck shop were mainly pies, pasties, sausage rolls and cream buns, which once every few weeks we could enjoy as an alternative to our packed lunch.

In grade six I became a milk monitor, being one of the students our teacher thought would not be troubled by missing 15 minutes of tuition a day. Two of us would leave class and set out the free bottles of milk to be consumed at morning break. We were lucky in that the milk was delivered just in time for the break so was still cold, whereas a number of friends have memories of their school milk being warm and causing them to gag. Being the 1960s, the school day always began with a whole school assembly, an address by the headmaster and then the singing of the National anthem, which at that stage was "God Save the Queen". This ritualistic start to the day was another defining difference to life in England where one simply turned up to the classroom each morning. After this nationalistic display, we would march off military style by twos in class order into our classrooms to the sound of a band playing a rousing Sousa march. The cane was still used for punishment, but only by the headmaster and I remember copping it once but have no recollection as to why it was administered. Generally, the teachers were kind and skilled, apart from one brute with a nasty temper who was eventually dismissed for throwing a grade four kid down the steps and breaking his arm.

At school, we boys generally stuck together and hung around as a crowd. By grade seven, I had hit the high spot and came top of the school, was appointed school captain and despite having only a one-hour session learning how to hold the racket and the basics of serving, became a member of the school tennis team. I suspect they were a bit desperate and the sports teacher, Mr Russell, was determined to get me off my butt and into a sport. I was too shy to have much to do with the girls but admired from afar the two who challenged me for top spot in the class. Joanne who had a very sunny disposition and who was everybody's favourite and Denise, an elegant tall girl who could run like the wind and later became one of Australia's top sprinters. A fourth contender for top of the class, Mark, joined us in year six and he and I became good mates. One of our major interests was blowing things up and initially we would satisfy the urge by buying fireworks and adapt them to enable the firing of missiles. After a while, we would catch the bus to "Selby's" where in those days you could purchase all sorts of chemicals and scientific equipment regardless of age. We managed to make our own gunpowder and rocket fuel with only minor injuries to ourselves. Our grade seven teacher (Miss McLachlan) memorably took a number of us out to the Cubana restaurant in town to celebrate our achievements at the end of our final year.

After a couple of years working at Chandlers, Dad, as usual, was looking for a new challenge and a way to advance his salary and prospects so he applied for a job as clerk/storeman at a firm called F.W. Buckham, situated in Charlotte Street, Brisbane city. The firm was in the business of making cast stereotypes for printing, which required an efficient system of dispatch to make the deadlines of the local newspapers. Luckily for Roy, the head of the firm, Laurie Buckham, was a relative of Bruce Buckham, a well-known 463 bomber pilot who carried out some remarkable exploits during the latter stages of World War 2. Bruce Buckham, who arrived at 463 Squadron just after the Trimble crew departed, took part in Lancaster raids to sink the battleship Tirpitz in a Norwegian fiord and witnessed the demise of Tirpitz by circling after the last raid to photograph the result of the bombing. With another example of Roy's luck, the link with 463 Squadron became apparent through the interview and Roy landed the position, which eventually led to him being managing director of the firm.

During his time at Buckhams, Roy's lucky streaks again showed up when he took over the role of running the Melbourne Cup sweep, a routine that was followed in most Australian work places like a religion. In the first year, 1966, he drew "Galilee" in the sweep and after the horse won, there were many groans about the organizer winning his own sweep. The following year he drew "Red Handed" which won to further groans from the shop floor. My grinning father explained that he always put $10 (five pounds prior to 1966) on the horse he drew and so was always financially well off after the Melbourne Cup. In the third year, he drew "Rainlover" so the whole workforce placed money on the horse, which won, making everyone happy. In year four he again drew "Rainlover" and almost everyone believed his luck had run out because in the more than 100 years of the cup only "Archer" had won the cup in successive years and those wins were in the first two years that the Melbourne Cup was run. Rainlover of course won for the second year in a row and my father was forever known at Buckhams as the "Lucky Pommie Bastard".

Dad's luck also worked on pub raffles and on Fridays he would often drop into the Stones Corner hotel on the way home from work. It was the closest pub that had a friendly atmosphere vaguely similar to an English pub and he would have a single beer and a chat with whoever was there. His major reason for dropping by was to buy a ticket in the Chook Raffle or meat tray draw and more often than not, he would come home with a chook or a tray of meat. He also had a habit of winning money when a major expense arose. After first winning the pools just before migrating to Australia, he won $5500 on the Lotto just before he and my mother had to go back to England to look after my grandfather in the 1970s. After Dad died, my brothers and I convinced ourselves that one of us must have inherited his luck, so we pooled money ($600) and "invested" it in the weekly Tattslotto draw. After a very short period of time the money had evaporated so we invested $300 more until we had to admit defeat and recognize that the luck had not been passed on and that we were all plain run of the mill "Pommie Bastards".

My first ever school holiday job was at Buckhams, where for a few months I was the delivery boy. I soon knew Brisbane city like the back of my hand, although in those days it was admittedly quite small. The workforce at Buckhams were highly skilled tradesmen, whose livelihoods were overtaken in the late 1970s by technological changes in printing techniques. They were a friendly lot with strong Australian accents and they had mostly accepted Roy, first as a fellow worker and then as the boss. I also learnt first hand about my father's moral stances and how his standards were acted upon in practise. In England, he had been a shop steward and trusted by all to look after the conditions and welfare of the workforce. He was also trusted by the management because he was capable of seeing both sides of an argument and recognised the necessity of management and workers compromising and working together to keep each other happy. He also took this philosophy into his managerial position.

At Buckhams, there was one particular middle-aged bloke who worked on the furnace, who would take a "sickie" every second or third week on a Monday with the result being that he never had any accrued sick leave owing. I overheard Dad having a chat with him about this habit and explaining how it was not just bad for management and his fellow workers when somebody else had to cover for him but that it defied the whole principle of sick leave, which was to cover salary when you were actually sick. He also stressed that the system relied on mutual respect to benefit both parties. It was made clear to the sickie taker that management would only cover the benefits he was entitled to and that if he was laid low with a serious illness then he would end up with no support the way he was rorting the system. A couple of years later the sickie taker did succumb to a serious illness, which required him to take three or four months off work. Needless to say, the firm did not come to the party with three months' pay on top of the sick leave he had taken over 20 years, and I heard my father out as he explained to me his and the firm's stance at the time. They did keep his job open whilst he was absent and he eventually returned to work a somewhat disgruntled employee, who received little sympathy from his mates. In contrast, another long-time employee was stricken with a serious cancer and had to take many months off work. He had taken very few sick days and the company supported him with a substantial number of extra paid sick days to ensure that their valued employee was financially OK.

I also learnt that working at the coalface of industry presented a few unique challenges. I was, like the rest of my family, an extremely fast walker and would finish my deliveries in apparently record time and be back on the lookout for more work. This caused a few of the people in the establishment to shake their heads and suggest I was working too hard and should slow down and take some time out whilst I was away on deliveries. They pointed out that everybody else worked at a steady pace and that I should do the same. At the time, I did not really twig to the realities of factory/workshop labour and the fact that they all wanted to present a united front regarding "the pace of work that people were capable of coping with." The philosophy was essentially to work at the pace of the slowest worker. My way around this problem was to take detours into interesting parts of the city on my way back from deliveries, browse the odd bookshop or ogle the girls in Queen Street.

It was only later during university when I had a Christmas holiday job at a small engineering firm that an extreme form of this brand of worker's philosophy struck me. I was to be at the workplace for three months and after the first few days was put on a piece of "problematic" machinery that was used to make multiple 90 degree bends from straight flanged metal tubes. The metal tubes had to be located precisely on a number of jointed metal fingers around which they were bent and this machine broke down two or three times a day, leading to a section of the shopfloor having 20-25 minutes rest while the engineers sorted the problem out. In my hands however, the machine did not breakdown and at the end of the first day there were a few mutterings in the change rooms after work and a few unfriendly glances coming my way. At the end of a second day, again with no breakdowns, it was decidedly frosty in the change rooms and a small delegation came over to "have a chat." It was made abundantly clear to me that; firstly, as a university educated person I was unlikely to have to work in such positions for the rest of my life and, secondly, that that I should consider my fellow workers, who were there for the long haul and, thirdly, that the bending machine was obviously flawed and WOULD break down at least twice a day. Industrial sabotage was not for me so I spent an evening wondering how to approach this problem and whether at the end of the next day I would be physically encouraged to co-operate with my fellow workers. I suspect one of the older heads in the workforce had a chat to management about the situation that was brewing and I was relocated to another job the following morning. Consequently, I never found out just how far they would have gone in their encouragement. The bending machine broke down three times the next day though.

The job at the engineering factory was in Melbourne during one of its stinking hot summers. On particularly hot days, and there were many, the guy whose job consisted of using long heavy tongs to take red hot metal formers out of a blazing hot furnace and placing them in an equally hot stamping machine, was always a no show. I was allocated eight hours in front of this hell hole with arms outstretched and learned firsthand the benefits of a sickie for the taker and the drawbacks for those who then had to step up. I looked upon this situation as character and body building and would usually finish a day on the furnace with a five to eight km run down by Elwood beach. By the time March came around, I was super fit, cash rich, relieved to go back to university, and preconditioned for the upcoming rugby season. I was also a tad wiser about industrial relations and how some parts of the world operated.

During the 1960s and 70s there was essentially a shortage of workers and obtaining holiday jobs whilst at school or university was easy. All of these jobs in one way or another informed me about work and life practices. The year following my messenger boy job, my holiday job was at "The George" cinema as a "lolly boy". Garbed in a short white starched coat, I would carry a tray of drinks, ice creams and lollies into the theatre before the start of the film and again during interval. I sometimes felt that I had a bit part in "The Sentimental Bloke". It did not pay very well but there was a lot of downtime to chat with the usherettes or watch the movie. In the 1960s, movies always had a long run in cinemas seating between 1,000 – 2,000 people and apart from small sections either side of interval, I can almost recall verbatim the dialogue of "Paint Your Wagon", "Casino Royale" and "The Battle of the Bulge". As for chatting up the usherettes, in 1966 I was a little young and shy for them at the time and it was the older "lolly boy" who occasionally ended up snogging with one of the girls in the empty back seats. The girls were just as bored as I was though and in retrospect with a little more bravery, I could have started my practical sex education a lot earlier! After that job I obtained a scholarship from the government and flush with funds didn't trouble the workforce until 1969 when after my final exams through my Mum's cousin Mary, I wangled a job in the Myers store where the toy department was short on staff and extremely busy over Christmas.

At the end of 1964, I was ready to leave primary school and head to the local high school at Camp Hill. Camp Hill High was not an appealing prospect so my new mate Mark and I cooked up a scheme to get into the selective high school, Brisbane State High, where my older brother had studied on our arrival in Brisbane. Without bothering our parents, we arranged for an interview with the deputy headmaster and took along our academic records. Thanks to our good results at Carina State School and the family history of elder brother Alan attending the school we were accepted and went home to inform our respective parents that we would be travelling 30 minutes on the trolley bus each day to "State High" near the city rather than walking to Camp Hill. My parents, particularly Dad, took it very well and I think they were happy that their quiet, shy son had at last showed some initiative. My high school years were thus quite different to what they might have been at Camp Hill.

State High was the oldest high school in Brisbane and a member of the GPS (Greater Public Schools) system. It consequently acted like a private school with Saturday sport, highly qualified teachers and a cohort of very smart kids. There were approximately 2200 students with more than 400 in my year alone, so it was also easy to blend in and get lost in the crowd. South Brisbane, where the school was located, was also full of migrants and because the school had to accept local kids there were many nationalities, so a rather different demographic to outer suburban Camp Hill. There were of course virtually no Asians at the time but South Brisbane had a large Greek population so plenty of kids of Italian and Greek background attended and a couple of my friends were from the Netherlands and the USA. The school was just over the river from Brisbane city so there were also a multitude of distractions just a short walk over the Victoria Bridge, an old narrow iron bridge that took trams. In year 8, I sat next to my mate to be, Rod, and we went through high school together, frequenting the snooker halls of Brisbane and becoming excellent snooker players. We were originally in the "top class" of 13 classes and sat with 40 of the smartest kids in the state. Despite obtaining reasonably good marks, I was in the bottom half of the class along with Rod, so we ended up in the second top class for the rest of our schooling with the bonus of forever after being in the top 10th percentile of the class. This move did a lot over the following years for our egos!

State High was ostensibly a co-educational school but operated like two independent schools. The old-fashioned girl's head mistress Miss McCorkill, a strict Seventh Day Adventist known by all behind her back as Dot, spent a lot of her time trying to ensure that the two sexes did not mix and the girls skirts were well below the knee. The girls would receive detentions for being seen walking to the bus with a boy, not wearing their gloves or hats or arriving at school with a skirt that showed their knees. Towards the end of the 60s as the mini skirt arrived on the scene, many of the girls received detentions for the latter crime and poor old Dot was having conniptions trying to keep 1940s rules in place. Once Dot or one of her informants realised that a girl was consistently observed in the company of one of the boys, she would be detained after school until her "boyfriend" became bored and went home without her. The classes were also split up along gender lines and the only class I ever had that included girls was Geography in my final year, where the student numbers enrolled in the subject were so low that the boys and girls from a number of classes had to be combined for the lessons.

In Geography class, Rod and I did not actually notice the girls much, because Ms Ammerlahn, our teacher, was only a couple of years older than we were and she was a gorgeous, tall, blond German woman who sat at the front of the class in the shortest of short miniskirts. She was also a good sport and once "caught" Rod and me skiving off after lunch and heading for town for a game of snooker. Rather than report us to the deputy head as most teachers would have done she gave us a lift to the snooker hall in her VW beetle and I can still remember the mental anguish of sitting close beside her as her long legs, hardly covered by the shortest of skirts, operated the clutch and brake. The highest mark I achieved in the final school exams was in Geography so she must have also imparted some knowledge. The advantages of a co-educational school were certainly not realised at State High in the 1960s and I grew up more ignorant of the female of the species than the boys that attended all boys' schools.

There were a number of other memorable teachers apart from Ms Ammerlahn, the only female teacher in my whole high school education. Mr McDonnell did a sterling and professional job of teaching German in the two years I attempted to learn it in preference to French and although I didn't progress very far it enabled me years later to breeze through a course in Science German at University and to get by on many trips to Germany. Mr Diamond was a gifted English teacher who managed to enthuse us, whilst our form teacher in the senior years who took Maths I and II and Chemistry, Mr Simpson, was knowledgeable, enthusiastic and appreciated by most. In our final year we had no Physics teacher for the first half of the year and an ancient retired teacher, Mr Heenan (Pud), was called back to teach us two years of Physics in four months. In my case, he succeeded and Physics was my second highest mark in the "Senior" exam.

Unlike most Australian high schools, the school had little space for recreation and a lot of our time at "play" was spent in the adjacent Musgrave Park and with South Brisbane being a decaying industrial area the other occupants of the park were usually the down and outs, drunks and the local Indigenous population. It was my first interaction of any sort with Aboriginals since arriving in Australia and my only knowledge of them was that incredulously they had only recently been granted the right to vote and a referendum was coming up to give them essentially the same rights as everybody else. There was no real connection with them, other than observing their journeys from the local pub to the park and observing what seemed to be constant arguments. Certainly, with nobody having any education about them or their culture, they were essentially left alone. It is no wonder that most people grew up with little knowledge of them and little empathy with them. The only discussion I remember about the upcoming referendum was the fact that nobody of our age seemed to be previously aware that the indigenous population did not have the same rights as everybody else and the consensus was that it was obviously wrong.

State High's main focus seemed to be sport, which was treated as essentially compulsory so I of course ignored it and apart from a short stint with the under 15B cricket team and a couple of rugby games in the fifths to accompany my mate Rod, during which I had absolutely no clue what was going on, I avoided it. One of the few sports that was not an official school sport was soccer, so I occasionally joined in lunchtime games of that with the Wogs, Clogs and Poms, which was more of a protest than a sporting endeavour. In England, I had studiously avoided soccer partly because it was the school sport and partly because I thought

I was lousy at it and did not want to embarrass myself. Mr Russell, who had tried to get me interested in playing sport at Carina, turned up as a teacher at State High and it was he who inveigled me into playing cricket for a short time. With a couple of thousand kids who actually wanted to play sport his time was taken up with them and he was in his element so after a short period I drifted quietly back to just backyard cricket and ball games with the local kids after school – non "compulsory" sport.

One of the activities I did get involved in at high school was theatre, where I teamed up with two outgoing fellow students Adrian and Terry, of Dutch and American heritage respectively. Like me, they were relatively recent immigrants and unlike everybody else that I knew at school, they were of the minority who were not labouring through two Maths, two sciences, English and a sixth subject for light relief. They were in the one class studying economics and "arts" subjects and seemed to have a lot of spare time on their hands. They were hence exotic friends and Terry was an out and out aspiring thespian who acted in the local Shakespearian group and already had a network in the Brisbane entertainment arena. Adrian, one of the clogs who played soccer during lunchtimes, was determined to be something big in the theatre. We were all three heavily involved in the year 11 production of "Calamity Jane", me of course as a backroom boy involved in the staging. Being part of the production allowed the participants to miss an hour or two of lessons and that was a large part of my interest. I learnt recently that both Terry and Adrian scurried off overseas to the USA after we all left school and whilst Terry continued on with his love of Shakespearian theatre he also branched into the politics of environment, became Arnie Schwarzenegger's secretary of the California Environmental Protection Agency "Climate change" and was last heard of heading Leonardo De Caprio's foundation. Adrian after a few years in the US moved to Europe and did become something big in European theatre. At that time, Australia was still something of a backwater for people aspiring to roles in the arts area so these two recent immigrants both departed Australia for overseas to pursue their dreams.

I managed to "waste" a lot of my time in the final two years of school on not just snooker but taking part as the lead in a play written by Terry and hanging around the theatre both at school and in the amateur theatres around Brisbane. Close to the end of school, Terry wangled us a spot on a local television show "I've Got a Secret". The segment involved a panel of four show biz people questioning a team of three to determine in our case "who is the real Terry T, aspiring young American actor". Despite Terry having an obvious American accent, Adrian an unusual strain of Aussie/Dutch and me an oddball mix of "elocution English", Geordie and Strine, two of the panel concluded I was Terry and only one picked the real Terry. My elocution English came about from sitting next to my well-spoken mate Rod for five years. His mother, understandingly some may say, disliked the strong Queensland accent and made sure Rod went to weekly elocution lessons. I benefitted from these lessons to the point that many people pick me as a Pom not for the single remaining sign of my Northern English accent – the short "a" for words like "castle" but for my "cultured" accent. From my television exposure, I brought home half a dozen plastic drinking mugs as a prize. Terry and Adrian tried to convince me after our TV exposure that they could make me into the next James Bond if we teamed up for a shot at stardom. Despite the fame at school after the airing of the television program, I figured that being paid in plastic mugs was probably not a good way to make a decent living. The theatre experience did contribute to some degree to me slowly overcoming my debilitating shyness.

1960s school days were long before Al Grassby and the Whitlam government introduced the concept of a multicultural Australia and dismantled the last vestiges of the White Australia policy, so apart from Adrian and Terry, everybody else I associated with at high school was a dinky di Aussie, hence social life was generally a bit one dimensional. In my final year class of 35, there were three students with Greek, Italian and central European surnames and everybody else was of Anglo-Saxon-Celtic heritage. These numbers were representative of the whole school population and in the 400 odd students of my year, there was only one student of Asian origin. At home, we tended to have many English, Scots and Irish visitors, either our relatives or their friends, people we had met on the boat, or fellow Brits who had gravitated towards people from the same background. The most exotic visitors were an American couple who my parents had met through jazz and they came over so that the husband Gordon could play double base to accompany my piano playing mum.

We were introduced to alternative food before most others though, with one of Dad's work mates Bill specializing in cooking Chinese food. He had a huge wok and many ingredients sourced from Chinese friends. This Chinese influence, along with an Italian repertoire that mum had picked up ensured that our food choices were not always the same as the meat and three veg of most of our neighbours and our staples included both rice and pasta on top of the good old English spuds. We had though never heard of what are now everyday vegetables such as zucchinis, aubergines and capsicums, spices were almost unheard of and the herbs were generally basic parsley and mixed herbs. Garlic though did appear on our menu in the pasta dishes. Dad of course started to grow the

Australian garden staples of silverbeet, pumpkin and chokos along with lettuce and tomatoes. Mum could never get any taste into the bitter silverbeet or the strange tasteless chokos and they did not last more than one outing on the menu. Pumpkin she managed to master quite quickly, although my older brother Steve was resistant to its charms. The biggest successes in the garden were ladyfinger bananas, mandarins and pawpaws once Dad had figured out which pawpaw variety to grow. Every now and then we were inundated with bananas and would fry them up in butter for breakfast morning after morning to experience the caramelised sweet flavour.

Like many immigrants, we missed our relatives and in those days, the cost of international telephone calls was prohibitive so like others we resorted to recording audio tapes to send back and forwards to England. We would describe some of the new taste sensations (good and bad) on these audio tapes as well as outline the different sort of life we were living and day-to-day events. The accents on the return tapes from England sounded broader and broader to our ears as the years went by. Now, in these days of Skype, Zoom, mobile phones and instant communication, it all seems rather primitive but in the 1960s it was high tech. Our family kept this tape exchange correspondence up for quite a while and then converted to videotapes when videotape recorders came on the scene. One instance in particular keeps the short-lived videotape exchange in mind. After my wife and I had children, we would send videotapes to my parents in Brisbane and overwrite any old tape that was hanging around. My wife, Liz, a doctor, had a number of short medical education tapes and we would overwrite those regularly. One day Doctor Liz managed to record the kids at the end of an education video on venereal disease rather than overwriting the original video. My parents were more than surprised on playing the video and my older brother took great delight in describing in graphic detail the moment when they switched it on to see surprising and confronting images.

Although we regularly had family holidays whilst living in England, I do not remember any holidays as a child/teenager in Australia, just occasional days out. The reasons for this were not financial but I think more related to our life in Australia being less structured, freer and fuller than in England, even though we were one of those rare families that did not possess a car. The fact that we kids were all now grumpy teenagers also may have had an impact. There was warm weather, lots of space, beaches a bus ride away, art galleries and museums in the city and hence much more life on hand than in Darlington. I think my parents no longer had a great desire to get away from their day-to-day environment. Carina and the surrounding local area however had very little going for it apart from the sports fields, bowls club and the local cinema, "The Planet" at Camp Hill, which was equipped with deck chairs rather than seats. Movies were watched whilst lying back in comfort and many young couples found that you could easily squeeze two people into one deck chair and become otherwise engaged during boring movies.

In my penultimate school year, the travel experiences of our journey to Australia surfaced and I felt the need to explore some of the vast country I had emigrated to and decided to take a holiday myself. Along with my mate Rod, I signed up for a bus and camping trip to central Australia with the YMCA. This trip came about through Rod, who was a rower and heavily into bodybuilding, convincing me that I was a skinny runt and needed to build some muscle. So twice a week, usually before or after a game of snooker we would attend the YMCA gym over the river in the city. This project did not succeed in developing my skinny body very much and gave me a lifetime dislike of smelly, enclosed gyms, but we did see a poster advertising YMCA activities through the school holidays, one of which was the central Australia trip. We duly signed up for a two week camping trip in August by bus through New England and central New South Wales to Melbourne, Adelaide, Coober Pedy, Ayers Rock (now Uluru), Alice Springs, Tennant Creek, Mt Isa and Charleville. As it turned out, we were away for almost three weeks after a number of adventures extended the trip.

The bus that we were allocated, an old Pioneer clipper with a rounded tail, was well past its prime so at the end of the first day we found ourselves sleeping on the cold floor in a church hall in Glen Innes, northern NSW whilst the bus underwent repairs. The repairs required a part to be shipped up from Sydney so we spent a second night in the church hall where, given the altitude and the winter temperatures, we froze. We arrived in Melbourne a day behind schedule to find that the bus now required a new axle and so a further 24 hour delay ensued and another couple of cold nights on the floor of another church hall were required. The YMCA were brilliant at finding cold, draughty church halls to put us up so as well as learning about Australia, I was being hardened up.

By Adelaide we were running two days late but the 30 passengers were now all good friends, having faced adversity together and bonded. At Ayers Rock, there was a primitive camping ground next to the pub and another cold night prior to climbing the rock (an activity recently banned). A couple of days later whilst travelling along the highway just south of Alice Springs the bus driver (there was only one) dozed off and missed the only bend in the road in hundreds of miles. We all woke up to nasty scraping noises, with the bus bouncing through the scrub. Large rocks or stumps in an otherwise flat desert ripped out various crucial parts under the bus and we all evacuated to get away from the smell of the diesel that now soaked the desert. The excitement of the crash culminated in a tow into Alice Springs and an extra three days in Alice Springs whilst parts were again located and flown in.

The main fun started on our arrival in Alice Springs when the first person came down with a nasty flu-like illness, which eventually affected 80% of those in the bus. By now five days late, we set off for Tennant Creek, leaving four of our number behind in Alice Springs hospital and with most of the rest of us developing nasty coughs. The remainder of the trip was essentially uneventful apart from a constant attrition in the numbers of passengers. We left a few people in Tennant Creek hospital and a couple more in Mt Isa. By Charleville I was in a bad way and in some pain but put my acting skills to work, emulated a not so sick person and refused to be left behind with a couple of others when within striking distance of home. Sleeping on the ground in a sleeping bag on that last night was definitely "character building".

By this stage of our adventure, Rod and I had become very friendly with two girls from one of the all-girl schools in Brisbane. They were a year ahead of us at school so normally would not have given us a second glance but after more than two weeks they were determined to explore our mutual attraction. Rod and his friend spent the last two days exploring each other in the back seat whilst I, and a very nice Californian blonde, attempted the same. Despite meeting one of the first girls who wanted to kiss me and get personal, I was in such a bad way health wise that kissing was interrupted after a few seconds for coughing and my body was in enough pain to preclude most other activities. My inability and lack of focus was a distinct frustration for my companion because all I was capable of was holding hands. I often wondered afterwards whether she caught the bug and suffered as I did.

On arrival in Brisbane we were met by my parents and the look on my mother's face as she took in the fact that my face was cadaverous and my 9½ stone body had dropped by about a stone in the last three weeks was something to remember. I eventually returned to school 2½ weeks later after a course of antibiotics and a good lie down. The 7,000km road trip had opened my eyes to the vastness of Australia and the desert like nature of large parts of the country.

There was a follow up to this adventurous trip. The next year Rod was still persevering with my bodybuilding at the YMCA when we noticed a poster for the 1969 winter camping trip – two weeks to Tasmania and back. I was up for that and went home to tell my parents. My mother, being a doom and gloom person who thought that one bad experience should put you off similar activities for life, was horrified and vehemently against it. I expressed the view that lightning was unlikely to strike twice and pursued the idea. A reluctant mother fought a rear-guard action but against my stubbornness and with my father as an ally she had to give in. The result of the previous year's trip had obviously put most people off the idea of bus/camping trips and the YMCA had to cancel the trip that year through lack of numbers. The few of us who had signed up for the adventure ended up joining an identical trip with the Kelvin Grove Teacher's College so I finished up, without Rod, heading to Tasmania with a group of people a year or two older than me. The trip, although following an identical itinerary to the YMCA version, would be rather different, both geographically and socially.

As we crossed the Victorian border at the end of day one, the budding teachers, all well over 18, noted that the drinking age in Victoria was 18 unlike the 21-year barrier of Queensland and convinced the bus driver to stop at the first available pub. At this stage of life, I had been to a few parties where alcohol magically appeared but thought, unlike many of my friends, that alcohol and particularly beer with its bitter taste, was not for me and I was also a law-abiding citizen. It was however my 18th birthday the very day we crossed the Victorian border and that information was on the passenger list for all the rest to see, so what could I do? My first and second beers were consumed in the beer garden of a majestic old country pub on the banks of the Murray River.

Over the next two weeks, with an older cohort for company and a desire to fit in, I learnt that a taste for beer did not take too long to acquire. Unlike the previous year, there were no breakdowns and no sickness making its way through the bus, apart from almost everyone getting seasick on a violent ferry crossing to Tasmania. With my training in surviving sea voyages some eight years earlier on the Oriana I was one of the few left standing on the ferry. My mother was relieved to see me hop off the bus back in Brisbane a fit and healthy character. She would have been less impressed if she knew that I now had a taste for beer, although being a law-abiding, and very young looking citizen, I did not touch the stuff until I was once again in Victoria. My period of abstinence did not last long because by January of the following year, I had joined the RAAF and was a Melbourne resident and apart from a "cultured" accent thought I was a dinky-di Aussie. That proved eventually to be not exactly true. But my experience in having to emigrate to Australia for a second time is quite another story.

By the time of my last year at school my mother and father were very much settled in Brisbane, although in 1968, seven years after arrival we of course moved house. Apart from meeting up with Jack and Merle Lawrence, Roy showed no interest in making contact with anything like the Returned Serviceman's League (RSL) or RAAF associations. It was only after many years of studiously ignoring Anzac Day that my father, when in his early 60s, decided to involve himself with the 463-467 Squadron Association. His two Aussie aircrew mates had passed away and he at last felt the need to connect with people who had had similar experiences to his in World War 2. By that time, the Brisbane branches of the 463 and 467 Associations had combined because of dwindling numbers and there was nobody in the association who he knew previously and nobody who had served at Waddington in the four months that he was there. Once they had determined that this Pommie was actually on the level he was well accepted and acted as the association secretary until shortly before his death in 1997. He even marched on Anzac Day with the association. He attended a number of joint reunions of the Australian 463-467 associations and discovered that there was nobody left in the whole of Australia who had flown at the same time as him. So at the age of 62, when he at last felt the need to share his experiences with old comrades, there was nobody he knew who went through similar experiences in the worst period of the war for Bomber Command. They had all perished through the war or gone to an early grave.

He also renewed contact with Jim Marles and the 207 Squadron Association in England and corresponded with them regularly until his death. Through the 207 Association, he connected with the Canadian pilot Bill Baker with whom he and Jim Marles flew one op, so he and Bill exchanged letters and photos. The 1944 visit of the Trimble crew to the Castle Bromwich aircraft factory also triggered some activity around this time. After the war the Birmingham factory was converted to the production of Jaguar cars and was (and is) still proud of its heritage. In 1991 the city and the factory were celebrating the extensive Spitfire production during WW2. Castle Bromwich produced approximately 12,000 Spitfires between 1939 and 1945. Jim Marles and the English branch of the 463/467 association were keen that the Lancaster production should also be remembered, so they arranged to attend the celebration and present a framed collage based around the Trimble crew's visit in 1944 and the first Lancaster produced.

In 1991 for this celebration, Mr Barry Hope[1] wrote "A Short History of Lancaster Production at Castle Bromwich" and recognised that the 50th anniversary of the first Lancaster produced would be in 1993. In order to celebrate that occasion he organised for a copy of a painting that he had commissioned of Lancaster HK535, to be ready and arranged with Jaguar for a presentation ceremony. The painting, "Dive Port Skipper", by Geoff Bell, is shown in chapter 7 and is of Lancaster HK535, Naughty Nancy, over Brunswick on the night the Trimble crew were lucky to survive. The original painting is signed by Alex Henshaw, the test pilot who first flew HK535 and by Jim Marles, amongst others. Roy subsequently sent a signature to England to be retro-fitted and obtained a copy after that for himself.

At Roy's funeral and life celebration, a dozen 463-467 association members attended and the president, Max Johnson, a flight lieutenant pilot on 467 Squadron, who was posted into Waddington two months after the Trimble crew finished, gave a speech and laid an Australian flag over his coffin. The last post was played by one of Roy's grandsons. He died aged 72 and was sent off as an Aussie comrade in arms.

Despite being an assimilated Australian, Dad had very fond memories of his childhood in Durham and expressed a desire to have his ashes scattered beside the River Browney. My older brother, Alan, being the dutiful first son, took his surprisingly heavy ashes to England and we met up in Durham to carry out his wishes. In and around Cornsay there was no evidence of its mining history and the village now sits in a pleasant green English landscape. We found a shady glade by the river outside the village and proceeded to scatter his ashes. Despite the sheltered position, the breeze caught the fine ashes and scattered them far and wide. The ashes that made it into the Browney joined the River Wear and passed through Bishop Auckland, Durham city, Chester-le-Street and Sunderland, all places where my mum had lived in the many pubs that my Granda worked in. We thought of the many times we knew of that Dad had been near death. Skidding under a truck on his sled as a child, walking away from three crashed Lancaster bombers, somewhere between 27 and 29 ops over Europe, living through a botched appendix operation and relatively unscathed after three major car accidents. He was definitely a "Lucky Pommie Bastard".

---

[1] Barry Hope has subsequently written a huge number of books on Bomber Command squadrons under the banner "In the Morning". They and the remaining copies of the painting of Naughty Nancy are available from him. The AWM library has copies of his books on the RAAF bomber squadrons.

13 JUST HOW LUCKY?

The Three Lancaster Crews.

Pilot	Fl Off Victor Herbert Trimble DFC (RAAF)	Plt Off Arthur Heap (RAAF)	Fl Off John Welch (RAAF)
Navigator	Fl Off Arthur Wilfred Herriott (RAFVR)	Fl Off Robert Gall (RAFVR)	Fl Off Hugh McCulloch (RAAF)
Flight Engineer	Sgt James (Jim) Marles (RAFVR)	Sgt Bill Carter (RAFVR)	Sgt Les Reynolds (RAFVR)
Wireless Operator	Sgt W. (Ron) Nixon (RAFVR)	Sgt Leo Ryan (RAAF)*	Flt Sgt K Charles French (RAAF)
Bomb Aimer	Sgt Bill Tom (Ginger) Aldworth (RAFVR)	Sgt Daniel McCreadie (RAFVR)	Flt Sgt Geoffrey Lynch (RAAF)
Mid Upper Gunner	Sgt Roy McNaughton (RAFVR)	Sgt Fred Tunnicliff (RAFVR)	Sgt Jim Seddon (RAFVR)
Rear Gunner	Sgt John (Jack) Patrick McKenna Lawrence (RAAF)	Flt Sgt Ken Glover (RAAF)	Sgt Arthur Whetton (RAFVR)
	All survived.	Shot down and all killed 24 December 1943. 463 Squadron Buried: GWGC Berlin	Shot down and all killed 27 August 1943. 207 Squadron. Buried: CWGC Durnbach

*The Original WOP was Sgt. Tony Boultbee (RAAF) who switched crews and survived the war.

Fellow trainees

The Trimble crew were the lucky crew of the three crews who moved on to 207 Squadron from 14OTU, being the only crew to survive. The members of the Heap and Welch crews were only a small number of the friends they made through their journey into Bomber Command. Very few of their other mates made it through the war, showing just how lucky Roy and the Trimble crew were when compared to their cohorts, and just how dangerous Bomber Command was in 1943/44.

Of the contingent of Australian pilots who arrived in Bournemouth from Sydney with Vic, Arthur and John, a number accompanied them to South Cerney to carry out their UK pilot training. At least eight of these Australian sergeant pilots were also transferred to 14OTU with Vic, Arthur and John. There they formed crews, with a number picking up rear gunners who had travelled from Australia in the company of Jack Lawrence. They also all picked up MUGS who had trained at Dalcross with Roy and seven of the eight went on together to 1654HCU. Five of these Aussie led crews were posted together to 57 Lancaster Squadron, RAF Scampton, where they started their ops at the same time as the 207 Aussie led crews. The sixth crew were posted to 61 Squadron at RAF Syerston, together with another Australian pilot who accompanied Vic to England, trained with John French, but progressed through a different HCU. The seventh was posted to 467 Squadron, a RAAF unit. The eighth crew went to 1661HCU and 50 squadron. The majority of these nine other crews did not survive.

Robert James Ratcliffe (RAAF), was killed on 10/11 August 1943, only one day after his arrival at Scampton. He flew as second pilot with Flt Lt Wilson on a raid to Nuremberg and all were killed[1].

Jack Smithers completed one op as a second pilot and one op with his own crew to Milan on 16 August 1943. On return from Milan, they lost an engine and then overshot the runway and attempted to go around. The aircraft crashed with five killed, including Smithers and his rear gunner, R. G. Haskins (RAAF), who had travelled to England with Jack Lawrence. The mid upper gunner, H. A. Burgess, one of the Dalcross 68 MUG Course graduates, survived the crash[2].

Gordon Alexander Duff (RAAF), completed three ops in addition to a trip as a second pilot. On return from his fourth op, a trip to Hannover on 22/23 September 1943, his aircraft was attacked in the circuit by an

---

[1] https://losses.internationalbcc.co.uk/loss/119355
[2] https://highgate-rsl.org.au/afcraaf-roll/haskins-ronald-henry-415789/

Me410 long-range night fighter and set alight. The bomb aimer and flight engineer managed to parachute to safety from 2,000 feet before the Lancaster dived into the ground. The other five crew members were killed, including Flt Sgt William Pryde, another of the rear gunners who had travelled all the way from Australia with Jack Lawrence. Whilst Gordon Duff stuck to the controls William Pryde kept firing to the end[3].

So, after just five weeks on 57 Squadron, three of the five Aussie led crews were gone or wounded. Sgt Leon Harvey Cooper, the normal MUG with the Duff crew and another graduate of 68 MUG course at Dalcross, had that night transferred to the crew of Fred Perrers, a New Zealand pilot. The Perrers' crew subsequently moved to 630 Squadron and completed a total of 19 ops before being shot down on their 20th, a trip to Berlin on the night of 23/24 November 1943. The rear gunner and WOP bailed out and became POWs. The others, including Leon Cooper perished[4].

Keith Cumming McPhie (RAAF, DFC), operated with 57 Squadron until he and his crew were shot down and killed over Berlin on 29/30 January 1944. The crash site was in the Russian zone, so the whole crew were not identified until 1951 when the Russians allowed CWGC staff into their sphere of influence[5].

The fifth pilot was Stanley George Townsend (RAAF, DFC). Townsend and his crew survived a full tour of ops. His MUG was A Hughes, another graduate of 68 MUG course, Dalcross.

Of the two crews who went to 61 Squadron, Flt Sgt Vidler (RAAF) carried out two ops as second pilot. He returned from the first of these, a trip to Milan but on 17/18 August just a week after arrival he and the crew of Flt Sgt Docker were killed on an op to Peenemunde. It was a bad night for 61 Squadron and three crews failed to return. The rest of Vidler's crew were then split up, with the Australian rear gunner, Ron Lowe, who was another of those who travelled with Jack Lawrence, going on to 57 Squadron. Lowe was shot down on 2 January 1944 and became a POW. The MUG of the Vidler crew, N Harris, was from 68 course, Dalcross.

The second of these two crews, led by Ronald James Mortimer (RAAF, DFC), completed a number of ops with 61 Squadron before being posted to the newly formed 463 Squadron at the same time as Vic Trimble and Arthur Heap. Mortimer and his crew were shot down on the 21/22 February 1944 on a raid on Schweinfurt. Mortimer was killed but

---

[3] https://highgate-rsl.org.au/afcraaf-roll/pryde-william-417232/
[4] https://630squadron.wordpress.com/2019/03/10/november-1943
[5] **National archives of Australia NAA: A705, 166/26/356.**

the two gunners, G Lloyd, yet another 68 MUG course graduate and Maxwell Dease, the Australian rear gunner and yet another travelling and training companion of Jack Lawrence, became POWs.

Douglas Chapman Dunn (RAAF), was posted to 467 Squadron along with his RAAF rear gunner Edward Gloster (another fellow traveller with Jack Lawrence) and Harry Deakin (RAFVR), another 68 course MUG. After a number of ops on 467 they were transferred to 463 when it formed and joined their mates in the crews of Trimble, Heap and Mortimer. The Dunn crew were shot down on 30/31 January 1944 on an op to Berlin and six were killed. The bomb aimer bailed out and became a POW[6].

So, well before the Trimble crew had finished their tour of ops, nine of their ten Australian pilot mates were dead, four of the seven Australian rear gunner mates were dead and two were POWs and four of their seven MUG mates were dead and one was a POW.

The 8th Australian, South Cerney pilot Lewis Arthur John McLeod, together with his 68 MUG course gunner, C Baker, was posted to 50 Squadron. They completed a tour and went on to a second tour with 97 Pathfinder Squadron. They were shot down on 22 June 1944. Lewis McLeod was killed and Baker bailed out and became a POW. Of the 13 pilots that I have tracked who travelled out with Vic and went on to Bomber Command Vic and Stan Townsend survived the war unscathed and George Grimbly was shot down over Berlin and became a POW. Of the 16 graduates of 68 MUG course at Dalcross, eight died, three became POW, one survived a crash and was injured, two (including Roy) definitely survived and the other two are presumed to have survived.

The Aircraft and fellow Aircrew on 207/463

The Trimble crew flew in at least 11 different Lancaster aircraft on ops and a 12th (W4952), that they pranged and destroyed just after their arrival at 207 Squadron. Only one of these aircraft survived the war. They also flew 17 different Lancasters on training flights at HCU, on the squadrons and at Lancaster Finishing School. Individual members of the crew additionally flew a number of ops with other crews. The stories of these aircraft and of their crews provide a microcosm of the myriad stories of the Bomber Command crews and their fates in World War 2 and help put the survival of the Trimble crew in the context of the overall Bomber Command losses during 1943/44.

Six of their eight 207 Squadron ops from RAF Langar were carried out

---

[6] https://losses.internationalbcc.co.uk/loss/106665

in LM326 –EM-Z, Z-Zebra. This aircraft was shot down and destroyed during a raid on Hannover on the night of 18 October 1943 during the first 207 Squadron op carried out from RAF Spilsby and whilst the Trimble crew were still on leave. The pilot was Sgt. Geoff Taylor, an Australian, who along with his crew of four Brits, a Canadian and an Australian rear gunner bailed out at low altitude and became prisoners of war. Their aircraft was one of the 140 allied victims of the German ace night fighter pilot Friedrich-Karl Müller, who eventually died in 1944 in an accident when his fighter stalled just before landing. Geoff Taylor authored a book about his final experiences on 207 Squadron, his capture and subsequent captivity in Stalag 4B, entitled "Piece of Cake"[7]. The book title ironically recalls the final words of the Commanding Officer at the end of the operational briefing, it being the RAF slang for "easy operation". The author, an excellent professional writer, captures the atmosphere of the times and the descriptions and prose are second to none. Much of the book concentrates on life in POW camps, where close to 11,000 Bomber Command airmen finished up after surviving crashes or bailing out. This is one of the most readable and insightful books to come out of this arena of war and a delight to read. In the 207 Squadron post war records on this loss it is stated, "Cause of loss not established. Crash landed 2030 onto the Reim-Reinerbaech Arzen Road, SW of Hamelin." Geoff Taylor's book certainly sets the record straight on exactly what happened that night and despite Geoff worrying for months that some of his crew did not manage to bail out, they all survived.

Two of the Trimble crew ops at 207 were carried out in ED601 EM-N, one from Langar and one from Spilsby. This Lancaster carried out 15 ops with 83 Squadron before being assigned to 207, where it survived at least another six successful ops until it crashed on its fifth trip to Berlin in a row. Pilot Officer Arthur Mann and his crew took off from Spilsby on 3 December 1943, just after the Trimble crew were posted to 463 Squadron. The aircraft crashed near Saalow, six km SW of Zossen and about 30 km south of Berlin with all crew members killed. The crew were originally all buried at Saalow, but were subsequently re-interred in the Berlin 1939-45 War Cemetery operated by the CWGC.

The crew were *Plt Off A. Mann, RAFVR aged 23; Sgt S. Martin, RAFVR aged 24; Fl Off H.F.C. Bonner, RAFVR; Plt Off E.V. Harley, RAF aged 21; Sgt A.S. Rushby, RAFVR, Sgt F.L. Brisco RCAF; Sgt N.F. Petty, RAFVR aged 29.*[8]

---

[7] "Piece of Cake" – Geoff Taylor, published by George Mann (1978).
[8] http://www.rafcommands.com/database/wardead/details.php?qnum=92161

The British Occupation Authorities and CWGC officials selected the site of the Berlin 1939-45 Commonwealth War Cemetery in 1945 after the end of the war almost immediately after hostilities ceased. Graves were re-interred in the cemetery after transfer from the general area around Berlin and from eastern Germany. The greater majority of those buried there, approximately 80% of the total, are Bomber Command airmen who were lost in the many air raids over Berlin and the towns and cities of eastern Germany. The remainder were men who died as prisoners of war, some of them in the forced marches into Germany from camps in Poland as the Russians advanced. The cemetery contains 3,595 Commonwealth burials of the Second World War, 397 of them unidentified.

This cemetery, like all those of the CWGC, is beautifully maintained and in the warm months of the year flowers bloom around the neat and tidy gravestones. It is situated in an extremely quiet, solemn garden setting close to the 1936 Berlin Olympic Games Stadium, the colossal imposing stadium built by the Nazis and used by the British after the war as their administration centre until 1996. The stadium was reconstructed in 2004 as one of the major unified Berlin stadiums. The cemetery is far enough away from the stadium and housing to be isolated from the normal activities of modern life and a walk around the graves is a moving experience, with almost all the grave markers displaying the air force badges of Commonwealth nations and showing the remarkably early age of most of those killed. The long rows of white crosses, whilst short in comparison with the World War 1 grave cemeteries, starkly illustrate the large number of aircrew lost over Berlin. In a small area of the cemetery, there is a section for the British who died during the occupation after World War 2 with a number of young children interred.

The crew carried out just one 207 op in W4959 EM-S, an aircraft like ED601 that had also been flown previously by 83 Squadron. This aircraft was lost on the night of 23 November 1943 when piloted by Flt Lt. Derek Edward Reay on a raid to Berlin. The Trimble crew also took part in this raid just before leaving 207 Squadron. Reay and all his crew died and their bodies never found. Their names are recorded along with 20,456 others at the Runnymede memorial, dedicated to those aircrew who died with no known grave.

The crew *were Flt Lt Derek Edward Reay, RAFVR aged 22; Sgt Cyril Burton, RAF; Sgt Leonard James Lewis, RAFVR; Fl Off Robert Edward Mair, RAFVR; Sgt Cornelius O'Connor, RAFVR; Sgt John Richardson, RAFVR, aged 22; Flt Sgt Alfred John Charles Williams, RAFVR aged 29.*

Reay's younger brother, Fl Off Geoffrey Reay, also in the RAF, was killed a year later on an op to Bochum in a Halifax and the two brothers are commemorated in Northern Ireland at their old school.

Only Roy and Jim Marles flew with Plt Off Bill Baker in DV361 EM-V. The Trimble crew had had yet another incident of some sort, most likely in training and four of the seven crew members were not allowed to fly. DV361 underwent a number of eventful ops before being lost. Only a week after Roy and Jim flew with them to Modane, DV361 piloted again by Bill Baker, collided with the rear of a 9 Squadron Lancaster over Berlin. The 9 Squadron Lancaster was piloted by Plt Off Frank Lees and he and his crew were forced to bail out. Apart from the rear gunner, Sgt L.N Harris, who died, they were all captured and imprisoned. DV361 had severe damage to the nose and port propellers and the bomb aimer Flt Sgt E. H Shimeild (RAFVR) fell to his death when the forward escape hatch directly underneath him was dislodged in the collision. Shimeild is buried in the Hamburg War Cemetery. Bill Baker and crew flew the damaged aircraft back to Spilsby on three engines with a freezing gale streaming through the damaged nose and had to corkscrew when coned by searchlights over the Netherlands. Despite wearing both silk gloves and flying gloves his hands froze to the control column and Bill lost all his fingers to frostbite but retained his thumbs. He was awarded the DFC, which was presented to him by Guy Gibson of Dambuster fame. Bill Baker survived the war to marry a station WAAF and emigrated to Canada. The other three members of the crew on the night Jim and Roy flew with them all survived the war.

The aircraft DV361 itself was repaired and subsequently lost when an engine caught fire on a cross-country test flight whilst flown by another Baker, Plt Off Geoff A Baker. Three of the crew died and are commemorated on a local memorial and on the Runnymede memorial whilst the other four bailed out.

Flt Sgt Cecil Ryall, WOP/AG, RAAF; Sgt Thomas Higgins, Rear Gunner, RAF(VR); Sgt George O'Neill, MUG, RAF(VR) all died.

The remaining crew members were later killed in action, whilst the pilot Geoff Baker was shot down and killed during a raid on Wesserling on 21/22 June 1944 with 619 Squadron. He is buried in the Rheinberg War Cemetery with four of his crew, the other two becoming POWs. The Wesserling raid was an extremely bad night for 619 Squadron with six out of 16 aircraft failing to return.

Four of the Trimble crew ops on 207 Squadron were carried out in LM383 EM-R. This aircraft was shot down, or hit by flak, on the night of 14 January 1944 over Brunswick, the same night that the Trimble crew had their most difficult op and flew home on two engines. The pilot was

Plt Off Patrick Kingston, an Australian from Murwillumbah NSW who enlisted in the RAAF on 11 October 1941. After training in both Australia and Canada, he sailed to the UK and was attached to 207 Squadron with his crew on 12 October 1943. He and all but one of his crew were killed over Brunswick. The bomb aimer, Sgt T Bowskill RCAF, bailed out and finished the war as a POW.

The main escape hatch for the crew was a door in the bomb aimer position on which the bomb aimer lay for the bombing run and this gave the bomb aimer a slightly better chance of survival. The Lancaster, despite its better record for taking punishment and surviving attacks, was narrow and contained many obstacles to movement making the two gunner positions the most difficult for escape routes. In 1943, the survival rate of aircrew in Lancaster aircraft shot down over Germany was 11%, compared to 29% for aircrew in Halifax aircraft. Many of the Halifax crews, shot down at a greater rate, preferred their aircraft because the width of the aircraft and larger escape hatches made it easier to exit a damaged aircraft and become a POW.

The others in the Kingston crew were *Sgt Geoffrey Walton, RAFVR aged 21; Sgt Stanley Rattray, RAFVR aged 21; Sgt Ronald Swann RAFVR, aged 21; Sgt John Morrish, RAFVR aged 19 and Sgt Gordon Ferguson, RCAF.*

Patrick and his crew now rest in Hannover War Cemetery, another Commonwealth war gravesite heavily occupied by bomber crews. The cemetery is located just out of the city of Hannover and is again a well-kept, contemplative site with copious flowers in summer. Patrick Kingston trained with Vic Trimble's 51st Battalion mate Bill Barbour in Canada and they are two of the 29 trainees in a photograph taken in Canada in 1942[9]. The 29 trainees in the photo were transferred to war zones in Europe, the Middle East, India, the Pacific and North America. 12 of those in the photo died on ops and one in training, three became instructors and stayed in Canada, two were injured in the UK and repatriated to Australia, two were shot down and became POWs, one was shot down and evaded, one was shot down and interned in Switzerland.

The first raid of the Trimble crew from Waddington was in Lancaster EE191, JO-F a brand new aircraft that had just been delivered to the newly formed 463 Squadron. This aircraft was lost on a bombing raid to Frankfurt on 18 March 1944 after it had completed 25 ops. The Trimble crew also took part in this raid as the final op of their tour. Nothing was heard of EE191 once it had taken off and it never returned to base, the

---

[9] http://www.rquirk.com/wargraves/4SFTS/course58raaffates.html
https://www.awm.gov.au/collection/C1007802

only one of the 18 aircraft from 463 Squadron that failed to return. The aircraft crashed into a suburb of Offenbach (four miles east of Frankfurt) and all the crew were killed.

The crew were *Plt Off J.W. Gardner, aged 28, RAAF; Flt Sgt H Perkins, RAFVR; Fl Off M.C Grevstad, aged 23, RCAF; Sgt J Cuthbertson, RAFVR; Sgt D Brotherton, aged 21; RAFVR; Sgt R J Mottram aged 22 RAFVR; Flt Sgt J R McGrath, aged 21, RAAF.*

They are buried in Durnbach War Cemetery, a CWGC site containing mostly aircrew shot down in Germany south of Munich.

For their second op with 463 Squadron, the Trimble crew were again allocated a brand new aircraft, HK535 JO-N, Naughty Nancy. They crewed this on its first four ops and thought of it as their own. At this time, my father was engaged to my mother, Anne (Nancy) Brown whose name possibly triggered the aircraft's nickname. She might not have appreciated the "Naughty" part or the pair of panties that were drawn on to signify each completed op. The aircraft's motif on the port side was a drawing of Jane, the popular cartoon woman of the Daily Mirror standing beside a farm gate dressed only in bra and panties. Wing Commander Kingsford Smith also did not appreciate the nose drawing and succeeded in removing the "artwork" when the aircraft returned to the squadron after repair. It was only under the Trimble crew that it had the naughty nose art. They successfully flew "Naughty Nancy" back on two engines after the Brunswick raid.

By the time a repaired Naughty Nancy came back from the factory the Trimble crew were already flying Uncle Joe and so were happy to hand the aircraft on to another crew. The aircraft, now named the "Nazi Neutralizer", carried out a number of further raids and was shot down by flak and crashed between Lezennes Hellemmes Forest and Marques Annapes on an op against Lille railway station on 10 May 1944.

The crew *were Flt Lt Eric McLaren Scott, RAAF, aged 22; Sgt Raymond Herbert Boulton RAFVR, aged 19; Flt Sgt. Ivan Chapple, RAAF, aged 24; Plt Off Walter Thomas Peters, RAAF aged 24; Sgt Leonard Edgar Pringle, RAFVR; Flt Sgt. Richard William Ash, RAAF, aged 20; and Flt Sgt William Allen Slade, RAAF, aged 23.*

All the crew are buried in Forest-sur-Marque communal cemetery, a CWGC site, along with two other crews lost the same night over Lille. This Lille raid was the worst night of the war for the Waddington based 463/467 Squadrons. Thirty-one Lancasters departed and seven failed to return. One of the aircraft carried an eighth crew member, so 50 men of the combined squadrons died that night. The crew list above consists of five Australians and two British. By this stage of the war in 463 Squadron crews Australians were starting to predominate, so the nationality distribution probably reflects that of the squadron aircrew at that time.

During their last months at Waddington, flying mostly in Uncle Joe, the Trimble crew carried out one op in an alternative aircraft, ED606 JO-E. Lancaster ED606 JO-E with Plt Off Graham as pilot, took off from Waddington on the night of 15/16 March 1944 to bomb Stuttgart, Germany. Seventeen aircraft from the Squadron, including the Trimble crew in Uncle Joe, took part in the raid and one of these failed to return. ED606 successfully completed the op but whilst circling the RAF Waddington aerodrome preparatory to landing, it collided with aircraft 'L' of 625 Squadron RAF (Captain Flt Sgt Bulger, RCAF). ED606 crashed near Branston, four miles southeast of Lincoln, UK. The crews in both aircraft were killed. Plt Off Graham, RAAF, aged 25 was on his first solo op.

The other crew of ED606 were: *Sgt J A Coates, aged 21, RAFVR; Sgt J G B Jameson, aged 21 RAFVR; Sgt H A Baxter, aged 22, RAFVR; Sgt D McA Munro, aged 21, RAFVR; Sgt T H Jones, aged 22, RAFVR; Flt Sgt A S Humphreys, aged 20, RAAF.*

Because they all died in the UK, the five British crew were buried in their hometowns, whilst the two Australians are buried in the RAF cemetery, Cambridge, UK. Sgt Munro is buried in the Campbelltown (Kilkerran) Cemetery, Argyllshire, UK, Sgt Coates in Shildon (St John) Churchyard, Durham, UK, Sgt Jameson in Newcastle-upon-Tyne (all Saints) Cemetery, Northumberland, UK, Sgt Baxter in Brookwood Cemetery, Surrey, UK., and Sgt Jones in Deptford (Grove Park) Cemetery, London, UK[10].

The Trimble crew's final aircraft as a full crew was ED611 JO-U, Uncle Joe. At this stage of the war, the Russians were allies and respected for their role on the Eastern Front, where they were taking the lion's share of the fighting. Many of the British and Dominion troops were politically left leaning, so naming an aircraft after Stalin was not at all surprising. This was the aircraft that they always considered in post war years to be their own, primarily because they successfully finished their tour in it. The aircraft had already carried out numerous ops with 44 Squadron before being assigned to 463 Squadron and the Trimble crew. In 44 Squadron, its call sign was U -Uncle so with the JO squadron identifier unique to 463 the name Uncle Joe possibly came after it arrived at 463.

---

[10] The story of its last flight is adapted from AWM 64 1/342 (1) AWM 237 (63) (64) and Commonwealth War Graves records. AWM is Australian War Memorial.

One of the few photographs of the Trimble crew, taken in February 1944, shows the aircraft with 43 bombs painted on beside the caricature of Joe Stalin. These 43 bombs signified the ops carried out with 44 Squadron. The two stars on the other side of the cockpit show the two ops of the Trimble crew carried out at 463, so the photograph must have been taken soon after 20 February 1944. Sgt Fussell, who was in charge of their dispersal area, took the photograph. Vic Trimble considered taking photos would be bad luck, hence the sparsity of photos of the crew. Jim, the flight engineer, described Uncle Joe as a wonderful old aircraft but that he could never get the four engines to remain synchronised despite constant adjustment. The aircraft eventually successfully took part in 115 ops, becoming one of a select group of 35 Lancasters to survive 100 ops or more. It was scrapped on 22 June 1947[11].

Sgt Ronald Codling, RAFVR aged 21, the gunner who took Roy's place as MUG when he was sick and also accompanied Roy and Jim on the op with Plt Off Baker, was killed along with the rest of the crew of R5895 when it was shot down by a night fighter. This 207 aircraft was flown by Plt Off J M Read RAFVR aged 22, on a raid on Magdeburg, 21/22 January 1944. The aircraft crashed on the outskirts of Danningkow, Germany and all the crew were recovered and buried there before being re-interred in the Berlin War Cemetery.

The other crew were *Fl/Eng Sgt. Leslie Francis Abel RAFVR aged 21; Nav Fl Off. Robert Walter Sharp RAFVR aged 19; Bomb aimer Fl Off. Charles Travers J RCAF aged 29; WOP/A/G: Sgt. Ronald Arthur Blake Boydon RAFVR aged 21; Rear Gun. Fl/Sgt. Eric Clark Clunas RAAF aged 26.*

That night Bomber Command lost 49 aircraft, mainly to night fighters when diversionary raids did not fool the German controllers.

Plt Off Jack Childs, the New Zealander rear gunner who took Jack's place in the Trimble crew for their first op after the Brunswick raid, was killed on the night of 15 March 1944 on a raid to Stuttgart. ME573, piloted by Fl Off J. Roberts RAAF, DFC, crashed near Kornwesheim, approx. seven miles north of Stuttgart. Roberts was very close to the end of a tour having carried out 28 ops. All the crew were killed and they are buried in the Durnbach War Cemetery, Germany some 48 km south of Munich.

The other crew were *Plt Off P.C.R. Brown, RAFVR (Nav); Flt Sgt J M Benzie, RAAF (B/Aimer); Flt Sgt S J F Palmer, RAAF (WOP); Sgt J Wilby, RAFVR (Fl Eng), Plt Off J. L. Childs, DFC RNZAF (MUG); Sgt*

---

[11] See "Ton-up Lancs" - Norman Franks, Octopus Publishing Group, for more information on Uncle Joe.

R. Pead RAFVR (RG).

Plt Off Brown also had an association with the Trimble crew, because his first operational trip was carried out as second navigator with the Trimble crew on the 16 December 1943 raid to Berlin. In 463 Squadron ORBs, Childs is recorded as a flight sergeant when he flew with Trimble and also when he flew with Roberts, so his promotion was in the pipeline at the time of his death. He was awarded a DFC, which also must have been in the pipeline as a DFM, but converted to DFC on his commissioning. Childs flew mostly with the crew of Geoff Baker on both 467 and 463 Squadrons from early June 1943 –January 1944. After this he flew with a number of other crews as well and was very close to the end of his tour. Geoff Baker, his original pilot, completed his tour six weeks before Childs was killed but went on flying, eventually completing a total of around 50 ops on Pathfinders.

Fl Off Fryer, who Roy reportedly flew with as a second gunner on two occasions, failed to return on the night of 3 May 1944 on a raid on Mailly, just after the Trimble crew left 463 Squadron. It was the 19th op of what was described in squadron records as a "difficult tour". Taking off at 2151 from Waddington their Lancaster III (LM458 JO-G) was shot down on the approach to the target and crashed at Poivres (Aube), 20 km NNE of Arcis-sur-Aube.

The crew were *Pilot Fl Off G Fryer RAAF; Fl Eng Sgt R J Gracey RAFVR; Nav Flt Sgt J B Ward RAFVR; B/Aimer Flt Sgt J Healy RAFVR; WOP Flt Sgt E A Stone RAFVR; MUG Sgt K W Owen RAFVR;, RG Fl Off H E Williams RAAF* and all were killed.

They are buried in Poivres churchyard, together with 30 other aircrew who were shot down and killed over the target that night.

Plt Off Kevin Harold McKnight, the pilot who carried out an op as second pilot with the Trimble crew, died with the rest of his crew on their seventh op. DV274 took off to attack Augsburg on 26 February 1944 and crashed near Liesse, 15 km NE of Laon (Aisne, France) with the loss of all seven crew.

The crew *Plt Off K.H. McKnight, RAAF; Fl Off S.A. Isham RAFVR; Fl Off C.J. Johnson RAAF; Flt Sgt Nelson, RAAF; Sgt L.W. Roberts, RAFVR; Sgt T. Winn RAFVR; Sgt K. Linford RAFVR* are all buried in Liesse communal cemetery close to Calais, a CWGC site where 52 aircrew are buried.

Plt Off P. E. Hanson, flew as second pilot with the Trimble crew on 20/21 December on a raid to Frankfurt. Hanson and his crew were one of the many inexperienced crews to be killed early on in their tour. On the night of 30 January 1944, they took off for Berlin in JA973 and did not return along with three other crews from 463 Squadron. "Following post war enquiries it was believed that the aircraft crashed at Repente, a small village north east of the Grosser Zecchlinersee, 12kms south of Mirow."[12] Sgt Hughes (RAF) became a POW and the other six crew members were killed.

PO Hanson, Sgt Bligh and Flt Sgt Wilson are buried in the Berlin 1939-1945 War Cemetery. The other three members Sgt M A Stevens, Flt Sgt G E Edgecombe and Sgt L Bowes are listed as missing and their names are commemorated on the Memorial to the Missing, Runnymede, Surrey, UK.

A 1947 report by the No. 4 Missing Research and Enquiry Unit, declared 'parts of the aircraft were discovered on the shore of Zecchlinersee near the village of Repente. A local resident stated that the aircraft fell into the lake at night after an explosion in the air and the fuselage, wing and engine were in the lake about 1.5 miles north west of Repente. The rear turret fell away before the aircraft hit the water. In 1983, the Hemsdorf diving group discovered aircraft parts in the lake but because the area at that time was in East Germany it was not until 1987 that further parts were discovered. Eventually in May 2000, a whole engine and parts were recovered and the aircraft was determined to be JA973.

Fl Off D. R. Pettit, who replaced navigator Arthur Herriott for a trip to Stuttgart and Flt Lt A Williams who replaced him on the following trip to Leipzig most likely survived the war, there being no remembrance details for either of them.

Some of the Trimble crew carried out ops as spare or replacement crew members on arrival at 207 Squadron, prior to starting their own tour. Jack Lawrence flew as rear gunner with Plt Off Gordon Moulton-Barrett and his crew on a raid on Nuremberg on 10 August 1943 in Lancaster DV191. Arthur Herriott also flew an op with this crew as navigator on 10/11 November 1943, the same night Jim and Roy flew with the Baker crew.

Moulton-Barrett and his crew were shot down over Berlin on the same night as Arthur Heap, Christmas Eve 1943, crashing at Luckenwalde, SSW of Berlin. Plt Off Moulton-Barrett, together with Sgt. Gladders, Fl Off Roberts, Flt Sgt Burl, Flt Sgt Sherlock, Flt Sgt Robinson bailed out and were taken prisoner. This crew had many different rear gunners and it was Sgt David Oswald Davies RAFVR that night who died. Davies has no known grave and is commemorated on the Runnymede memorial. The aircraft was DV188 EM-J, the Lancaster that Vic Trimble flew in as

---

[12] https://highgate-rsl.org.au/afcraaf-roll/hanson-peter-edward-415528/

second pilot on his arrival at 207. The aircraft DV191 was lost over Brunswick, the same night that the Trimble crew lost two engines and struggled to make it home. The aircraft was piloted by Fl Off G.W. James and crashed near Hannover at Bakede, north of Hameln of Pied Piper fame. The pilot and Sgt. E.W.H Johnston were killed and are buried in the Hannover War Cemetery. The other five crew bailed out and were taken prisoner.

Jim Marles flew as flight engineer with Flt Sgt SWG Hall in Lancaster ED498 on 12 August 1943 on a raid to Milan. Hall and his crew transferred to 83 Squadron, a Pathfinder squadron, so extending their 30 op tour to 45. They were subsequently lost without trace on 20 October 1943 on a raid on Leipzig. The aircraft ED498, flown by Sgt RG (Bob) Pearcey, was lost four nights later on the night of the Trimble crew's first op on Milan. The aircraft was attacked by a night fighter on the way to the target and after extinguishing an engine fire continued with the op on three engines. On their return after bombing the target the aircraft was set on fire through further enemy action and crashed near Houlgate, 25km north east of Caen, France. Six of the seven crew died and the navigator Fl Off George Blakeman miraculously bailed out, so survived the crash and was taken prisoner.

The other crew members, *Sgt. R.W. Wilcockson, Sgt. J.S. White, Plt Off R. G. Pearcey, Sgt. J.C. Cunningham, Sgt. J. Kerkman and Sgt. H. Clement* are buried in Houlgate (Beuzeval) Communal Cemetery in France.

Arthur Herriott flew as a second Navigator with Plt Off J.A.C Stephens in Lancaster ED586 EM-F to Nuremberg on 10 August 1943. Stephens must have been close to the end of his tour as he and his crew were posted out to training units in early October 1943. He and three of his crew survived the war but ED586 was lost near Stettin on a raid on 6 January 1944. The aircraft was flow by Fl Lt George Henry Ebert (DFC) on his 29th op. Ebert was the pilot of the aircraft on Vic Trimble's first op as second pilot. All the crew, including Wg Cdr Ashley Jackson, flying as second pilot, were killed and are buried in the Poznan old garrison cemetery. This cemetery also contains the graves of many of the aircrew killed after the "Great Escape" from Stalag Luft III, the bodies being re-interred in Poznan post World War 2.

The Ebert crew were: *Pilot – Flt Lt George Henry Ebert DFC RAF; second Pilot aboard for experience Wg Cdr Ashley Duke Jackson MiD, RAF; Fl Eng Sgt Bernard Owen Greenhill RAF; Nav Flt Sgt Fred Thomas Murray Sidebotham RAFVR; Air Bomber Fl Off Peter Noel Hodgson RAFVR; WOP Flt Sgt Jack Thomas Toplis RAFVR; MUG Sgt Aubrey Harris Miller RAFVR; RG Flt Sgt Alfred John Simmons RAFVR.*

Wg Cdr Jackson had been attached for operational experience ahead of being given command of another squadron. It was in this aircraft 'F for Freddie' that Wynford Vaughn Thomas flew on a trip to Berlin on 3 September 1943 to make the famous BBC recording, broadcast on the Home Service on 4 September 1943 and many times since, of a Lancaster crew on a bombing raid[13].

Of all the 17 Lancaster aircraft that the Trimble crew flew in training or on test flights only one survived the war. The others were all lost in accidents or on ops with very few crew surviving the losses. One of them was DV1840, the aircraft Vic flew in as second pilot with Flt Lt Ebert. It was also the aircraft that Plt Off Jack Bremner was killed in during an aborted take-off at Langar, described in chapter four.

Those killed were: *Fl Off Archibald Bremner, buried in Glasgow Cardonald cemetery; Sgt Robert Appleton; Flt Sgt Roland Woodhouse; Flt Sgt Arthur Archer; Sgt John Horsley, all commemorate at Runnymede; Sgt Arthur Smith buried Allerton cemetery. Liverpool; Flt Sgt Frederick Dyde buried St Swithun church Long Bennington.*

The brief details in this chapter outline the fates of many aircrew directly associated with the Trimble crew who died during 1943/44, as well as the few who survived. The stark numbers underline the luck that the Trimble crew had in surviving the war and the chance nature of death or survival in such an environment. It was no wonder that the aircrews became closely bonded mates who kept mostly to themselves as a mechanism to cope with the constant losses surrounding them. Naming the crews and their fates I hope contributes to commemorating their lives, their bravery and their sacrifice and the lives of all Bomber Command aircrew in World War 2 who lived through the experience or died.

---

[13] The recording can be heard at https://www.awm.gov.au/collection/C276375

RESOURCES

Australian War Memorial:
https://www.awm.gov.au/visit/events/conference/air-war-europe/nelson
Access to the "guest Books" of "Cogers", London 1940-1945.
Biographical details of RAAF aircrew AWM 65
RAAF World War 2 fatalities / compilation Alan Storr. Royal Australian Air Force World War 2 fatalities RAAF WW2 fatalities – used as the source for the fates of a number of aircrew.

The following three websites were also accessed to provide detail on aircrews.
https://internationalbcc.co.uk/
http://aircrewremembered.com/
http://www.rafcommands.com/

National Archives, UK. For squadron Operational Record Books for 57, 61, 207 and 463 Squadrons (AIR27-538, -578, -1234 and -1921)
Training base Operational Record Books for 14OTU (AIR 29/653) and 3ACRC (AIR 29/477/4)
Combat reports (AIR50-232-36, 232-42, 232-55, 232-56, 232-237,232-249, 266-1, 266-32).

National Archives, Australia for military records of RAAF personnel, photographs and archived articles.
NAA: A9300, TRIMBLE V H
NAA: A9300, LAWRENCE J P M
NAA: A9300, HEAP K A
NAA: A9300, HEAP E T
NAA: A9300, HEAP A W
NAA: A9300, BARBOUR W M
NAA: A9300, ROYES G H

NAA: A9300, BOULTBEE A P
NAA: A9300, MCCULLOCH H J
NAA: A9300, KINGSTON P N
NAA: A9300, DUFF G A
NAA: A9300, MORTIMER R J
NAA: A9300, McPHIE K C
NAA: A9300, GRIMBLY G L P
NAA: A9301, 420875 - Ken Glover
NAA: A9301, 414130 - Alfred William Emslie
NAA: A9301, 415518 - Keeble Charles French
NAA: A9301, 405974 - Gordon William Ingram

Commonwealth War Graves Commission website for details on crew KIA and burial, remembrance sites.

463/467 website – archived in TROVE on the National Archives Australia website. https://webarchive.nla.gov.au/tep/25490

630 Squadron history
https://630squadron.wordpress.com/2019/03/10/november-1943/

207 Squadron Royal Air Force History
http://www.207squadron.rafinfo.org.uk/default.htm

RAF Waddington Heritage centre and in particular Jimmy Tarbox who showed me around and explained the material.

The Bomber Command War Diaries
http://webarchive.nationalarchives.gov.uk/20070705230246/http://www.raf.mod.uk/bombercommand/index.html
    Unless otherwise stated the brief descriptions of the Bomber Command raids (in bold in the text and normal in the appendix) accompanying each op of the Trimble crew are taken from this source. In some instances extra material has been added and the English expression changed for clarity and consistency.

Personal letters, photographs and records of Roy McNaughton

Flying Logbook and letters of Vic Trimble. Kindly supplied by the Trimble family.

APPENDIX

TRIMBLE CREW OPERATIONS

The numbering is for the ops of the Vic Trimble and confirmed with Vic's logbook. Jim Marles, who I talked to in 2010, declared that the crew had actually carried out 28 ops and that their last op with 207 Squadron was never recorded. There are a variety of errors in the ORBs, mostly in the names of crews flying but also including flights that were not recorded. There is no evidence in Vic Trimble's log book of extra flights so it is probable Jim was referring to flights by him with other crews. Crew post raid intelligence reports taken from ORBs and Combat reports from National Archives, UK AIR50, are in italics. The descriptions of the raids on each city are derived from the Bomber Command War diary and squadron ORBs.

207 Squadron RAF Langar
1. 10/11 August 1943   **Nuremberg**   DV188 J-Joe

Flt Lt Ebert   Sgt Greenskill   Sgt. Sidebottom   Sgt Toplis   Sgt. Miller
Plt Off Hodgson   Sgt. Simmons   **Flt Sgt Trimble – second pilot**.

NB. In the ORBS the name is Heap V. H. – an error – Vic's logbook shows it was him and Heap did his second pilot trip the night before with the same crew. The I/O was probably doing a copy and paste from the previous night.

DA191 Q-Queenie
Sgt. Moulton-Barrett   Sgt.Gladders   Fl Off Roberts   Sgt. Burl
Sgt. Robinson   Sgt.Sherlock   **Sgt. Lawrence**

ED586 F-Freddie
Plt Off Stephens   Sgt.Bury   Sgt. Love   Sgt. Fegrum   Sgt. Barfoot
Sgt. Bate   Sgt. McDavitt   **Fl Off Herriot second navigator**

653 aircraft - 318 Lancasters, 216 Halifaxes, 119 Stirlings to Nuremberg. The Pathfinders attempted to ground-mark the city and, although their markers were mostly obscured by cloud, a useful attack developed in the central and southern parts of Nuremberg. The Lorenzkirche, the largest of the city's old churches, was badly damaged and about 50 of the houses in the preserved Altstadt were destroyed. There was a large 'fire area' in the Wöhrd district. 16 aircraft - 7 Halifaxes, 6 Lancasters, 3 Stirlings - lost, 2.5% of the force.
9 Mosquitos to the Ruhr, 18 Wellingtons minelaying off Texel and in the Frisians. No losses.

12/13 August 1943   **Milan**

ED498 D-Dog
Flt Sgt Hall   **Sgt Marles**   Sgt. Boardman   Sgt. Ball   Sgt. Richard
Sgt. Bird   Sgt. Martin

504 aircraft - 321 Lancasters and 183 Halifaxes despatched to Milan and carried out a successful raid. 2 Halifaxes and 1 Lancaster lost.
152 aircraft of 3 and No 8 Groups - 112 Stirlings, 34 Halifaxes, 6 Lancasters to Turin. 2 Stirlings lost.
7 Mosquitos to Berlin, 24 Wellingtons minelaying off Brittany ports, 9 OTU sorties. 1 Mosquito and 2 Wellington minelayers lost.

2.   14/15 August 1943   **Milan**   EMZ LM326

Flt Sgt Trimble   Sgt Marles   Fl Off Herriott   Sgt Nixon
Sgt Aldworth   Sgt McNaughton   Sgt Lawrence

Up 2122 down 0557 target attacked at 0124 from 15,000 ft with 4,000 lb and 4 Small Bomb Containers (SBCs) 8 × 30 +5 SBCs 90 × 30 lb incendiaries, large fires concentrated, window dropped, Pathfinder flares a great help to navigation.

140 Lancasters of 1, 5 and No 8 Groups carried out another attack on Milan, claiming much further damage. 1 Lancaster lost.
7 Mosquitos carried out a nuisance raid on Berlin without loss.
As a critical industrial centre of Italy, Milan was the target of continuous

carpet bombing during World War 2. The city continued to be heavily bombed even after Marshal Pietro Badoglio surrendered to the allied forces in 1943, due to Milan being an integral part of Mussolini's Italian Social Republic puppet state, an important command centre for the German Army and a centre of heavy engineering. When the war in Italy was finally over on April 25, 1945, Milan was heavily damaged and entire neighbourhoods in the vicinity of the engineering works such as Precotto and Turro were destroyed. After the war, the city was reconstructed and has again become an important financial and industrial centre of Italy. More than 30% of the buildings were completely destroyed and another 30% were so heavily damaged that they were demolished in the first years after the war. For the most part those buildings were located in the city centre and hundreds of historic buildings built over the previous 1,000 years were lost.

3. 22/23 August 1943   **Leverkusen**   EMZ LM326

Flt Sgt Trimble   Sgt Marles   Fl Off Herriott   Sgt Nixon
Sgt Aldworth   Sgt McNaughton   Sgt Lawrence

Up 2125 down 0206 attack at 19,000 feet, 4,000lb + incendiary, bombed on ETA green TI, window dropped - raid not a success. TIs scattered.

COMBAT REPORT
While in position 5106W 0617N on a course of 305°N at 0032 hrs at a height of 19,000ft one unidentified twin-engine enemy aircraft was sighted on the port quarter down, at 700 yards; the enemy aircraft did not attack but as the Lancaster made a diving turn to port the mid upper gunner opened fire at 600 yards and closed at 400 yards when the E/A was lost.
No claims are made and there was no damage to the Lancaster as E/A did not open fire. At the time there was no visible ground or searchlight cooperation and visibility was good with 10/10 cloud at 10,000 feet and half-moon.

Leverkusen: 462 aircraft - 257 Lancasters, 192 Halifaxes, 13 Mosquitos. Leverkusen, situated on the outskirts of Cologne, housed the giant IG Farben chemicals factory, which was chosen as the aiming point for this raid. It was hoped that some of the bombs would hit this important industrial site. There was thick cloud over the target area and there was a partial failure of the OBOE signals. At this time Bomber Command were essentially trialling OBOE as a guidance technique with limited success. Bombs fell over a wide area; at least 12 other towns in and near the Ruhr recorded bomb damage. 3 Lancasters and 2 Halifaxes lost, 1.1% of the force. The raid could only be described as a failure. Leverkusen was targeted twice more in 1943 with greater success.

12 Mosquitos to the Ruhr and 6 to Hamburg, 47 aircraft minelaying in the Frisians and off Texel, 7 OTU sorties. No losses.

4. 27/28 August 1943 **Nuremburg** EMZ LM326

Flt Sgt Trimble   Sgt Marles   Fl Off Herriott   Sgt Nixon
Sgt Aldworth   Sgt McNaughton   Sgt Lawrence

2130 – 0453 bombed from 18,000 at 0054, 4,000lb + incend, no cloud good visibility, A pretty good prang, Pathfinder flares and MC very good, many fighters in area all carrying white light.

COMBAT REPORT
While in the target area, flying at 19,000' on an IAS (indicated air speed) of 170mph on a magnetic course of 354° three unidentified enemy aircraft were sighted between 00.57 and 01.00 hours.
The first was sighted at 600 yards on the starboard up and flew over the Lancaster. Both gunners fired short bursts.
The second enemy aircraft approached from the port quarter down. The rear gunner opened fire at 700 yards and the E/A sheared off.
The third enemy aircraft passed underneath the tail of the Lancaster from starboard to port. The rear gunner fired a short burst.
No claims are made for any of the attacks.
Each of the E/A carried a white light in the nose. At the time, visibility was good and there was no apparent ground cooperation.
MONICA was useless, owing to the number of enemy aircraft in vicinity, it was registering continuously.

674 aircraft - 349 Lancasters, 221 Halifaxes, 104 Stirlings - to Nuremburg. 33 aircraft - 11 of each type on the raid - lost, 4.9% of the force.
Nuremberg, the city where the Nazis held their major political rallies, was the symbolic centre of Nazi power and an important manufacturing city for aircraft, submarine and tank engines. It was bombed numerous times from August 1943 to April 1945 and was the scene of many unsuccessful RAF raids before it was almost totally destroyed by a January 1945 night raid which was followed up with daylight raids by the USAAF. Hundreds of thousands of people were made homeless and thousands died. The marking for this raid was based mainly on H_2S. 47 of the Pathfinder H_2S

aircraft were ordered to check their equipment by dropping a 1,000-lb bomb on Heilbronn while flying to Nuremberg. 28 Pathfinder aircraft were able to carry out this order. Nuremberg was found to be free of cloud, but it was very dark. The initial Pathfinder markers were accurate but a creep-back quickly developed which could not be stopped because so many Pathfinder aircraft had difficulties with their H_2S sets. The Master Bomber could do little to persuade the Main Force to move their bombing forward, because only a quarter of the crews could hear his broadcasts. Creep-back was a major problem caused by the natural inclination of the crews to let the bombs go as soon as they felt they were over the target. Given that they had to fly straight and level through night fighter infested skies with radar directed flak and searchlights probing for them it was an understandable inclination. 4.9% loss rate.

5. 27/28 September 1943   **Hannover**   EMN ED601

| Plt Off Trimble | Sgt Marles | Fl Off Herriott | Sgt Nixon |
| Sgt Aldworth | Sgt McNaughton | Sgt Lawrence | |

Up 1930 down 0013 20,000 ft at 2222 hrs 4,000lb and incendiaries, smoke up to 1,000ft, visibility good target identified by green TIs. Evasive action taken over target to avoid searchlights. Bombed centre of fires owing to being coned by 50 searchlights. Raid well concentrated and window dropped. The target was bombed in concentration although some bombs dropped short. Much smoke but no individual fire seen.
Coned in searchlights (also master) lost 8,000ft in escaping.

Hannover: 678 aircraft - 312 Lancasters, 231 Halifaxes, 111 Stirlings, 24 Wellingtons. 5 B-17s also took part. 38 Bomber Command aircraft - 17 Halifaxes, 10 Lancasters, 10 Stirlings, 1 Wellington - lost, 5.6% of the force, and 1 B-17 also lost. The use by the Pathfinders of faulty forecast winds again saved the centre of Hannover. The bombing was very concentrated but fell on an area 5 miles north of the city centre. No details are available from Germany but RAF photographic evidence showed that most of the bombs fell in open country or villages north of the city.
21 Lancasters and 6 Mosquitos of No 8 Group carried out a diversionary raid on Brunswick, which was successful in drawing off some night fighters. 218 people were killed in Brunswick - 51 Germans and 167 foreigners. 1 Lancaster lost.
9 Mosquitos on another diversion to Emden, 5 Mosquitos on OBOE tests to Aachen (3 were successful), 19 aircraft minelaying in the Kattegat and the Frisian Islands, 4 OTU sorties. No losses.

LUCKY POMMIE BASTARD

The B-17 aircraft, chosen because of their ability to fly well above the bomber stream were radio counter measure aircraft equipped with numerous jammers.

6. 1/2 October 1943 **Hagen** EMZ LM326

| Plt Off Trimble | Sgt Marles | Fl Off Herriott | Sgt Nixon |
| Sgt Aldworth | Sgt McNaughton | Sgt Lawrence | |

1831 up 0006 down, target attacked 2107 from 19,000 ft with 4,000lb. 10/10 cloud flames visible thru clouds bombed on green and red indicators. Had to jettison 16x50lb incend to gain height. Success of raid doubted. NB. One a/c crashed on take-off with all killed.

COMBAT REPORT
43/9334 In position 52° 23' N 05° 20' E at 20:58hrs, flying at 19,000ft on a magnetic course of 125° at an IAS of 160 mph an unidentified twin engine enemy aircraft, burning a white light in the nose, was seen on the port quarter, up, at 600 yards after a warning had been received by MONICA.
The enemy aircraft came in as though to attack and at 600 yards a diving turn to port was made, both gunners opening fire until, at 500 yards the enemy aircraft broke away to the starboard quarter down, without firing.
No claims are made.
Visibility was good above cloud and as previously stated, MONICA was working very satisfactorily.

Hagen: 243 Lancasters and 8 Mosquitos. This raid was a complete success achieved on a completely cloud-covered target of small size, with only a moderate bomber effort and at trifling cost. The OBOE skymarking was perfect and severe damage was caused. 2 Lancasters lost, 0.8% of the force.
At the same time as the main attack on Hagen was ending, 12 OBOE Mosquitos were dispatched to attack a steelworks at Witten, north-west of Hagen, for training purposes. 8 Mosquitos bombed at Witten and 2, whose OBOE equipment failed, dropped their bombs on the fires burning in Hagen. No aircraft lost.

7. 2/3 October 1943 **Munich** EMS W4959

| Plt Off Trimble | Sgt Marles | Fl Off Herriott | Sgt Nixon |
| Sgt Aldworth | Sgt McNaughton | Sgt Lawrence | |

Up 1854 down 0250 target attacked 2234 at 18,000ft. Using green and yellow TIs Target not much alight when bombed but after left raid seemed more concentrated. Searchlights and fighters and numerous little flak.

COMBAT REPORT
Over the target at 22:41 hrs, flying at 18,000', on a magnetic course of 091° at an IAS of 165 mph, a Ju88 was sighted on the starboard quarter down at 300 yards. It made a climbing attack, opened fire simultaneously with the rear gunner of the Lancaster, and as a diving turn to starboard was made the Mid upper gunner also fired a short burst.
Fire from the E/A was ineffective but the Ju88 is claimed as damaged as tracer was seen to hit the fuselage.
Visibility at the time was good and the target was well illuminated by fighter flares. MONICA was not carried.

294 Lancasters of 1, 5 and No 8 Groups and 2 B-17s - to Munich. 8 Lancasters lost, 2.7% of the force. Visibility over the target was clear but the initial marking was scattered. Heavy bombing developed over the southern and south eastern districts of Munich but later stages of the raid fell up to 15 miles back along the approach route. Most of this inaccurate bombing was carried out by No 5 Group aircraft, which were again attempting their 'time-and-distance' bombing method independently of the Pathfinder marking. The No 5 Group crews were not able to pick out the Wurmsee lake, which was the starting point for their timed run.
8 Mosquitos to Cologne and Gelsenkirchen, 117 aircraft minelaying at various places from Lorient to Heligoland, 21 OTU sorties. 1 Halifax minelayer lost.

8. 7/8 October 1943   **Stuttgart**   EMZ LM326

Plt Off Trimble   Sgt Marles   Fl Off Herriott   Sgt Nixon
Sgt Aldworth   Sgt McNaughton   Sgt Lawrence

Up 2026 down 0300 target attacked at 0015 from 19,000 ft 4,000lb 10/10 cloud. Target identified by yellow and green TIs 3 main concentrations with centre being the biggest, window dropped, Route particularly good. Some large red fires were seen.

343 Lancasters were despatched to Stuttgart. The first aircraft to be equipped with ABC, from 101 Squadron operated on this night. The German night fighter controller was confused by the Mosquito diversion

on Munich and only a few night fighters reached Stuttgart at the end of the attack; 4 Lancasters were lost, 1.2% of the force. The target area was cloud-covered and the H_2S Pathfinder marking developed in two areas.
16 Lancasters of No 8 Group carried out a diversionary raid without loss and claimed hits on the Zeppelin factory at Friedrichshafen.
10 Mosquitos to Munich, 7 to Emden, 5 to Aachen, 79 aircraft minelaying from Brest to Heligoland, 14 OTU sorties. 1 Stirling minelayer lost.

207 Squadron RAF Spilsby

9. 20/21 October 1943 **Leipzig** EMN ED601

Plt Off Trimble   Sgt Marles   Fl Off Herriott   Sgt Nixon
Sgt Aldworth   Sgt McNaughton   Sgt Lawrence

Up 1730 down 0017 Target attacked at 2107 hrs from 19,000 feet with 1 × 4,000lb and 13 SBCs incendiaries. 10/10 cloud over target. Target was identified by fires and incendiaries. Scattered incendiaries but glow visible from presumed target for a long time. The captain reported this an effort wasted.

Leipzig: 358 Lancasters of 1, 5, 6 and No 8 Groups. 16 Lancasters lost, 4.5% of the force. This was the first serious attack on this distant German city. Weather conditions were very difficult - Bomber Command records describe them as 'appalling' - and the bombing was very scattered.
28 Mosquitos to Berlin, Cologne, Brauweiler and Emden, 12 Stirlings minelaying in the Frisians, 26 OTU sorties. 2 Mosquitos lost.
Leipzig was a distant target in the East of Germany and one that had not been successfully bombed. It was Germany's fifth largest city, a centre for trade fairs and important as a large industrial centre, aeroplane construction centre and railroad hub. This raid was again not decisive and the city was finally attacked with great success and loss of life, on 4 Dec 1943 when a firestorm was started. Leipzig was raided many more times by both the RAF and USAAF throughout the war.

10/11 Nov   **Modane**   EMV DV361
Fl Off Baker   **Sgt Marles**   Sgt Gedling   Sgt Castell   Sgt Shimeild
Sgt McNaughton   Sgt Skelton

DA191 Q-Queenie
Plt Off Moulton-Barrett   Sgt.Gladders   **Fl Off Herriott**   Sgt. Burl
Sgt Davies   Sgt. Robinson

Both Roy and Jim Marles took part in this raid with the Baker crew. Arthur Herriott went to Modane as navigator with the Moulton-Barrett crew. ORBs list only 6 crew members but the 7th was probably Sgt J Sherlock who was the normal bomb aimer.
Up 2045 down 0458 At 0111 hr bombed from 15,000ft in clear visibility, 4,000lb, 5x150x4lb, 1x9-x4lb, 3x12x3lb, 1x8x30lb incendiaries. Large explosion seen at 0113 and sheet of flame. Conc looked good. Moulton-Barrett report was similar.

313 Lancasters raided Modane. The four others in the Trimble crew were still recovering from injuries in a training accident where they had had another hard landing. Modane, a French railway centre on the Italian border was attacked twice in an effort to shut down rail traffic. This was the second attack and it was hoped to close the tunnel south of Modane. The results were similar to those of the first raid and it was not particularly successful.

10.   18/19 November 1943   **Berlin**   EMO DV383

| Plt Off Trimble | Sgt Marles | Fl Off Herriott | Sgt Nixon |
| Sgt Aldworth | **Sgt Codling** | Sgt Lawrence | |

This was the first raid of what has been termed the Battle of Berlin and the first of 8 trips to Berlin by the Trimble crew.
Last resort target Texel attacked at 1938hr from 18,000ft. Port inner engine unserviceable Sortie abandoned when port inner failed and behind by 30min. A flak position was bombed which was active on the island. After bombing a big explosion was seen and was followed by a red fire which lasted for 20minutes.

440 Lancasters and 4 Mosquitos were dispatched to Berlin. Few German fighters intercepted the force. 9 Lancasters were lost, 2.0% of the force. Berlin was completely cloud-covered and both marking and bombing were carried out blindly. Bomber Command could make no assessment of the results. The route out was a wide swing out over the North Sea and over the Dutch coast.
Major diversionary raids on Mannheim and Ludwigshafen by 395 aircraft - 248 Halifaxes, 114 Stirlings, 33 Lancasters - of Nos 3, 4, 6 and 8 Groups. German fighters successfully engaged the bomber force and 23 aircraft - 12 Halifaxes, 9 Stirlings, 2 Lancasters - were lost, 5.8% of the force.
Cloud was present over the target area and much of the bombing was scattered. 21 people were killed, 154 injured and 7,500 bombed out. Many bombs fell outside the city and the local report lists much damage and

loss at farms. This was the last major raid on the much-bombed city of Mannheim for 15 months. 798 ton of high explosive and 795 ton of incendiaries were dropped.
10 Mosquitos to Essen, 6 to Aachen and 6 to Frankfurt, 16 Wellingtons minelaying from Texel to St Nazaire, 7 OTU sorties.
Total effort for the night: 884 sorties, 32 aircraft (3.6%) lost.

11. 22/23 November 1943　　**Berlin**　　EMO DV383

Plt Off Trimble　　Sgt Marles　　Fl Off Herriott　　Sgt Nixon
Sgt Aldworth　　Sgt McNaughton　　Sgt Lawrence

Up 1648 down 2337. 2012 from 22,000ft. Good visibility over clouds 10/10 over target. One sky marker seen. A terrific explosion was seen at 2022. Route good. No interference by fighters.

Berlin attacked by 764 aircraft - 469 Lancasters, 234 Halifaxes, 50 Stirlings, 11 Mosquitos. This was the greatest force sent to Berlin so far but it was also the last raid in which Stirlings were sent to Germany. Bad weather again kept most of the German fighters on the ground and the bomber force was able to take a relatively 'straight in, straight out' route to the target without suffering undue loss. 26 aircraft - 11 Lancasters, 10 Halifaxes, 5 Stirlings - were lost, 3.4% of the force. The telling point of the raid and many previous ones was the 10% loss of Stirlings versus 2.3% of Lancasters and 4.3% of Halifaxes. The Stirling losses were unsupportable, hence their withdrawal from the battle. Berlin was again completely cloud-covered and returning crews could only estimate that the marking and bombing were believed to be accurate. In fact, this was the most effective raid on Berlin of the war. A vast area of destruction stretched from the central districts westwards across the mainly residential areas of Tiergarten and Charlottenburg to the separate suburb city of Spandau. Because of the dry weather conditions, several 'firestorm' areas were reported and a German plane next day measured the height of the smoke cloud as 6,000 metres (nearly 19,000 ft).
Bomber Command decided to make a maximum effort on this operation because of favourable weather in England and unfavourable weather for the night fighters over Europe. The simple straight in - straight out route was also chosen because of the weather conditions. The strategy worked on this occasion. Rather than waves of aircraft of the same type, for the first time they mixed the aircraft types with the more experienced crews bombing first and the inexperienced crews bringing up the rear. New

target marking techniques were also employed with sky markers plus ground flares. It was estimated that 175,000 people were bombed out on this night and some 50,000 men were diverted from other duties to assist with repairs.

The list of buildings destroyed or severely damaged included: the Kaiser-Wilhelm-Gedächtniskirche (the Kaiser Wilhelm Memorial Church) which is today, half ruined, half restored and a major monument and attraction in Berlin; the Charlottenburg Castle; the Berlin Zoo; much of the Unter den Linden; the British, French, Italian and Japanese embassies; the Ministry of Weapons and Munitions; the Waffen SS Administrative College; the barracks of the Imperial Guard at Spandau and; many industrial premises, including 5 factories of the Siemens electrical group and the Alkett tank works which had only recently been moved from the Ruhr to Berlin. The huge explosion seen by the Trimble crew and many others was the Nuekolln gas works going up. Hitler's private train was apparently destroyed in this raid.

12 Mosquitos to Leverkusen, 14 Wellingtons minelaying in the Frisians and off Texel, 12 OTU sorties.

12. 23/24 November 1943   **Berlin**   EMO DV383

| Plt Off Trimble | Sgt Marles | Fl Off Herriott | Sgt Nixon |
| Sgt Aldworth | Sgt McNaughton | Sgt Lawrence | |

Up 1712 down 2354. Target attacked at 2012 hours from 19,000ft. with 1× 4,000lb 16SBCs incendiaries. 8/10 cloud over target area. Conc of green TIs bombed. Fires developed well but were in 2 separate areas. The attack opened on time, then the Pathfinders moved the attack further North. It did not appear to be a good concentration. Flak was not as plentiful as previously.

383 aircraft - 365 Lancasters, 10 Halifaxes, 8 Mosquitos - to continue the attack on Berlin. The bombing force used the same direct route as had been employed on the previous night. The German controllers made an early identification of Berlin as the probable target; their single-engine fighters were gathered over the city before the arrival of the bombers and other fighters arrived a few minutes later. Fake instructions broadcast from England caused much annoyance to the German who was giving the 'running commentary'; the Germans started using a female commentator but this was promptly countered by a female voice from England ordering the German pilots to land because of fog at their bases. 'Spoof' fighter flares dropped by Mosquitos north of the bomber stream

also caused some diversion of German effort. Bomber crews noticed that flak over the target was unusually restrained, with the German fighters obviously being given priority. 20 aircraft - all Lancasters - were lost, 5.2% of the bomber force. The target was again cloud-covered and the Pathfinders carried out skymarking, but many of the Main Force crews aimed their bombs through the cloud at the glow of 11 major fires still burning from the previous night. Much further destruction was caused in Berlin. The huge flak tower at the Tiergarten took a direct hit, which merely shook the structure and put out the lights.

6 OBOE Mosquitos attacked the Knapsack power-station near Cologne without loss.

13. 26/27 November 1943 **Berlin** EMO DV383

Plt Off Trimble Sgt Marles Fl Off Herriott Sgt Nixon
Sgt Aldworth Sgt McNaughton Sgt Lawrence

Up 1726 down 0045. Target attacked at 21.17 hours from 22,000ft with 1 x 4,000lb 12 SBCs incendiaries. One green TI bombed. Too early to form any opinion of the attack, but small fires from previous raid still visible. Pathfinder flares very scattered. Route quite good.

On this night, the new 3 cm H_2S radar was used by the Pathfinders.
443 Lancasters and 7 Mosquitos to Berlin and Stuttgart (diversion). Both forces flew a common route over Northern France and on nearly to Frankfurt before diverging. The German controllers thought that Frankfurt was the main target until a late stage and several bombers were shot down as they flew past Frankfurt. Only a few fighters appeared over Berlin, where flak was the main danger, but the scattered condition of the bomber stream at Berlin meant that bombers were caught by fighters off track on the return flight and the casualties mounted. 28 Lancasters were lost, 6.2% of the force, and 14 more Lancasters crashed in England. The weather was clear over Berlin but, after their long approach flight from the south, the Pathfinders marked an area 6-7 miles north-west of the city centre and most aircraft bombed there. Because of Berlin's size, however, most of the bombing still fell within the city boundaries and particularly on the semi-industrial suburb of Reinickendorf; smaller amounts of bombing fell in the centre and in the Siemensstadt (with many electrical factories) and Tegel districts. The Berlin Zoo was heavily bombed on this night. Many of the animals had been evacuated to zoos in other parts of Germany but the bombing killed most of the remainder. Several large and

dangerous animals - leopards, panthers, jaguars, apes - escaped and had to be hunted and shot in the streets.

The diversionary raid on Stuttgart was carried out by 157 Halifaxes and 21 Lancasters. 6 Halifaxes lost, 3.4% of the force. The bombing was very scattered and caused little damage but part of the night fighter force was drawn off from the Berlin operation.

19 Stirlings and 14 Wellingtons minelaying off Texel and in the Frisians, 5 OTU sorties.

Total effort for the night: 666 sorties, 34 aircraft (5.1%) lost.

The losses do not include those aircraft lost on return (they never did, meaning the real losses were higher). Fog covered most of the air bases and 30 aircraft force landed or crashed on return with 15 totally destroyed. 39 aircrew and 2 civilians were killed from these crashes. (total a/c losses were thus 7.4%)

463 Squadron RAF Waddington

14.   16/17 December 1943   **Berlin**: EE191- JO-F

Plt Off Trimble   Sgt Marles   Fl Off Herriott   Sgt Nixon
Sgt Aldworth   Sgt McNaughton   Sgt Lawrence   **Plt Off Brown P.O second nav.**

Up 1704 down 0005. 10/10ths cloud, green TIs cascading 19,000ft 2008 hrs 1x 4,000 HC 930x4 and 100x 4 XIBs 408x 30 incendiaries. Glow of fire beneath cloud. Some of the markers scattered. Cloud hampered observation. The route was quite good, very little opposition both in and out. Fighters were present at target. Searchlights were ineffective and flak was moderate. The PFF was concentrated with an occasional stray red, green and sky markers.

In squadron ORBs it is recorded that Plt Off Trimble was caught in searchlights on this trip and experienced concentrated flak. This does not correspond with the intelligence report of Trimble or anybody else that night.

COMBAT REPORT
At 20.08 hrs, 19,000ft over target heading 062°N. Airspeed 165 IAS. Mid upper gunner sighted Ju88 astern 500 yards up. When sighted E/A was starting to attack. MU gave order to corkscrew port and rear and mid upper gunners opened fire. E/A followed through and opened fire giving 3 bursts but was unable to get guns to bear. Both mid upper and rear gunners gave several short bursts but could observe no hits. E/A using wing machine guns but no tracer was used. E/A held off at 500 yards

throughout corkscrew and then broke away to starboard down and was not seen again. There does not appear to have been any cooperation with ground defences. Weather 10/10 ths cloud about 10,000' clear above. Fighter flares in vicinity. No hits claimed. Visual MONICA fitted but WOP was in astro hatch. MONICA worked satisfactorily throughout. 1500 rounds expended. No Claim.

463 Squadron sent 13 a/c to join the 483 Lancasters and 10 Mosquitos that carried out the main raid to Berlin. All 463 a/c returned. Five further Mosquitos dropped decoy fighter flares south of Berlin. The bomber route again led directly to Berlin across Holland and Northern Germany and there were no major diversions. The German controllers plotted the course of the bombers with great accuracy; many German fighters were met at the coast of Holland and further fighters were guided on to the bomber stream throughout the approach to the target. More fighters were waiting at the target and there were many combats. The bombers shook off the opposition on the return flight by taking a northerly route over Denmark. 25 Lancasters, 5.2% of the Lancaster force, were lost. Many further aircraft were lost on returning to England. Berlin was cloud-covered but the Pathfinder skymarking was reasonably accurate and much of the bombing fell in the city. In the city centre, the National Theatre and the building housing Germany's military and political archives were both destroyed. The damage to the Berlin railway system and to rolling stock, and the large numbers of people still leaving the city, were having a cumulative effect upon the transportation of supplies to the Russian Front; 1,000 wagon-loads of war material were held up for 6 days. The sustained bombing had now made more than a quarter of Berlin's total living accommodation unusable. On their return to England, many of the bombers encountered very low cloud at their bases. The squadrons of 1, 6 and No 8 Groups were particularly badly affected. 29 Lancasters (and a Stirling from the minelaying operation) either crashed or were abandoned when their crews parachuted. The group with heaviest losses was No 1 Group with 13 aircraft lost; the squadron with heaviest losses was 97 Squadron, No 8 Group, with 7 aircraft lost.

47 aircraft - 26 Stirlings, 12 Mosquitos, 9 Lancasters - carried out raids on 2 flying-bomb sites near Abbeville. Neither raid was successful. The larger raid, by the Stirlings on the Tilley-le-Haut site, failed because the OBOE Mosquito markers could not get any closer than 450 yards from the small target. The 9 Lancasters of 617 Squadron which attacked the second site, in a wood at Flixecourt, dropped their 12,000lb bombs accurately on the markers placed by the only OBOE Mosquito operating at this target, but the markers were 350 yards from the flying-bomb site and none of the

617 Squadron bombs were more than 100 yards from the markers. No aircraft lost.

2 Beaufighters and 2 Mosquitos of 141 Squadron, recently transferred from Fighter Command to No 100 Group, inaugurated Bomber Command's Serrate operations in patrols near the routes of the Berlin raid. (Serrate was a radar device which homed on to the radar emissions of a German night fighter.) One Mosquito made contact with an Me110 and damaged it with cannon-fire. The crew of this first successful Bomber Command Serrate patrol was Squadron Leader FF Lambert and Flying Officer K Dear.

5 Mosquitos to Duisburg, 35 aircraft minelaying in the Frisians and off Biscay ports. No losses.

On this 4th altercation with German night fighters the crew escaped without any damage. The fighter was observed before it attacked and the corkscrew commenced to evade its attentions. Just after this operation, on 19 Dec Vic had his logbook endorsed by the base commander Gp Cpt Elsworthy for "Gross Negligence when taxying".

15. 20/21-12-1943 **Frankfurt** HK535 JO-N Naughty Nancy

Plt Off Trimble Sgt Marles Fl Off Herriott Sgt Nixon
Sgt Aldworth Sgt McNaughton Sgt Lawrence **Plt Off Hanson P. second pilot**

Up 1722 down 2318, 10/10ths cloud bombed on ETA. No markers visible at the time. One green TI seen to go down after bombing. 21,000ft 19.44 hrs. 1x 4,000HC, 1350x4 50x4 XIBs 80 x 30. Fires seen through cloud. Very scattered, but appeared to be more concentrated as aircraft left the target area. The raid seemed very scattered and PFF were prominent by their absence. The gunners saw some good fires after we left the target.

463 Squadron sent 9 aircraft to join 650 bombers attacking Frankfurt and all returned. There were many combats on the way to the target. 6.3% were lost.

Frankfurt: 650 aircraft - 390 Lancasters, 257 Halifaxes, 3 Mosquitos. The German control rooms were able to plot the bomber force as soon as it left the English coast and were able to continue plotting it all the way to Frankfurt. There were many combats on the route to the target. The Mannheim diversion did not draw fighters away from the main attack until after the raid was over but the return flight was quieter. 41 aircraft - 27 Halifaxes, 14 Lancasters - lost, 6.3% of the force. The bombing at

Frankfurt did not go according to plan. The Pathfinders had prepared a ground-marking plan on the basis of a forecast of clear weather, but they found up to 8/10ths cloud. The Germans lit a decoy fire site 5 miles south east of the city and also used dummy Target indicators. Some of the bombing fell around the decoy but part of the creep-back fell on Frankfurt causing more damage than Bomber Command realised at the time. Part of the bombing somehow fell on Mainz, 17 miles to the west, and many houses along the Rhine waterfront and in southern suburbs were hit.

44 Lancasters and 10 Mosquitos of 1 and No 8 Groups carried out a diversionary raid on Mannheim but most of the bombing fell outside the city. No aircraft lost.

8 Lancasters of 617 Squadron and 8 Pathfinder Mosquitos attempted to bomb an armaments factory near Liege but the Mosquito marking was not visible below the clouds and the Lancasters did not bomb; 1 Lancaster lost. 6 Mosquitos to Rheinhausen and 5 to Leverkusen, 8 RCM sorties, 2 Beaufighters on Serrate patrol, 23 Stirlings minelaying in the Frisians, 38 OTU sorties. 1 Stirling minelayer lost.

16.   23/24-12-1943   **Berlin**   HK535 JO-N Naughty Nancy

Plt Off Trimble   Sgt Marles   Fl Off Herriott   Sgt Nixon
Sgt Aldworth   Sgt McNaughton   Sgt Lawrence

Up 0017 down 0751, Clear up to run in but 10/10ths thin cloud over aiming point up to 12,000ft. 21,000ft 0403hrs Bombed 1 green TI cascading at 0402hrs. 1 x 4,000lb mine. 840x4 150x4 XIB 48x30. A red glow just to SSW of aiming point. Many fighter flares SE of target area. We were in first wave and raid was not concentrated very much when we bombed. However, it seemed a good concentration as we left the area. The broadcast winds were a great aid to the navigation. The Leipzig spoof seemed a great success and Frankfurt had their share of fighter flares.

463 Squadron sent 12 a/c to join 379 Lancasters attacking Berlin. The target was cloud-covered and marking was by H_2S, with fair results. 4.2% lost. Plt Off Heap and his crew who moved from 207 Squadron with the Trimble crew were shot down on this operation. All were killed.

Berlin: 379 aircraft - 364 Lancasters, 8 Mosquitos, 7 Halifaxes. The bomber casualties were not as heavy as on recent raids, partly because German fighters encountered difficulty with the weather and partly because the German controller was temporarily deceived by the Mosquito diversion at Leipzig. The main force of fighters only appeared in the target area at the end of the raid and could not catch the main bomber stream. 16 Lancasters were lost, 4.2% of the force. The Berlin area was covered by cloud and more than half of the early Pathfinder aircraft had trouble with their H_2S sets. The markers were scattered and sparse.

12 Mosquitos to Aachen, 9 to Duisburg and 7 to Leipzig, 4 RCM sorties, 3 Beaufighters on Serrate patrols, 7 OTU sorties. 1 Beaufighter lost.

17.   1/2-January 1944   **Berlin**   HK535 JO-N Naughty Nancy

Plt Off Trimble   Sgt Marles   Fl Off Herriott   Sgt Nixon
Sgt Aldworth   Sgt McNaughton   Sgt Lawrence   **Plt Off McKnight, K H second pilot**

Plt Off Trimble, bombing BERLIN. Sortie completed. Up 2359 down 0734. 10/10 cloud, tops about 16,000ft, Hazy up to 22,000ft. Incendiary fires. On running in 6 Wanganui flares could be seen, these however had gone out before a/c got to them. Some further Wanganui flares went down some distance from the first. These also had gone out on arrival. The bomb aimer bombed a patch of fire being the only thing left to see. After bombing three Wanganui flares went down. These, however were some distance North of the second lot. 21,000ft 0310 hr 1x 4,000HC, 900 x 4, 48x30lbs Inc. No results could be seen, neither was there the usual glow below cloud. Weather conditions over target seemed to prevent a concentrated raid. Route markers were not the navigational aid they usually are. Quite a number of combats sighted, but very few fighter flares were seen.

463 Squadron sent 10 a/c to start the new year for Berlin, joining 421 Lancasters in a very effective raid. There are no specific details in the post-war bombing assessment, the raid is simply listed as very effective. 463 Squadron lost Flt Sgt Lawson and crew: 7 KIA.

421 Lancasters despatched to Berlin. Despite a Mosquito 'spoof' raid on Hamburg, German fighters were directed on to the bomber stream at an early stage and were particularly active en-route to Berlin. 28 Lancasters were lost, 6.7% of the force.

15 Mosquitos to Hamburg, 11 to Witten, 7 to Duisburg, 4 to Bristillerie and 1 to Cologne, 6 RCM sorties, 14 OTU sorties. No losses.

By this stage of the war various code words were being used for the target markers, the main ones being Whanganui, which were parachute supported sky markers dropped above clouds, Parramatta, blind dropped ground flares, and Newhaven, blind dropped marker flares employing H_2S followed by visual markers. The code names were simply the original hometowns of three aircrew (a New Zealander, an Australian and an

Englishman) who happened to be in the in the operations room when the system was devised.

18.   14/15-1-1944   Brunswick   HK535 JO-N Naughty Nancy

| Fl Off Trimble | Sgt Marles | Fl Off Herriott | Sgt Nixon |
| Sgt Aldworth | Sgt McNaughton | Sgt Lawrence | |

Fl Off Trimble, bombing BRUNSWICK. Sortie completed. Up 16.52 hours. Down 22.30 hours. 8-10/10 cloud, tops 10,000ft. Green TIs, 20,000ft. 19.50hrs. 1 × 4,000HC. 1500 × 4. 80 × 30 incendiaries. Red glow on port side under cloud. Attacked by fighter leaving target, causing much damage. R/G unconscious due to damaged oxygen M/U fired at E/A 6 sec burst, E/A temporarily lost to sight, but next seen through thin cloud layer to burst on ground. A/B hit by splinter. Crew suffered from lack of oxygen. Landed at Wittering for long runway due to no brake pressure.

COMBAT REPORT
1922 hrs course 299N Height 25,000ft speed 160 IAS position 52.05N 10.08E First indication of fighter, crew saw tracer from port quarter down which smashed elevators and port rudder. Rear gunner then sighted FW190 breaking away to starboard up. Enemy aircraft then positioned himself on port quarter level and turned to attack at 400 yards. Rear gunner gave dive port but was unable to fire due to lack of oxygen, pipe had been severed in first attack. Mid upper gunner gave 6 sec burst at 300 yards and fighter was lost to sight starboard down for 5 secs and was then seen to dive to starboard in flames. E/A was seen by mid upper gunner to dive through layer of cloud and blew up on ground. 400 rounds ammo expended. Visual MONICA U/S throughout trip. Rear gunner unconscious through lack of oxygen throughout second attack. No fighter flares or searchlight cooperation.
GROUP CAPT commanding: As the attacking aircraft was lost to sight for 5 secs after the 6 sec burst from the mid upper gunner, I do not consider that the aircraft seen going down in flames can definitely be established as the same aircraft. Claimed; probably destroyed.

496 Lancasters and 2 Halifaxes on the first major raid to Brunswick of the war. 38 Lancasters lost, 7.6% of the force. The German running commentary was heard following the progress of the bomber force from a position only 40 miles from the English coast and many German fighters entered the bomber stream soon after the German frontier was crossed near Bremen. The German fighters scored steadily until the Dutch coast was crossed on the return flight. 11 of the lost aircraft were Pathfinders.

Brunswick was smaller than Bomber Command's usual targets and this raid was not a success. The city report describes this only as a 'light' raid, with bombs in the south of the city, which had only 10 houses destroyed and 14 people killed. Most of the attack fell either in the countryside or in Wolfenbüttel and other small towns and villages well to the south of Brunswick.

82 aircraft - 59 Stirlings, 13 Halifaxes, 10 Mosquitos - attacked flying bomb sites at Ailly, Bonneton and Bristillerie without loss.

11 Mosquitos to Magdeburg and 6 to Berlin, 9 RCM sorties, 2 Serrate patrols, 29 aircraft minelaying off Brest and in the Frisians, 36 OTU sorties. No losses.

Total effort for the night: 673 sorties, 38 aircraft (5.6%) lost.

19.   15/16.2.44   Berlin   ED611 JO-U Uncle Jo

| Fl Off Trimble | Sgt Marles | Fl Off Herriott | Sgt Nixon |
| Sgt Aldworth | Sgt McNaughton | **Flt Sgt Childs** | |

Fl Off Trimble, bombing BERLIN. Sortie completed. Up 1733 down 0032. 10/10 cloud 10,000ft. Vis good 1 green TI seen to cascade at 2124hrs 23,000ft 2123 hr. 1 x 4,000HC. 900 x 4. 60 x 30, 150x4 "I" Inc. Red TIs seen on approach to target and followed by Wanganui flares and green TIs in fair concentration. Observation difficult but faint fire glow visible for approx. 20 minutes after leaving target. Attack seemed scattered at first. "Spoof" on Frankfurt was late in starting. Fighters seemed to be more concentrated on route TO rather than FROM target.

463 Squadron sent 17 a/c to join the 891 bombers attacking Berlin, dropping 2,642 tons of bombs on the city.

After a rest of more than two weeks for the regular bomber squadrons, 891 aircraft - 561 Lancasters, 314 Halifaxes, 16 Mosquitos - were dispatched to Berlin. This was the largest force sent to Berlin and the largest non-1,000 bomber force sent to any target, exceeding the previous record of 826 aircraft (which included Stirlings and Wellingtons) sent to Dortmund on the night of 23/24 May 1943. It was also the first time that more than 500 Lancasters and more than 300 Halifaxes were dispatched. The German controllers were able to plot the bomber stream soon after it left the English coast but the swing north over Denmark for the approach flight proved too far distant for many of the German fighters. The German controller ordered the fighters not to fly over Berlin, leaving the target area free for the flak, but many fighters ignored him and attacked bombers over the city. The diversion to Frankfurt-on-Oder failed to draw any fighters. 43 aircraft - 26 Lancasters, 17 Halifaxes -were lost, 4.8% of the force.

Berlin was covered by cloud for most of the raid. Heavy bombing fell on the centre and southwestern districts and some of Berlin's most important war industries were hit, including the large Siemensstadt area. This was really the end of the true 'Battle of Berlin' with only one more raid on the city in this period and that was not for more than a month.

23 OBOE Mosquitos attacked 5 night fighter airfields in Holland, 43 Stirlings and 4 Pathfinder Halifaxes carried out minelaying in Kiel Bay, 24 Lancasters of No 8 Group made a diversion raid on Frankfurt-on-Oder, 9 aircraft made RCM flights and 14 Mosquitos carried out Serrate patrols. A Serrate Mosquito was the only aircraft lost.

2 Mosquitos to Aachen, 6 Stirlings and 6 Wellingtons minelaying off Bayonne and Lorient, 48 aircraft on Resistance operations. 1 Stirling lost from a Resistance flight.

Total effort for the night: 1,070 sorties, 45 aircraft (4.2%) lost.

For the Trimble crew this was their eighth and final trip to Berlin and their first trip since the near disaster over Brunswick a month earlier. Apart from Jack Lawrence, who was in hospital for the month, they had all had leave. Jack had not been discharged from hospital, so the rear gunner was an experienced New Zealander, Flt Sgt Jack Childs.

20.   19/20.2.44 **Leipzig**   ED611 JO-U Uncle Joe

| Fl Off Trimble | Sgt Marles | **Flt Lt Williams** | Sgt Nixon |
| Sgt Aldworth | Sgt McNaughton | Sgt Lawrence | |

Fl Off Trimble, bombing LEIPZIG. Sortie completed. Up 2357 down 0731. 10/10 S.C. 10,000ft Green with red stars: single flare, 21,000ft 0409 hrs 1 × 4,000HC, 1200×4, 36×30 Inc. Red glow could be seen through clouds, and could be seen 100 miles from target. The raid seemed to be highly successful and well concentrated. The northern route home was quite good. Most of the ground defences remained quiet and did not identify themselves. No fighters were seen on this route.

463 Squadron sent 18 a/c in the 823 bombers attacking Leipzig. The German controller correctly estimated the target and massed his fighters en route. The bombers were under attack all the way. No damage report is available from Germany, and cloud prevented PRU assessment. 463 Squadron lost Plt Off F. Fayle and crew: 7 KIA.

Leipzig: 823 aircraft - 561 Lancasters, 255 Halifaxes, 7 Mosquitos. 78 aircraft - 44 Lancasters and 34 Halifaxes - lost, 9.5% of the force. The

Halifax loss rate was 13.3% of those dispatched and 14.9% of those Halifaxes which reached the enemy coast after 'early returns' had turned back. The Halifax IIs and Vs were permanently withdrawn from operations to Germany after this raid.

This was an unhappy raid for Bomber Command. The German controllers only sent part of their force of fighters to the Kiel minelaying diversion. When the main bomber force crossed the Dutch coast, they were met by a further part of the German fighter force and those German fighters, which had been sent north to Kiel hurriedly returned. The bomber stream was thus under attack all the way to the target. There were further difficulties at the target because winds were not as forecast and many aircraft reached the Leipzig area too early and had to orbit and await the Pathfinders. Four aircraft were lost by collision and approximately 20 were shot down by flak. Leipzig was cloud-covered and the Pathfinders had to use skymarking. The raid appeared to be concentrated in its early stages but scattered later.

45 Stirlings and 4 Pathfinder Halifaxes minelaying in Kiel Bay, 16 OBOE Mosquitos bombing night fighter airfields in Holland, 15 Mosquitos on a diversion raid to Berlin, 12 Serrate patrols. 1 Mosquito lost from the Berlin raid. 3 Mosquitos attacked Aachen and 3 more bombed flying-bomb sites in France without loss.

Total effort for the night: 921 sorties, 79 aircraft (8.6%) lost.

This was the heaviest Bomber Command loss of the war so far, easily exceeding the 58 aircraft lost on 21/22 January 1943 when Magdeburg was the main target. Almost 100 of the aircraft sent to Leipzig turned back before the target. Arthur Herriott was unavailable so the navigator on this operation was Flt Lt Williams. Fl Off Pettit fulfilled the navigator role on the next operation.

21.   20/21.2.44   **Stuttgart**   ED606 JO-E

| Fl Off Trimble | Sgt Marles | **Fl Off Pettit** | Sgt Nixon |
| Sgt Aldworth | Sgt McNaughton | Sgt Lawrence | |

Fl Off Trimble, bombing STUTTGART. Sortie completed. Up 0004 down 0659. Hazy, no cloud 23,000ft 0401hrs 1x4,000HC 60x30lb inc, 1100x4lb inc ,100x15. Centre of pattern all green T.T.s visible Streets could be seen burning on leaving target. The most concentrated attack for a long time.

463 Squadron sent 14 a/c to join 598 bombers attacking Stuttgart. The most important factory in Germany, the Bosch works making dynamos,

injection pumps and magnetos, was badly damaged. Only 1.5% of the bomber force were lost. This was the second time the Trimble crew went to Stuttgart and was one of the most successful Stuttgart raids.

598 aircraft - 460 Lancasters, 126 Halifaxes, 12 Mosquitos - to Stuttgart. The North Sea sweep and the Munich diversion successfully drew the German fighters up 2 hours before the main bomber force flew inland and only 9 aircraft - 7 Lancasters and 2 Halifaxes - were lost, 1.5% of the force. 4 further Lancasters and 1 Halifax crashed in England.

156 aircraft - 132 from training units and 24 from squadrons - flew a large training exercise across the North Sea as a preliminary feint; 24 Mosquitos attacked airfields in Holland; 7 Mosquitos made a diversionary raid on Munich and there were 7 Serrate patrols. No aircraft lost.

28 Stirlings and 6 Wellingtons laid mines off French ports. 1 Wellington lost.

Total effort for the night: 826 sorties, 10 aircraft (1.2%) lost.

22.   24/25.2.44   Schweinfurt   ED611 JO-U Uncle Jo

Fl Off Trimble   Sgt Marles   Fl Off Herriott   Sgt Nixon
Sgt Aldworth   Sgt McNaughton   Sgt Lawrence

Fl Off Trimble, bombing SCHWEINFURT. Sortie completed. Up 2049 down 0445. No cloud – haze and smoke. TIs had finished going down on arrival. Centre of fire as near as it could be assessed in relation to where TIs had been seen previously to go down was used as a point of aim. 21,000ft 0121hrs 1x4,000HC 650x4. 100x4 XIBs 80x30. Area of fires appeared large compared with size of target. There was also a noticeable trailback of incendiaries.

463 Squadron sent 14 aircraft in the two-part attack on Schweinfurt. The first wave of 392 bombers encountered the fighters and losses were 5%. The second wave two hours later were better off, losses were 3.2%. An overall loss of 4.5%. 463 Squadron lost Flt Lt. R. Mortimer and crew: 2 KIA, 5 POW and Flt Lt. C. Martin and crew: 6KIA, 1 POW. Flt Lt. Bill Marshall's aircraft was hit by heavy flak and damaged. The crew managed to fly it back to Waddington.

734 aircraft - 554 Lancasters, 169 Halifaxes, 11 Mosquitos - carried out the first Bomber Command raid on Schweinfurt, home of Germany's main ball bearing factories. 266 American B-17s had raided the factories the previous day.

Schweinfurt was one of the most famous bomber targets of World War 2. The ball bearing factory there supplied 50% of the German needs through four factories and so the city was targeted 22 times – particularly by the USAAF. The USAAF, flying in daylight, could more easily target specific sites and so employed a strategic bombing strategy that differed from that of the RAF. This strategy resulted from the much stronger defensive armament of the B17, the lack of navigational training to allow night bombing and later in the war the availability of long-range fighters to accompany the bombers. The heavy armament and design of the B17 meant that the bomb loads were almost half that of the Lancaster. Thus, the USAAF often attempted to knock out critical components of German industry like ball bearing plants or oil facilities. The RAF concentrated more on area bombing but some raids were directed at specific sites. The Germans combatted the bombing offensive by decentralizing their ball bearing manufacturing plants (and other industries) because of the bombing and by importing such items from neutral countries. Bomber Command introduced a novel tactic on this night. The Schweinfurt force was split into two parts - 392 aircraft and 342 aircraft, separated by a 2-hour interval. Part of the German fighter force was drawn up by earlier diversions. The first wave of the Schweinfurt bombers lost 22 aircraft, 5.6%; the second wave lost only 11 aircraft, 3.2%, and it is believed that night fighters shot down only 4 bombers from the second wave.

Total losses were 33 aircraft - 26 Lancasters, 7 Halifaxes - 4.5% of the force.

179 training aircraft on a diversionary sweep over the North Sea, 60 Halifaxes and 50 Stirlings minelaying in Kiel Bay and the Kattegat, 15 Mosquitos to airfields in Holland, 8 Mosquitos to Kiel and 7 to Aachen, 12 Serrate patrols. 2 Stirlings were lost from the minelaying operation and 1 Serrate Mosquito of No 141 Squadron was lost, the first Serrate aircraft to be lost under Bomber Command control. 5 Wellingtons laid mines off Lorient without loss.

Total effort for the night: 1,070 sorties, 36 aircraft (3.4%) lost.

23.   25/26.2.44   **Augsburg**   ED611 JO-U   Uncle Jo

Fl Off Trimble   Sgt Marles   Fl Off Herriott   Sgt Nixon
Sgt Aldworth   Sgt McNaughton   Sgt Lawrence

Fl Off Trimble, bombing AUGSBERG. Sortie completed. Up 1840 down 0208. No cloud, slight haze 2 red TI markers 21,000ft 22.41hrs 1x4,000GP – 36hrs. delay. 630x4, 100x4 XIBs 92x30 inc. Good fires were seen starting as aircraft left the target area. Red explosion seen at 22.52hrs. in target area. Red spot fires were not seen but many enemy red flares were seen scattered along part of track. The raid seemed concentrated after we had bombed. Fighter flares encircled target and searchlights numerous. No evidence seen of US air force daylight raid. Yellow TIs were far too bright.

463 Squadron sent 11 aircraft to join 594 bombers attacking Augsburg. 2,000 tons of bombs were dropped on the city in the first major attack of the war. The raid was in clear weather and very accurate. The industrial area was severely damaged. The German propaganda news was now referring to these raids as 'terror bombing'. 463 Squadron lost Plt Off K. McKnight and crew: 7 KIA.

In February 463 Squadron had flown 74 sorties to 5 targets for the loss of 4 crews: 23 men KIA, 5 POW. Both 463 and 467 Squadrons had been snow bound for most of the month and flying and maintenance at Waddington had been very difficult. Often night flying was impossible, as sufficient snow could not be shovelled from dispersals and runways.

594 aircraft - 461 Lancasters, 123 Halifaxes, 10 Mosquitos - on the first large raid to Augsburg. The various diversions and the splitting of the main bomber force into 2 waves again reduced casualties still further with the second wave arriving when most of the night fighters were refueling. 21 aircraft - 16 Lancasters, 5 Halifaxes - lost, 3.6% of the force; at least 4 of these casualties were due to collision.

The bombing at Augsburg was outstandingly successful in clear weather conditions and against this 'virgin' target with only weak flak defences. The Pathfinder ground-marking was accurate and the raid became controversial because of the effects of its outstanding accuracy. The beautiful old centre of Augsburg was completely destroyed by high explosive and fire, with much less than the usual spread of bombing to the more modern outer areas, where some industry was located. There were 246 large or medium fires and 820 small ones; the temperature was so cold (minus 18" Celsius) that the River Lech was frozen over and many of the water hoses also froze. The Germans publicised it as an extreme example of 'terror bombing'.

131 aircraft minelaying in Kiel Bay, 22 Mosquitos to airfields in Holland, 15 Mosquitos on diversionary raids to 4 towns to the north of the Augsburg routes, 5 RCM sorties, 10 Serrate patrols. 3 Halifaxes and 1 Stirling lost from the minelaying operation.

Total effort for the night: 777 sorties, 25 aircraft (3.2%) lost.

24.   1/2.3.44   **Stuttgart**   ED611 JO-U   Uncle Jo

Fl Off Trimble   Sgt Marles   Fl Off Herriott   Sgt Nixon

Sgt Aldworth   Sgt McNaughton   Sgt Lawrence

Fl Off Trimble, bombing STUTTGART. Sortie completed. Up 2307 down 0636, 10/10 cloud, tops 14,000ft. Centre of 2 green TIs just disappearing into cloud. 22,000ft 0308, 1x4,000HC, 800x4, 100x4 XIBs, 72x30. Glow on clouds. Wanganui few and scattered. Attack was scattered but a huge explosion was seen south of target. Heavy predicted flak was seen over the target

463 Squadron sent 13 aircraft to join the 557 bombers attacking Stuttgart. The weather was still freezing and heavy cloud all the way prevented the fighters from getting into the bomber stream. Cloud over the target covered the markers. Pathfinders could not keep the target marked, and crews could not assess the results. Post-war German records say the city was heavily hit, with the Bosch and Daimler-Benz works badly damaged. Losses were 0.7%, none from Waddington.

The third trip to Stuttgart for the Trimble crew. Because of the southerly position of Stuttgart the Lancaster must have been coming home through France to land at Tangmere in west Sussex, an airfield famous as a fighter station.

25.   15/16.3.44   Stuttgart   ED611 JO-U   Uncle Jo

| Fl Off Trimble | Sgt Marles | Fl Off Herriott | Sgt Nixon |
| Sgt Aldworth | Sgt McNaughton | Sgt Lawrence | |

Fl Off Trimble, bombing STUTTGART. Sortie completed. Up 1922 down 0330, 6-7/10 cloud 8/9,000ft. Centre of all red TIs visible. 22,000ft 2320hrs. 2x1,000HC, 96x30. 900x4. 150x4 XIB. Incends were the only thing to be seen. There were no large fires starting at this time. PFF not seen to start before 2309hrs. Aircraft held back as much as possible. TIs were scarce. Numerous incends were seen burning on ground on run in. These were short of target. On leaving target impression was that attack generally fell short. Flare green with red stars believed enemy were seen 20 miles approx. S of target. These were seen when on leg F-G.

463 Squadron sent 17 aircraft to join 863 bombers attacking Stuttgart, despite clear weather. Strong winds upset the markers and only part of the force actually bombed the centre of the city. Fighters were active. 4.3% were lost. 463 Squadron lost Plt Off Roberts and crew: 6 KIA, 1 POW. Flt Sgt W. Graham collided with a 625 Squadron aircraft in the landing circuit at Waddington, all the crew were KIA.

863 aircraft - 617 Lancasters, 230 Halifaxes, 16 Mosquitos - ordered to attack Stuttgart. The German fighter controller split his forces into 2

parts. The bomber force flew over France nearly as far as the Swiss frontier before turning north east to approach Stuttgart. This delayed the German fighters contacting the bomber stream but, when the German fighters did arrive, just before the target was reached, the usual fierce combats ensued. 37 aircraft - 27 Lancasters, 10 Halifaxes - were lost, 4.3% of the force. Two of the Lancasters force-landed in Switzerland. Adverse winds delayed the opening of the attack and the same winds may have been the cause of the Pathfinder marking falling back well short of the target, despite the clear weather conditions. Some of the early bombing fell in the centre of Stuttgart but most of it fell in open country south west of the city. The Akademie was damaged in the centre of Stuttgart and some housing was destroyed in the south western suburbs.

140 aircraft - 94 Halifaxes, 38 Stirlings, 8 Mosquitos - attacked railway yards at Amiens. 2 Halifaxes and 1 Stirling lost.

22 Lancasters of No 5 Group to an aero-engine factory at Woippy, near Metz. 10/10ths cloud caused the attack to be abandoned before any bombs were dropped. No aircraft lost.

17 Mosquitos to 5 German targets and 10 Mosquitos to airfields in Holland, 2 RCM sorties, 11 Serrate patrols, 2 Stirlings minelaying off Texel, 31 aircraft on Resistance operations, 18 OTU sorties. 1 Serrate Mosquito lost.

Total effort for the night: 1,116 sorties, 41 aircraft (3.7%) lost. The number of sorties flown on this night was a new record.

26. 18/19.3.44 **Frankfurt** ED611 JO-U Uncle Jo

| Fl Off Trimble | Sgt Marles | Fl Off Herriott | Sgt Nixon |
| Sgt Aldworth | Sgt McNaughton | Sgt Lawrence | |

Fl Off Trimble, bombing FRANKFURT. Sortie completed. Up 1906 down 0121. Thin cloud at almost own height. (22,000ft). Numbers of red TIs burning on ground. 20,000ft , 2203 ½ hrs 1x4,000HC1200x4, 150x4 XIB 58x30 Inc. Target consisted of pattern of red TIs and incendiaries which were reasonably well placed in relation to the TIs. There was some evidence of creep back. Route good. Considering there were far too many aircraft over the target at one time. This was a real nuisance on making bombing run with other aircraft close at either side it was necessary to bomb the western most markers missing chance of aiming point.

463 Squadron sent 18 aircraft on the 846 bomber attack on Frankfurt. German reports list 99 industrial firms destroyed, 55,000 people left homeless, a military train hit and 20 soldiers killed, 80 wounded. Fighters

were active. 2.6% were lost. 463 Squadron lost Plt Off J. Gardner and crew: 7 KIA.
846 aircraft - 620 Lancasters, 209 Halifaxes, 17 Mosquitos - to Frankfurt. The German fighter force was again split. One part was lured north by the Heligoland mining operation but the second part waited in Germany and met the bomber stream just before the target was reached, although cloud made it difficult for these fighters to achieve much success. 22 aircraft - 12 Halifaxes, 10 Lancasters - were lost, 2.6% of the force. The Pathfinders marked the target accurately and this led to heavy bombing of eastern, central and western districts of Frankfurt. The later phases of the bombing were scattered but this was almost inevitable with such a large force; new crews were usually allocated to the final waves.
17 Mosquitos to airfields in Holland, Belgium and France, 98 aircraft on minelaying diversion in the Heligoland area, 11 Mosquitos on a diversion raid to Kassel, 4 RCM sorties, 13 Serrate patrols. No aircraft were lost and the Serrate Mosquitos claimed 3 Ju88s destroyed.
19 Lancasters of No 5 Group (including 13 aircraft from No 617 Squadron) on an accurate raid of an explosives factory at Bergerac in France, 12 Mosquitos to Aachen, Dortmund and Duisburg, 8 aircraft on Resistance operations, 18 OTU sorties. No aircraft lost.
Total effort for the night: 1,046 sorties, 22 aircraft (2.1%) lost.

22/23.3.44   **Frankfurt**   LM458

Fl Off Fryer R. McNaughton rear gunner or spare MUG?

NB. Roy appears in two unofficial records as a gunner with Fl Off Fryer on this raid but not in ORBs. The missing gunner's logbook of Roy would confirm or deny this record.
463 Squadron sent 15 a/c and all returned.
Frankfurt: 816 aircraft - 620 Lancasters, 184 Halifaxes, 12 Mosquitos. Again, an indirect route was employed, this time crossing the Dutch coast north of the Zuider Zee and then flying almost due south to Frankfurt. This, and the Kiel minelaying diversion, confused the Germans for some time; Hannover was forecast as the main target. Only a few fighters eventually found the bomber stream. 33 aircraft - 26 Lancasters, 7 Halifaxes - were lost, 4.0% of the force.
The marking and bombing were accurate and Frankfurt suffered another heavy blow; the city's records show that the damage was even more severe than in the raid carried out 4 nights earlier. Half of the city was without gas, water and electricity 'for a long period'. All parts of the city were hit

but the greatest weight of the attack fell in the western districts. The report particularly mentions severe damage to the industrial areas along the main road to Mainz. 162 B-17s of the Eighth Air Force used Frankfurt as a secondary target when they could not reach Schweinfurt 36 hours after this RAF raid and caused further damage. The Frankfurt diary has this entry: "The three air raids of 18th, 2second and 24th March were carried out by a combined plan of the British and American air forces and their combined effect was to deal the worst and most fateful blow of the war to Frankfurt, a blow which simply ended the existence of the Frankfurt which had been built up since the Middle Ages."

20 Mosquitos bombing night fighter airfields, 128 Halifaxes and 18 Stirlings minelaying in Kiel Bay and off Denmark, 22 Mosquitos on diversion and harassing raids to Berlin, Dortmund, Hannover and Oberhausen, 16 RCM sorties and 16 Serrate patrols. 1 Halifax minelayer lost.

20 OTU Wellingtons carried out leaflet flights to France without loss.

Total effort for the night: 1,056 sorties, 34 aircraft (3.2%) lost.

30/31.3.44   **Nuremberg**   LM458
Fl Off Fryer R. McNaughton rear gunner or spare MUG?

NB. Roy appears in two unofficial records as a gunner with Fl Off Fryer on this raid but not in ORBs. The missing gunner's logbook of Roy would confirm or deny this record.

This would normally have been the moon stand-down period for the Main Force, but a raid to the distant target of Nuremberg was planned on the basis of an early forecast that there would be protective high cloud on the outward route, when the moon would be up, but that the target area would be clear for ground-marked bombing. A Meteorological Flight Mosquito carried out a reconnaissance and reported that the protective cloud was unlikely to be present and that there could be cloud over the target, but the raid was not cancelled. Although this was the worst raid for Bomber Command losses in the war, 463 Squadron sent 18 a/c and all returned.

795 aircraft were dispatched - 572 Lancasters, 214 Halifaxes and 9 Mosquitos. The German controller ignored all the diversions and assembled his fighters at 2 radio beacons which happened to be astride the route to Nuremberg. The first fighters appeared just before the bombers reached the Belgian border and a fierce battle in the moonlight lasted for the next hour. 82 bombers were lost on the outward route and near the target. The action was much reduced on the return flight, when

most of the German fighters had to land, but 95 bombers were lost in all - 64 Lancasters and 31 Halifaxes, 11.9% of the force dispatched. It was the biggest Bomber Command loss of the war.

Most of the returning crews reported that they had bombed Nuremberg but subsequent research showed that approximately 120 aircraft had bombed Schweinfurt, 50 miles north-west of Nuremberg. This mistake was a result of badly forecast winds causing navigational difficulties. 2 Pathfinder aircraft dropped markers at Schweinfurt. Much of the bombing in the Schweinfurt area fell outside the town and only 2 people were killed in that area. The main raid at Nuremberg was a failure. The city was covered by thick cloud and a fierce cross-wind which developed on the final approach to the target caused many of the Pathfinder aircraft to mark too far to the east. A 10-mile-long creep-back also developed into the countryside north of Nuremberg. Both Pathfinders and Main Force aircraft were under heavy fighter attack throughout the raid. Little damage was caused in Nuremberg.

49 Halifaxes minelaying in the Heligoland area, 13 Mosquitos to night fighter airfields, 34 Mosquitos on diversions to Aachen, Cologne and Kassel, 5 RCM sorties, 19 Serrate patrols. No aircraft lost.

3 OBOE Mosquitos to Oberhausen (where 23 Germans waiting to go into a public shelter were killed by a bomb) and 1 Mosquito to Dortmund, 6 Stirlings minelaying off Texel and Le Havre. 17 aircraft on Resistance operations, 8 OTU sorties. 1 Halifax shot down dropping Resistance agents over Belgium.

Total effort for the night: 950 sorties, 96 aircraft (10.1%) lost

ABOUT THE AUTHOR

Don McNaughton was born in Darlington, Co. Durham and emigrated with his family to Australia in 1961 at the age of 9. After attending school in Brisbane he joined the RAAF in 1970 where he trained as an Aeronautical Engineer. After 4 years that he wouldn't have missed for quids, he resigned from the air force and commenced a science degree, majoring in chemistry and then carrying out a Ph D in physical chemistry. As an academic his research areas are molecular spectroscopy underpinning the understanding of interstellar chemistry and analytical micro and nano-spectroscopy aimed at understanding biochemical change at the micro and nano level. He retired in 2017, and is Emeritus Professor of Molecular Sciences at Monash University, Melbourne, Australia. He retains his interest in the air force and aircraft and has always maintained an interest in 20th Century military and social history. *Lucky Pommie Bastard* is his first foray into writing anything other than scientific papers and book chapters.
Don is married to Elizabeth, a General Medical Practitioner and together they have two children.

TRIMBLE CREW OPS

LUCKY POMMIE BASTARD

www.ingramcontent.com/pod-product-compliance
Lightning Source LLC
Chambersburg PA
CBHW021402290426
44108CB00010B/353